Sponsored Identities

litics in Puerto Rico

In the *Puerto Rican Studies* series,
edited by
Luz del Alba Acevedo,
Juan Flores, and
Emilio Pantojas-García

SPONSORED IDENTITIES

CULTURAL POLITICS

IN PUERTO RICO

Arlene M. Dávila

TEMPLE UNIVERSITY PRESS
Philadelphia

TEMPLE UNIVERSITY PRESS, PHILADELPHIA 19122

Printed in the United States of America

☉ The paper used in this book meets the requirements of the
American National Standard for Information Sciences—
Permanence of Paper for Printed Library Materials,
ANSI Z39.48-1984

Text design by Gary Gore

Library of Congress Cataloging-in-Publication Data

Dávila, Arlene M., 1965–
    Sponsored identities : cultural politics in Puerto Rico /
Arlene M. Dávila.
        p.   cm. — (Puerto Rican studies)
    Includes bibliographical references and index.
    ISBN 1-56639-548-8 (cloth : alk. paper). —
    ISBN 1-56639-549-6 (paper : alk. paper)
    1. Puerto Rico—Cultural policy—History—20th century.
    2. Culture—Economic aspects—Puerto Rico. 3. Popular culture—
    Puerto Rico—Marketing. 4. Ethnocentrism—Puerto Rico—
    History—20th century. 5. Politics and culture—Puerto
    Rico—History—20th century. 6. Instituto de Cultura
    Puertorriqueña. I. Title. II. Series.
    F1976.D38 1997
    306′.097295—DC21   97-1942

To my father,
un jíbaro de verdad

CONTENTS

ILLUSTRATIONS

PREFACE

This study of Puerto Rico's cultural politics began in 1992 when I conducted preliminary fieldwork, although its development has long been in the making. As an island-born and U.S.-based Puerto Rican with a background in museum work, I have had a deep interest in the struggles involved in the public representation and definition of Puerto Rican culture. Issues of identity are key concerns for both Puerto Ricans in the States and on the island, and my work in culturally specific museums in New York City had heightened my interest in the role of cultural institutions in shaping definitions of collective identity.

This research is also informed by the current academic milieu and the plethora of studies questioning nationalisms and the construction of national identities as tools of colonial and post-colonial liberation. These studies guided my interest in the polit-ical implications of current debates over the island's national identity and the hierarchies embodied and reproduced in con-structions of identity. Finally, this work is anthropological, in that it presents an ethnographic case study of some of the intersections between global processes and local-level cultural politics, issues at stake in Puerto Rico and beyond.

The result is a study that, in hindsight, I recognize as part of my own quest to come to terms with Puerto Rican cultural politics. For a so-called "native anthropologist" this involved going against the advice of more than one senior scholar who warned me about studying "my own culture," as well as having to rationalize and legitimize working on a popular and coveted topic within Puerto Rican Studies. This task also involved overcoming early fears about writing on Puerto Rican culture, considering that the knowledge of U.S.-based Puerto Ricans and their right to speak about Puerto Rican culture (and even their Puerto Rican identity, for that matter) are often questioned on the island. In the process I came to understand a little more about my simultaneous involvement in and distance from Puerto Rican cultural politics. After all, it was because of my years in the States and my impending return there following the completion of my research that I was able to move freely among the same political groupings that serve as bases for social and political distinctions on the island, and to write about issues that many friends and informants may find difficult to address. Unlike me, they are the direct actors and agents in a continuing story that is loaded with implications for the island's political future. I was nevertheless encouraged repeatedly by my informants to write and publish this book and was thus reassured that this work would shed at least some light on what is a larger and evolving story. The following pages are therefore not meant to address all of the nuances and implications of contemporary cultural politics; that would be an excessively ambitious, if not impossible, task. Rather, my aim is to highlight some of the opportunities and contradictions involved in contemporary cultural politics on the island, as experienced by those who shared with me their interests, frustrations, and experiences in cultural work in Puerto Rico. Ultimately I hope this work provides a window into some of the debates and discourses developing around Puerto Rican culture and an opportunity for further debate on the everyday dimensions of cultural struggles on the island.

This study is based upon fieldwork conducted in Puerto Rico during the summer of 1992 and from July 1993 to July 1994. During this time, Puerto Rico changed administrations and language policies and held a plebiscite. More changes are likely to come by the time this book is published: The centennial of U.S. occupation of the island is upcoming, and Congress's eradication of tax exemptions that have benefited U.S. companies on the island and the possibility of yet another political status plebiscite are likely to have an impact on local politics and debates over culture on the island. In fact, as I go over the page proofs for this book, among other issues, there is growing debate over a proposed educational reform by the current pro-statehood administration to promote bilingual education in Puerto Rican public schools. The proposal, which has been publicly linked to this party's growing awareness of the United States's unyielding opposition to the incorporation of a culturally and linguistically distinct state, evidences that it is in the realm of cultural policies and programs that status options and definitions will continue to be contested on the island. Because of the ongoing nature of cultural politics, I have tried to address the changes in the island's cultural policies, legislation, and political events that have taken place since my original fieldwork. My discussion, however, draws mostly from my priority research period, which I use to analyze what emerged as recurring themes within Puerto Rican cultural politics.

Two areas of interest guided the research design for this work: the character and constitution of Puerto Rico's cultural policy at the government level and the popular notions of Puerto Ricanness through which people express their identity in everyday life. I was interested particularly in the rise of grassroots groups that are organizing events with cultural overtones and the ways they affect and are shaped by dominant definitions of Puerto Rico's national identity.

I initiated my research by examining the requirements of the government cultural policy and definitions of "culturally relevant projects" and by conducting interviews with representatives of government cultural institutions, such as the Culture Division of the Tourism Office, the Folk Arts Division of Puerto Rico's Economic Development Administration (Fomento), and the Cultural Commissions at the Puerto Rican legislature. However, I focused mainly on the Institute of Puerto Rican Culture, whose explicit governmental mission is the promotion and dissemination of Puerto Rican culture. I interviewed representatives working at different levels in the Institute, paying particular attention to those most directly involved with the local cultural groups, such as the cultural advisers and the regional supervisors. I also conducted archival research on the historical development of Puerto Rico's cultural legislation at the Institute of Puerto Rican Culture, the National Archives, and the Library of the Puerto Rican Senate.

Realizing that corporate interests constitute important funders of the cultural groups, I decided to focus on the companies with the greatest visibility at the island's cultural festivals, such as Bacardi, R. J. Reynolds, and Anheuser-Busch. During the course of my research, I held interviews with representatives of these companies and with their publicity and public relations agents. I also conducted some twenty-two interviews that included representatives of other advertising agencies and of the publicity industry generally, in order to compare the advertising strategies of the three companies with those of the industry at large.

With a background of the major entities involved in the composition of Puerto Rico's cultural policy at the national level, I then moved to analyze some of the issues involved in the organization of cultural activities and the micropolitical dynamics between funders and organizers. For these purposes, I interviewed over twenty organizers of such events and attended various activities to meet organizers, funders, and members of the attending public. In order to analyze in greater depth the historical and political variables affecting these groups, I decided to focus on one regional area. I chose the southeastern town of Caone (pseudonym), because it is one of the first cities to found a cultural center and because it is the site of one of the Institute's regional offices for the promotion of culture, which is in charge of advising, funding, and supervising the work of cultural centers in the area. This role facilitated my research on the local and national aspects of the government's cultural policy. In addition, as a large metropolitan center, Caone provided easy access to a variety of independent organizers of cultural activities. This new regional emphasis added another dimension to my research: issues of place, identity, and politics in the work and development of these cultural groups. "The community" surfaced as an important source of identification for the work of these groups.

The concept of "community" has been challenged in the anthropological literature for its association with uniformity, parochialism, homogeneity, and consensus. Yet space and place continue to serve as important loci of struggle, and "the community," as spatially recognized, provides an important referent for the construction of memories and identities. In this light, my emphasis is not on overt and fixed regional characteristics but rather on how different community-based cultural groups are related to state structures and to their local communities (Jones 1987) and how these relationships inform the work and development of the local groups.

Thus, I conducted interviews with present and past leaders and members of grassroots organizations in Caone and observed their activities and planning meetings to investigate the relationship between local organizers and government and corporate funders. I assessed public reception of the groups' activities by observing the level of participation in these activities and by interviewing the attending public. I conducted interviews in Spanish, and except for material excerpted from English news articles, I translated all quotes myself. I used pseudonyms for individuals in this work, except for politicians and other public figures. All towns and communities are identified by their actual names, except for the city of Caone. Although many informants urged me to use the city's real name, there was disagreement on this point among some of the parties involved in the research. The city's history and that of its municipalities has not been changed.

Finally, as is often the case with long-term projects, this work has received the help of many friends, colleagues, and institutions, who all deserve acknowledgment and appreciation. This research was facilitated by grants from the Wenner Gren Foundation for Anthropological Research, the National Science Foundation, and the City University of New York/University of Puerto Rico Academic Exchange Program. With regard to the numerous individuals who assisted me during the publication of this book, I will start by thanking my mentor, Delmos Jones, who encouraged me from early on to pursue this project and challenged and supported my ideas. Acknowledgment is also due to June Nash, who provided continuous feedback, and to Antonio Lauria and Brackette Williams, who provided insightful comments on an earlier draft of this manuscript. I am especially grateful to Juan Flores for his vision and faith in this project from its earliest inception. I also want to thank the members of the Department of Anthropology at the Graduate Center of the City University of New York, particularly Terri Vulcano for her continuous encouragement.

Many friends and colleagues in Puerto Rico made my research a fruitful and enjoyable experience at the personal, social, and intellectual levels. My greatest gratitude goes to the Vega family, especially William, Mallín, Toña, and Ana, and to Juan and Iris Soto as well as to the many grassroots cultural workers I met throughout my research who face "cuesta arriba" (uphill) conditions in preparing their activities. I am grateful to more cultural organizers and activists than can be mentioned in these pages, but I will point out the help of Maria Pou, Haydee Torres, Mariano Rodríguez, Carlos Padilla, Juan Troncoso, Evelyn Torres, Ivor Hernández, Felix Rivera, Josilda Acosta, and Miriam Vargas, who, among others, helped me understand the complexities of everyday cultural issues and taught me so much in the process. The interpretations presented in this book are, of course, my own and are not necessarily shared or endorsed by those who helped me with this project.

I am also grateful to the staff of the National Archives, the Institute of Puerto Rican Culture, the Fundación Luis Muñoz Marín, Fomento, and Puerto Rico's Tourism Office, among other governmental offices I visited. At the University of Puerto Rico, I received assistance from Angel Quintero Rivera and from Jorge Duany, who was a source of continuous support.

I also benefited from the comments of Yvonne Lassalle and Maureen O'Dougherty, with whom I have discussed this project from the start. This work was also improved by the comments of Bonnie Urciuoli, Dan Segal, Ruth Glasser, Debora Pacini-Hernández, and the anonymous reviewers of the manuscript. Marvette Pérez, Agustín Laó, Linda Alcoff, Teresa Vega, Ara Wilson, Nicole Toulis, Francisco Scarano, Cristiana Bastos, Gerald Creed, Jonathan Hearn, Kate McCaffrey, Caroline Tauxe, Karin Rosemblatt, Marcela Clavijo, and other colleagues also provided valuable insights and a forum for the equal exchange of critical thinking and ideas. My appreciation goes to all of them as well as to Flora Kaplan, with whom I learned the political significance of cultural institutions, and Stuart Ewen, for his original approach to all scholarship. I also want to thank all my colleagues at Syracuse University who helped me in multiple ways toward this endeavor. I am also obliged to the many people involved in the production of this book, particularly Murphy Halliburton, who provided much advice and unlimited support through the long processes of researching and publishing. Thanks are also due to Jennifer Holladay, who provided editorial support, to Doris Braendel for all her valuable advice, and to Marilú Montalvo. Last, while I have benefited from the advice of all the aforementioned people, I alone am responsible for any flaws in the content or analysis of this book.

ABBREVIATIONS

AFAC   Administración para el Fomento de las Artes y la Cultura (Administration for the Promotion of the Arts and Culture)

ARECMA   Asociación Recreativa, Educativa, y Cultural del Barrio Mariana (Recreational, Educational, and Cultural Association of the Mariana Barrio)

DIVEDCO   División de Educación de la Comunidad (Division of Community Education)

Fomento   Administración de Fomento Ecónomico (Puerto Rico's Economic Development Administration)

ICP   Instituto de Cultura Puertorriqueña (Institute of Puerto Rican Culture)

PIP   Partido Independentista Puertorriqueño (Puerto Rican Independence Party). Also referred to as the pro-independence party

PNP   Partido Nuevo Progresista (New Progressive Party). Also referred to as the pro-statehood party

PPD   Partido Popular Democrático (Popular Democratic Party). Also referred to as the pro-commonwealth party

Making and Marketing National Identities

"**N**ow everybody loves Puerto Rican culture," observed a Puerto Rican schoolteacher and festival organizer, "but that's exactly the problem. Now you have people that don't know culture but are putting together events because it's fashionable. That's why we need the Institute of Puerto Rican Culture, so people don't devalue our culture."

Culture is certainly fashionable in Puerto Rico. In addition to the hundreds of cultural festivals that are celebrated every year on the island, transnational corporations, well aware that culture sells, are drawing on images of Puerto Rican folklore and popular culture to advertise beer, cigarettes, and other products. Meanwhile, political supporters of U.S. statehood, of independence, and of commonwealth status variously claim to be pro–Puerto Rico and all things Puerto Rican.

The current emphasis on cultural identity in Puerto Rico, a U.S. colony that continues to debate its political status, represents a significant development considering that overt demonstrations of Puerto Rican identity were once regarded as subversive. Once limited and associated with pro-independence sectors of society, manifestations of cultural identity are now widespread: musicians sing nationalist songs on prime-time television, and nationalist symbols, such as the Puerto Rican flag, decorate advertisements

1

and private dwellings alike. Yet, as the teacher's comments suggest, these developments have raised contentions over what elements and which interests can legitimately represent Puerto Rican culture. These issues and their impact on contemporary politics and on shaping and expanding definitions of identity are the subject of this work.

This study examines the dynamics of cultural politics in contemporary Puerto Rican society.[1] It considers the debates regarding the use, definition, and representation of Puerto Rican culture as the terrain on which a variety of actors seek to advance and legitimize interests that range from selling products to promoting U.S. statehood or independence. I argue that such debates are actively involved in shaping conceptions of national identity and, ultimately, in reformulating the basis and the processes by which identities are constructed on the island. My analysis probes the scope and nature of cultural nationalism and the forces fueling its growth in contemporary society. In short, I attempt to show cultural nationalism to be far from a unitary movement but rather one that serves and generates divergent objectives, including those that sustain and others that challenge dominant frameworks about culture, identity, and political participation.

The case of Puerto Rico provides a good example of cultural nationalism and a unique entry point for examining the issues at stake in contemporary cultural struggles. A colony in a postcolonial world, Puerto Rico has remained in a colonial relationship with the United States since the U.S. occupation of the island in 1898. Puerto Ricans attained commonwealth status in 1952, which conferred self-governing authority under federal jurisdiction and rendered the island a "free associated state" of the United States. Under this arrangement, Puerto Ricans are subject to all federal laws, but they are not permitted to vote in U.S. elections or influence the political decisions that affect most aspects of their lives. Yet despite their lack of political sovereignty, most Puerto Ricans consider themselves a territorially distinct national unit, a nation defined by its cultural distinctiveness notwithstanding its political and economic dependency on the United States. In fact, while the average Puerto Rican now feels more pride than ever before in his or her identity, most favor the continuation of some type of political and economic relationship with the United States.

However, the lack of mass support for independence has led many island scholars to discount the heightened role of culture as a "light" nationalism or a neonationalism that has no significance for anticolonial politics. This view mirrors criticism of the widespread escalation of cultural movements in the current transnational context where the idiom of culture is increasingly rendered into one more tool to sell consumer goods.[2] Yet local cultural identities continue to be salient mediums for political mobilization and serve to promote a variety of other interests, not limited to issues of sovereignty and independence (Johnson 1994, Nash 1995, Young 1993). This work highlights these issues by considering the current growth of cultural nationalism not as an apolitical development but as part of a shift in the terrain of political action to the realm of culture and cultural politics, where the idiom of culture constitutes a dominant discourse to advance, debate, and legitimize conflicting claims. Through this focus I emphasize the variety of struggles that are currently being waged through culture, hoping to shed light on some of the opportunities and constraints involved in contemporary cultural and nationalist movements.

Contemporary cultural politics permeate many sectors of Puerto Rican society, from the media to government departments for tourism and education. In order to highlight the historical context of current conflicts, this study focuses on the Institute of Puerto Rican Culture, the governmental entity charged since the 1950s with defining and defending Puerto Rican culture, and on Puerto Rico's rapidly proliferating grassroots festival organizations. Varied in their goals and activities, which range from sports to environmental protection, these grassroots groups have a common interest in organizing public festivals and cultural celebrations. Their growth reflects the increased significance of culture in political discourse and provides examples of the range of interests that are promoted through culture on the island.

The government's initial attempts to promote cultural nationalism in the 1950s are the starting point of this discussion. While local debates over culture in Puerto Rico can be traced to the ideas of educated elites in the eighteenth and nineteenth centuries, it was only in the 1950s, after Puerto Rico attained local autonomy through commonwealth status, that the government first made a concerted effort to define an official cultural policy and stipulate what could rightfully represent Puerto Rican culture. At this time, the colonial government developed an "official nationalism" (Anderson 1983) that emanated from and served the colonial state. This involved emphasizing the island's cultural distinctiveness through a cultural nationalism that helped to disguise its politically dependent status and sought to reconcile diverse interests into a stable colonial project. Puerto Rico's separatist nationalism was contained by repression and co-optation, the nation was associated with the realm of the cultural, and views of national identity became "institutionalized" through cultural policies and government cultural agencies. The Institute of Puerto Rican Culture was founded at this time, with the official task of defining and disseminating the constituent elements of Puerto Rico's national identity. Shortly afterwards, cultural centers affiliated with the institution were established to replicate its mission at the local level. By the late 1970s, government-affiliated cultural centers had been founded in almost all of the island's seventy-eight municipalities, where they were intended to serve as extensions of the central institution.

The official discourse about what could rightfully represent Puerto Rican culture reproduced patterns of nationalist ideologies similar to those found in many other contexts (Domínguez 1990, Verdery 1991). First, culture was "objectified" as a set of distinct and identifiable traits and products defined as forming the essence of national identity (Handler 1988: 13–16, Friedman 1994: 88). It was constructed as something that could be lost or possessed, or be embodied in a fair, a piece of folk art, a tradition, or an object, rather than as a way of life and everyday culture. These products could then be assigned value as being more or less able to represent Puerto Ricanness or deemed more or less likely to provide the "content" of Puerto Rican identity. It is "culture" constructed as an element of self-identification that has formed the basis for struggle in Puerto Rico's cultural politics.

Moreover, within the official discourse about Puerto Rican culture, authenticity was defined through strict dichotomies such as that opposing a pure, utopian past and folklore to the impure and immoral influences of modernity. The United States, with its commercial culture, represented the "other" against which authentic Puerto Rican culture was defined. Thus, images of national identity became centered around a traditional agrarian past with its customs and folklore; and a romanticized and harmonious integration of the indigenous Taino, Spanish, and African components of society, under the rubric of Hispanic tradition, was set in opposition to the American invader.[3] In sharp contrast with this authenticated view of national identity, Puerto Ricans have long been geographically divided; 2.7 million Puerto Ricans currently live in the United States while island residents number 3.5 million. There is constant migratory traffic between Puerto Rico and the mainland, and American commercial culture touches every aspect of contemporary island life. Furthermore, 71 percent of the island's population lives in urban areas; unemployment stands at over 20 percent of the workforce; and services, manufacturing, and the civil sector, rather than agriculture, are the primary sources of employment (Negociado del Censo Federal 1990). In this context, contemporary folk artists are more likely the urban unemployed, Puerto Rican music is increasingly the result of the hybridization of musical rhythms, and ideas of Puerto Ricanness are more broadly disseminated by Budweiser than by political parties or government institutions.

Tensions between government-sanctioned images of national identity and people's lived social realities are not unique to Puerto Rico. Against the perceived threats represented by modernity, many nationalist ideologies have built images of bounded national entities eternally pitted against pollution and contamination (Handler 1988, Lloyd 1994, Olwig 1993). These tensions are increasingly evident in this age of transnational flows, where the media, commercial culture, and the growth of diasporic populations continue to challenge traditional constructs of culture and national identity. My interest, however, is in tracing the ongoing negotiations, ancillary creations, and practices in which people engage as they seek to maintain cultural distinctiveness. Such attempts are vividly displayed in Puerto Rico, where the island's cultural identity remains the most important basis for defining the national entity, and where the idiom of culture has historically served as a site for contesting power over the colonial state. These factors have sustained ongoing attempts by island intellectuals and political elites to maintain cultural authenticity by upholding officially constructed definitions of culture, or by renewing these definitions without challenging their "traditional" foundations.

In the realm of everyday life, however, new expressions of Puerto Ricanness are being generated by a variety of grassroots cultural organizers. Specifically, an assortment of independent groups, committees, and organizers of festivals are functioning as arenas for the definition of national identity and increasing the public space for cultural debate and contestation. These groups vary widely; I refer to them here as "independent" or "community groups" to highlight their regional and community orientation and their independence from the Institute of Puerto Rican Culture and all other government cultural entities. They include groups such as the Recreational, Educational, and Cultural Association of the Barrio Mariana, which started as a community-renewal organization, and the Christian Collegial Center in Jayuya, whose focus is on the local youth, as well as many other groups whose work is directed to their communities rather than at promoting a particular view of national identity. However, as they voice diverse interests through cultural claims and organize festivals and public events as part of their programs, these groups are also becoming involved in contesting and representing Puerto Rican culture in public life. In this process, most groups draw on the official cultural policy regarding Puerto Rico's traditional agrarian past and folklore as representative of what is distinctively Puerto Rican. Yet the extent of this borrowing varies. Rather than "authentic" folklore or other ethnic markers used by the government's cultural policy, increasingly it is popular and mass culture, as well as regional icons like the breadfruit, the cane worker, or the flat-bottom boat that dominate grassroots representations of Puerto Rican culture. This trend, in turn, highlights the dissemination of popular expressions of Puerto Ricanness that go beyond the official definitions of cultural authenticity. As a result, although they differ in their goals and activities, these groups are alike in being perceived as threats to the "homogeneity of the nation," which the official cultural nationalist project strives to project. Thus, their departure from government cultural policies will be analyzed as popular challenges to restrictive definitions of identity, and their work is viewed as part of larger attempts to rearticulate the discourse of culture toward specific ends.

Of particular interest in this context are corporate advertisers, especially those promoting such consumer goods as liquor, soft drinks, food, and tobacco. Aware of the marketing potential of the current popularization of cultural nationalism, these companies are also staking claims to Puerto Rican culture through their support of folk art fairs, festivals, and contests and their use of Puerto Rican folklore, history, and popular culture as background in their advertisements. Through an analysis of the background and motivations leading to the corporate turn to culture, I analyze some of the local contentions and contradictions ensuing from this development as corporate publicity strategies alternately reinforce and challenge dominant representations of culture. Thus, far from promoting homogenization, corporate sponsors contribute a new dimension to contemporary cultural politics. Considered by some a threat to the authenticity of the nation, commercial sponsors nevertheless add to the national dialogue over what can appropriately depict Puerto Rican culture. Specifically, grassroots activities and representations of Puerto Ricanness are increasingly distinguished as "cultural" or delegitimized as "commercial" and accepted or rejected on this basis. Ironically, however, corporate sponsors are simultaneously helping to market and showcase new ways of expressing Puerto Ricanness that are shunned by official definitions of Puerto Rican culture.

These are some of the developments that are central to my analysis of the constraints and possibilities for broadening the scope of representations and the interests that can be advanced in cultural terms. I attempt to broaden discussions of culture, politics, and nationalism by recognizing the contributions of local groups and private corporations to debates over definitions of national identity. In doing so, I address two issues central to present-day culture struggles—the ongoing tension between state-sponsored nationalist programs and alternative conceptions of group identity, and the nature of contemporary processes of identity formation in an increasingly mass mediated and transnational world.

Culture and the Creation of Nationalism

As ethnic and cultural identities acquire greater importance in present-day political movements, the study of nationalism and the cultural construction of national identities have come to the forefront of contemporary social analysis (Foster 1991, B. Williams 1989). This emphasis has led to a general awareness that forging a cultural identity, either from an ethnic past (Connor 1973, Smith 1986) or from recent inventions (Anderson 1983), is a central component of all nationalist programs.

Although they always entail the construction of a national identity, nationalisms have, nevertheless, taken many forms and been shaped by specific historical forces and agents.[4] This diversity has made defining and studying nationalisms a difficult task. Yet contemporary studies tend either to conflate all types of nationalism or to treat them, and other social categories of identity such as ethnicity, as "peoplehood constructs" (Fox 1990, Wallerstein 1991). These conceptualizations highlight the similarities among different types of nationalism, but they can also hide their historical specificity and social particularities.

While not arguing for a strict categorization among different types of nationalism, I find it useful to distinguish the case of Puerto Rico as an example of cultural nationalism in order to highlight the particular historical circumstances that led to the current emphasis on cultural distinctiveness, over concrete political boundaries and definitions, as the primary determinant of national identity. Accordingly, the distinction lies in the "loci of political identity," whether the relevant political unit is thought to be the cultural unit or the nation-state as recognized by the international community (see Barnett 1974: 240 quoted in Williams 1991: 16). The distinction between nations and states can be traced to Herder's eighteenth-century ideas of the "folk soul" in which nations are deemed to have a distinct essence rooted in history and tradition (Hutchinson 1987). This conception was later subverted by classical views of a nation as a political entity bounded by a state. Yet the distinction between nations and states is important in order to study types of nationalism that identify with something other than a nation-state, such as those encapsulated within a greater state or constrained by a colonial relationship, as in the case of Puerto Rico. In this context, national identity is defined not as identification with a nation-state as a juridically defined unit (Hylland Eriksen 1993) but in terms of identification with a culturally distinct community.

The conception of a national identity drawing on the identification with a culturally distinct unit, rather than on an independent nation-state, is particularly relevant for the case of Puerto Rico. Due to the politically divided nature of Puerto Rican society and to years of repression and persecution of separatists and pro-independence advocates, "nation" and "nationality" are highly contentious terms on the island. Many apply these categories to the United States or to Puerto Rico according to their particular political goals for the island—U.S. statehood, commonwealth, or independence—or according to whether they take as basis the island's cultural identity or politically dependent status. This was evident in demonstrations organized in 1996, prompted by a public comment by the pro-statehood governor to the effect that Puerto Rico is not a nation because it has never been a sovereign state. This statement led to a heated public debate and to the organization of three parallel marches in which thousands were mobilized to support different and competing goals: to affirm their nationality irrespective of the island's political status, to affirm their U.S. citizenship, or to express their desire for the political independence that would provide a legal basis for Puerto Rico's nationhood. References to the "national" are still politically loaded terms in everyday society, but the terms "culture" and "identity" are commonly used to express identification with Puerto Rico as a distinct collective unit. Specifically, discussions of culture and claims to be *pro cultura, culturalista,* or *puertorriqueñista* (pro–Puerto Ricanness and things Puerto Rican) are all statements of national identity or of self-identification with Puerto Rico as a culturally distinct unit.

This work argues that cultural nationalism in Puerto Rico is a direct result of the limits imposed by colonialism on the development of a politically defined nation-state, which led to the emphasis on culture as Puerto Rico's "domain of sovereignty"

(Chatterjee 1993), a realm wherein the local government could establish a degree of autonomy even under colonial control. It is this historical function of culture as the only institutionalized channel of nationalism that has since heightened the significance of the idiom of culture as a venue of self-identification and political debate. However, by focusing on cultural nationalism I do not mean to imply that it is the only type of nationalism operating on the island. Nationalism in Puerto Rico has been characterized as a heterogeneous movement (Carrión 1993) as it ranges from the more widespread cultural nationalism to a separatist nationalism that seeks political sovereignty for the island. However, it is cultural nationalism that has historically evolved into the dominant form of nationalist thought and that provides the framework for contemporary debates.

In the literature on nationalism, cultural nationalism is also known as the process of reinvigoration, authentication, and standardization of a country's national identity. This process has been documented as an integral part of the development of all nationalist movements, one that leads to the integration of a plurality of identities into a common national culture and the expression of a common identity.[5] As such, cultural nationalism is an ongoing and recurring process that can emerge and heighten at different historical stages: prior to the constitution of a state, as in the case of pre-independence India (Chatterjee 1993); long after statehood has been achieved, as in the case of Japan's *nihonjinron* movement of the 1970s and 1980s (Yoshino 1995); or as a recurrent force in times when national identity is perceived as threatened by internal or external forces—for example, as documented in the case of Irish cultural nationalism (Hutchinson 1992). Yet always, cultural nationalism serves as a key component in the constitution, renewal, and reinvigoration of a country's national identity and feeds a sense of political distinctiveness. Contrary to the emphasis of the above studies, these processes are not led only by intellectuals and governmental elites or by the "thinking elites" (Yoshino 1995), defined as those who formulate ideas of national identity through creative pursuits. Conceptions of identity are affected, directly or indirectly, by a variety of agents including those to whom these views are geared. I therefore draw on a broader conception of intellectuals as including "anyone whose social practice invokes claims to knowledge or to the creation and maintenance of cultural value and whose claim is at least partly acknowledged by others" (Verdery 1991: 16). In particular, I discuss the role played in shaping and authenticating a national identity by advertisers and local groups who may or may not be openly concerned with the creation and direction of ideas of national identity and whose participation in this realm may be largely unnoticed or unacknowledged.

This work addresses these two attributes associated with cultural nationalism: the emphasis on culture over other political boundaries, and the processes of shaping and constructing national identities. For my point of departure, however, I use the struggles involved in shaping views of national identity; hence my interest in contemporary cultural politics and struggles over definitions of culture and who and what are its most appropriate representatives.

The Politics of Culture and Authenticity

Pivotal to the constitution of a national identity are the containment and redefinition of difference into ideas of common peoplehood. These processes are characterized by contention and negotiation, through which a dominant standard of the nation is constituted. This, in turn, serves to demarcate who is and who is not part of the community as defined, and on what basis. Anthropologists examining these processes have analyzed the creation of meanings and ideas of common peoplehood in terms of nationalist ideologies, or ideologies for the "production of conceptions of peoplehood" (Fox 1990: 3) that provide ideas of common identity through which people define themselves as part of a given community and operate to produce, define, and contest ideas of national identity. In this way, nationalist ideologies provide the terrain upon which actors define or contest the ideas and meanings of the national community.[6] In turn, research on how people construct particular nationalist ideologies has found a preponderance of similar ideological precepts, such as the equation of a nation with a people (implying homogeneity, purity, and stability), which affect the development of constructs of cultural identity (B. Williams 1993: 146). These processes have been linked with nationalism's Western heritage; in particular, the Enlightment concept of nations as authentic and unique entities has led to the expectation of cultural distinctiveness as an intrinsic component to legitimize political demands in all nationalist ideologies (Breuilly 1982: 108-9). Accordingly, claims to national distinctiveness have since been justified as natural through affirmations of authentic and distinctive elements embodied either in a language, a unique history, or a people. This, in turn, explains the recurrence of tropes from nature, kinship, and myths of shared heritage among nationalist ideologies, used to naturalize the national community and to link it with a recent founding myth or a continuous and glorious past (A. Alonso 1994).

We should note, however, that not all myths of national identity place the same emphasis on homogeneity. Segal (1994) argues that, due to a history of colonization and the continual arrival of transplanted populations, nationalisms in the "New World," such as in the Caribbean, have often embraced ancestral diversity as a defining component of their national identities, celebrating the harmonious coexistence of different peoples who still remain culturally distinct. Puerto Rico's national myth emphasizes this kind of diversity and includes Spanish, indigenous, and African components, although, like many *mestizaje* myths in Latin America, Puerto Rico's embraces homogeneity and claims that these three strands have merged into a single ethnicity, the "Puerto Rican."

These differences in emphasis, however, do not make nationalist ideologies more inclusive, unbiased, or unaffected by inequalities of power. Whatever the model, the consolidation of ideas of national identity by nationalist programs is intrinsically involved in the unequal categorization of aspects and elements of a given society according to the dominant criteria for defining the national community. Some people and certain elements of the culture are valued as part of the community; others are shunned, excluded, and categorized as "ethnic" or foreign. It is in this sense that nationalist ideologies are composed of the hegemonic, or that which becomes, as result of cultural struggles, the dominant standard of the nation (B. Williams 1989). These processes often rely on transformist hegemonic processes by which the cultural products of different groups are appropriated, assimilated, and neutralized to create an image of national distinctiveness while forms of exclusions are being recreated (B. Williams 1991).[7]

These processes were evident in Puerto Rico in the 1950s, when the pro-commonwealth leadership first won political and economic power with the attainment of commonwealth status, which it legitimized by promoting the nation as a cultural community. Separatist nationalism was contained by repression and co-optation, and different elements of Puerto Rican culture and society were unequally incorporated into a culturalist definition of the nation embodied in folklorized images of a utopian agrarian past. Among other distinctions, this view emphasized the island's Hispanic heritage and deemphasized its African component.

It is important to note, however, that the commonwealth's cultural nationalist project was structurally limited from its inception by the island's colonial status. Political and economic activity has always been limited to coalitions that advance U.S. and local interests on the island. These constraints have not only affected the island's cultural nationalism: its development strategies and the constitution of the commonwealth itself have resulted from political projects that represented the consolidation of U.S.

interests and those of dominant local sectors (Pantojas-García 1990). We therefore need to make a distinction between hegemony as an ongoing process by which struggles are vested around the incorporation, intersection, and articulation of different interests in order to ally groups and advance particular goals; and hegemony as a condition, resulting from the successful completion of such a process through which a class or group is able to achieve consensus and provide intellectual and moral leadership to the rest of society (Mallon 1995, Roseberry 1994). Neither the pro-commonwealth party nor any other political faction in Puerto Rico has been able to secure local hegemony independent of U.S. interests, although domestic elites have established a degree of power over the colonial state through the containment and incorporation of competing groups and interests.[8] It is as a result of these processes that the pro-commonwealth party was able to attain political dominance in the 1950s and to direct efforts to disseminate the foundational elements that still form the backbone of most representations of Puerto Rican culture on the island.

Tropes of national identity, however, are always vulnerable constructs contingent on power relations and the maintenance or transformation of a given social order. State-developed myths of national identity, for instance, need to be constantly renewed, defended, updated, and articulated in all areas of society, ranging from historical and literary accounts of common peoplehood to cultural policies and official versions of history (Rowe and Schelling 1991, Sommer 1990). These processes are never smooth or cohesive; yet in Puerto Rico they are further complicated by the island's colonial status and, in particular, the historical ambiguity of commonwealth status. Specifically, the commonwealth has remained a "moment" rather than a permanent status, and has continued to be contested by other political interests also attempting to affect definitions of national identity and to link them to different status options for the island. This situation has further hindered the dissemination of an uncontested view of national identity and increased the significance of cultural struggles as a framework for debate and conflict. In particular, Puerto Rico's indeterminate colonial situation has perpetuated the creation of cultural policies and institutions that could never be fully popularized due to their symbolic significance for those that controlled them. As Pierre Bourdieu shows, claims to knowledge and authenticity are part and parcel of struggles over the monopoly of power in which those in dominant positions "operate essentially defensive strategies, designed to perpetuate the status quo by maintaining themselves and the principles on which their dominance is based" (Bourdieu 1993: 83).[9] In this context we see government cultural workers incorporating elements of popular culture and everyday life into official definitions of Puerto Rican culture while, for the most part, sanctioning these definitions through the standards of authenticity and restricting those who can take part in the cultural domain through cultural policies and legislation. In this context, I argue that the early policies for promoting cultural nationalism were able to generalize a cultural definition of Puerto Rican identity, center politics around culture, and contribute to the colonial premises on which views of Puerto Rican culture have since been grounded. Yet these processes were never devoid of struggle about the content of culture and its most appropriate representatives.

Alternative Authenticities

Against this already politicized and contingent background, we also need to consider how questions of identity in Puerto Rico are affected by global political economic processes. We need to account for the ways in which transnational corporations are making consumer products appear Puerto Rican as they tap into culture in order to sell their goods, as well as for the mass-mediated popular culture and hybrid representations of cultural identity displayed by a variety of grassroots groups. These developments are at the heart of contemporary research, which, aware that nationalism within the context of globalization is not a contradictory but rather a complementary process, increasingly focuses on the disparate processes through which cultural identities are promoted, hindered, or shaped (Featherstone 1995, Hall 1991, Miller 1995).

In this research a key question emerges about the relevance of "national identities" at a time when the intrastate system circumscribes the potential of nationalism to legitimize national spaces; a constant flow of peoples, images, and ideas challenge strict conceptualizations of identity; and ongoing processes of commodification affect cultural markers of identity (Basch et al. 1994, Friedman 1994, Gupta and Ferguson 1992). Under these conditions, new agents such as transnational corporations are joining nationalist elites in constructing images of collective identity, and modes of identification often elude traditional definitions of space, territoriality, and the objectification of the nation through material bases of authenticity while still expressing and demarcating the existence of a cultural community (Malkki 1992, Rosaldo 1989). It is these processes that have led many to advance constructs such as "hybrid culture" and "blurred" or "transnational" or "postmodern" identities to describe the new processes of identity formation that emerge as a result of the ongoing dislocation of national, state, and territorial boundaries (Appadurai 1990, García-Canclini 1992b, Basch et al. 1994, Featherstone 1995).

In turn, these new spaces and forms of identification are often perceived as opportunities that may potentially supersede the exclusionary nationalist forms of identification. Thus some suggest that the new forms of cultural identification and more flexible cultural affirmations directly challenge notions of cultural identity tied to patrimony and attachment to territory and may therefore be more resilient to appropriation (García-Canclini 1992a). In a similar manner, the mass media and the consumption of commodities and products are often regarded as sites for local strategies of self-definition that may provide alternatives to nationalist forms of identification and mediums for progressive politics (Garnham 1993, Shohat and Stam 1994).

Nevertheless, little attention has been given to how these processes actually operate in daily life, especially in relation to lingering nationalist precepts and processes and their ongoing attempts to objectify or essentialize forms of identity. These issues are particularly relevant considering evidence that points to the dual nature of global processes that lead both to homogeneity and to the recreation of difference, by fostering quests for authenticity, fixity, and determinacy. Postmodern theory emphasizes the end of meta-narratives, such as nationalism, but what we often see is the durability of the old paradigms of race, nation, and culture, albeit reconstituted in new guises, such as those of the new racism that speaks of the "insurmountability of cultural differences," (Balibar 1991: 21) or new nationalisms that prioritize cultural rather than civic ties (Friedman 1994). Even hybrid forms themselves, by necessity, are in a constant stage of becoming, or attaining some fixity to be rendered useful in strategic politics (Naficy 1993). In this context, engaging in cultural struggles inevitably involves not superseding but bridging and negotiating with established categories of identification and hierarchies of representation.

This study takes up these issues by considering the seemingly more fluid forms of identification at play in the case of Puerto Rico not in opposition but in relation to the island's nationalist discourse. I draw from the view that the alternative sites and expressions of Puerto Ricanness based on popular culture and everyday life evidenced in this work do not mark a demise of nationalism or nationalist forms of identification, for it is still in relation to lingering nationalist precepts that these practices operate.[10] It is not the idea of the nation that is being contested but its nature and range of representation. In fact, I argue that the emergence of more diverse representations of Puerto Ricanness has not challenged the discourse of authenticity and cultural identity but rather has shaped and helped reconfigure its scope and reach. In this way, my concern is with the conflicts and challenges that people confront in the process of rearticulating identities, not only in relation to external politico-economic constraints but also in relation to dominant frameworks for defining authenticity.

Thus, the new ways of representing Puerto Rican culture that are generated through the "reception" and "consumption" (de Certeau 1984) of official constructions of nationhood are an important aspect of this work. Cultural organizers are actively employing and manipulating official cultural policy and, in the process, simultaneously engaging in subsidiary productions, both through the adoption of imposed orders, spaces, and regulations and the incorporation of new materials for representing "Puerto Ricanness." Similarly, people are mediating the involvement of corporate sponsors in their work and reformulating what is meant by a "culturally meaningful activity" through the adoption of hybrid cultural expressions. However, while folk music is mixed with merengue, T-shirts showing salsa musicians displace traditional folk images, and the organizers of New York's Puerto Rican Day parade are staking a claim in discussions about the island's political fate, these developments still operate in relation to established hierarchies of authenticity. Thus my intent is to trace these developments but also to inquire about the extent to which the popular forms of resistance and manipulation of the government's cultural policies are displaced or compromised by lingering precepts for defining national identities. Specifically, I inquire into the processes by which oppositions to dominant views of national identity negotiate and come to terms with the exclusionary premises of nationalist discourse, and the extent to which popular claims to culture depart from, reproduce, or help expand the criteria on which cultural legitimacy is based. Moreover, I trace people's ability or inability to articulate alternative interests through such practices. Through this focus I seek to highlight the particular uses of nationalist discourse at work in Puerto Rico and thus transcend conceptualizations of nationalism as a unitary force or the ultimate "essentialized" identity. Instead, my concern is with the ongoing processes of incorporation as well as the alternative initiatives that are always involved and generated within any nationalist project.

These are the issues that guide my study of contemporary practices for representing Puerto Ricanness in relation to ongoing attempts by different sectors of Puerto Rican society to secure and maintain standards for the island's national identity through claims to knowledge and authenticity. It is through this analysis that contestations about issues of legitimacy and potential departures from dominant views of national identity are revealed. This results in conflicting developments that attest to the interaction of contrasting models for articulating collective identities in contemporary society.

Finally, my research adds to a long tradition of studies on Puerto Rico's national identity that have challenged the dominant conception that there is an identifiable, single "Puerto Rican culture" and that there is consensus on its meaning. Since local intellectuals first gave themselves to the task of identity formation, a quest heightened after U.S. occupation of the island, the issue of Puerto Rico's national culture has been the subject of continuous analytical inquiry. This emphasis is particularly evident in the literary production that has served as a key forum to define and debate the nature and content of Puerto Rico's national identity. For instance, the literary works of Puerto Rican elites in the 1930s and 1950s, which explored the themes of generation, paternalism, and the legacy of Spanish culture, have long been considered pivotal in elaborating the values and class interests of the Puerto Rican elite of the times (Flores 1979, Gelpí 1993). Similarly, literary works and historical reassessments since the 1970s have provided swift challenges to the dominant

Hispano-centered interpretations of Puerto Rican culture by highlighting issues of race, class, and gender (J. L. González 1987, Zenón Cruz 1975, Sola 1990). In fact, the importance of literature in nourishing and defining nationalisms (Bhabha 1990, Said 1993) is nowhere more evident than in the politically constrained context of colonial Puerto Rican society, where discussions of the island's national identity have long pervaded the literary and scholarly work.[11]

However, while debates on Puerto Rican national identity have been plentiful, the literary focus of most of this work has left us with little ethnographic description of the processes through which contestations over culture take place and the way in which dominant views of Puerto Rican culture are challenged or constructed. In fact, it is not until recently that studies have begun to address the everyday dimensions of struggles involved in definitions of Puerto Rican identity. Contemporary research has begun to bring attention to the varieties of expression—such as joking, beauty pageants, and cultural and language policies—through which people both challenge and define Puerto Ricanness in contemporary society (Flores and López 1994, Pérez 1994, Torres 1994, Morris 1995). Similarly, the transnational community of Puerto Ricans is beginning to be regarded as a pivotal element in definitions of Puerto Rican nationality (Laó 1997, Negrón-Muntaner and Grosfoguel 1997).

As a result, the issue of national identity is increasingly being placed in a "postnational" context in which cultural expressions of national identity, not tied to specific political aspirations, are finally rendered an appropriate subject of analysis. What follows is part of this larger quest to bring attention to the conflicts and challenges confronted by people in the processes of asserting and contesting "Puerto Ricanness." In so doing, I seek to go beyond traditional definitions of cultural nationalism as a transient ideology, a "lesser" form of nationalism, a literary movement, or a strategy designed by state bureaucrats in order to analyze it as it is actively manifested in contemporary society. In this context, while no longer overtly subversive, assertions of Puerto Ricanness remain forever contested, if not entirely controversial.

Overview

This book is organized into six chapters. The first, "Securing the Nation through Politics," begins by describing the emergence of cultural nationalism as a political tool for the consolidation of the commonwealth government. This development is traced to early cultural policies initiated by the local commonwealth government, including the creation of the Instituto de Cultura Puertorriqueña (Institute of Puerto Rican Culture, ICP). This chapter also traces the debates surrounding changes in cultural policy since the mid-1950s, which serve as a background to contemporary discussions about culture on the island.

Chapter II, "The Institute of Puerto Rican Culture and the Building Blocks of Nationality," turns to a discussion of the processes through which the "foundational" elements of Puerto Rican culture were established and officially disseminated through the government's cultural institutions. The chapter describes how these ideas are represented in and disseminated by the ICP's programming, and how these policies help reproduce the colonial foundations of Puerto Rican society.

The third and fourth chapters present case studies of the micropolitical dynamics at play among different groups involved in the public display of Puerto Rican culture on the island. These chapters draw on interviews with representatives of a variety of groups throughout the island, but the discussion centers mainly on three groups in a southeastern town I call Caone. Chapter III describes the ICP-affiliated center of Caone as an example of the repercussions of national cultural policy at the local level and the struggles that characterize ICP-affiliated centers. Chapter IV focuses on nonaffiliated groups as vehicles for the articulation of alternative views of Puerto Ricanness.

Chapter V, "Culture, Politics, and Corporate Sponsorship," focuses on the advertising and promotional strategies of R. J. Reynolds for Winston cigarettes and Anheuser-Busch for Budweiser beer, as the basis for a discussion of commercial interests as additional players contesting Puerto Rican nationality. I discuss how commercial interests draw on both the official cultural nationalist standards for representing Puerto Rican culture and on aspects of contemporary popular life. The chapter concludes with a discussion of some of the strategies through which people negotiate the involvement of corporate sponsors on the island.

The sixth chapter, "Contesting the Nation, Contesting Identities," pays particular attention to the ongoing tension between culturalist and commercial views of national identity resulting from the cultural policy of countering the "degeneration" of commercialization and its threat to authenticity. Through case studies of two cultural events, I argue that the dichotomization of culture, into the cultural (as authentic) and the commercial, is one more cloak for the subversion of alternative views of nationality. By analyzing how "commercial" expressions are continually subordinated and devalued in relation to the authenticated culture, I argue that this tension is most useful in legitimizing institutionalized views of Puerto Rican culture. The chapter ends by highlighting the compromises that people design to cope with these tensions.

The Conclusion explores the prospects for the creation of alternative views of nationality in the commercial, colonial, and national context of contemporary Puerto Rican society. The discussion reflects on both the constraints that associate the national culture and nationalism with a "proper" discourse, and the spaces that are opening up for the representation of difference and conflict within Puerto Rico's cultural and national discourse.

Chapter I

Securing the Nation through Politics

> It is not enough to try to get back to the people in that past
> out of which they have already emerged; rather we must join
> them in that fluctuating movement which they are just giving
> a shape to, and which, as soon as it has started, will be the
> signal for everything to be called in question.

—Frantz Fanon, *On National Culture*

In the 1993 plebiscite on the island's political status, the Puerto Rican Independence Party (PIP) won only 4.4 percent of the overall vote, trailing far behind the Popular Democratic Party (Partido Popular Democrático or the PPD, pro-commonwealth) and the New Progressive Party (Partido Nuevo Progresista or PNP, pro-statehood), which earned 48.6 and 46.4 percent of the vote respectively. Held independently from the U.S. Congress, which was not bound by its results, the plebiscite did not lead to any changes in the island's political status. However, the results confirm the dominance of the two political parties that seek the continuation of some type of political relationship with the United States. Yet Puerto Rico's political climate was not always so. In 1952 electoral support for independence was high, and the pro-independence party was the second most popular political option on the island.[1]

The decrease in electoral support for independence, however, does not reflect a decline in nationalist identification in Puerto Rican society but rather as a shift in its historical manifestation. It is this transformation in the predominant expression of nationalism that is the focus of this chapter. Inevitably, this task requires me to discuss in a few pages a complex process that is the subject of much research. I have nevertheless opted to provide a limited historical discussion in order to situate readers in local politics and then focus on the growth and development of the government's cultural policies. This chapter considers these policies an important locus for the historical transformation of Puerto Rico's nationalism and traces how those policies and the debates over their founding have shaped discussions over culture on the island.

A Curbed Nationalism

The traditional conception of nationalism as the principle that "the political and the national unit should be congruent" (Gellner 1983: 1) has faced major obstacles in Puerto Rico. Even under Spanish colonization, the island's economic privation, immigration policies instituted by the Spanish government to Hispanicize and strengthen its hold on the island, and Spanish political repression halted the growth of a separatist nationalism (Ferrao 1990).[2] Under these conditions economic concerns took priority over sovereignty as Puerto Rico's landowning elites sought to obtain from Spain more economic and political autonomy along with control of trade and tariffs.

The advent of American colonization in 1898 shattered Puerto Rico's aspirations for autonomy, but the early twentieth century saw an upsurge in local interest in the island's national identity. The catalyst was U.S. occupation of the island and the rapid and profound changes brought by American colonization. Among other changes, the local government was reconstituted with U.S. appointees, and the economy was transformed from an hacienda economy to one dominated by U.S. commercial agriculture, while the educational system evolved into a tool for the Americanization of the island. These transformations affected all sectors of Puerto Rican society, but they threatened most directly the interests of the formerly dominant landowning elite, who now turned to the island's Hispanic legacy in response to U.S. colonialism. Spanish civilization, metaphors derived from the landowning economy (such as the nineteenth-century image of Puerto Rico as an all-encompassing family, which had helped bridge the class relations of the hacienda economy), and the Catholic legacy provided bases for asserting a distinct spirit common to all Puerto Ricans (Flores 1979, Gelpí 1993).

This Hispanophile emphasis prevailed in the island's most important institutions of the time, such as the Union Party, which dominated local politics until the late 1920s, and the Ateneo Puertorriqueño, the stronghold of island intellectuals. It would also dominate the literary production of what is known as the 1930s generation, most of whose writing was pervaded by the search for Puerto Rican identity (Ferrao 1990: 53).[3] This identity project regarded *hispanidad* as the embodiment of civilization and contrasted it to the "Nordic barbarism of the invader." Puerto Rican culture was associated with the "positive values" of strong kinship bonds, hospitality, respect for elders, and a strong sense of Christian religiosity, traits that were contrasted to the invading American culture rather than that of the previous Spanish colonizers.[4]

Against this backdrop, independence was discussed and desired by many on the political scene. However, it was not until the founding of the Nationalist Party in 1922 that independence became the single priority of a political party on the island.[5] By the mid-1920s and early 1930s, under the leadership of Pedro Albizu Campos, the Nationalist Party had adopted a non-negotiable anti-imperial and anticolonial stance. Its campaign for independence employed a variety of means that included exposing the illegality of U.S. colonization of the island, calling attention to Puerto Rico's situation in international forums, promoting Puerto Rican national symbols such as the flag and the national anthem, and engaging in armed struggle (Rodríguez Fraticelli 1992, Tirado 1993). Yet the party's emphasis on national liberation over any other issue, including economic restructuring, along with its Hispano-centered conception of nationhood and petit bourgeois political base, limited the scope of its popular support and therefore its threat to U.S. rule. Thus, the Nationalist Party did not present a significant threat to U.S. interests in Puerto Rico until its involvement in the sugar strikes of 1934 showed its potential to attract greater popular support (Pantojas-García 1990).[6]

Repression of the Nationalist Party peaked during the 1930s, with the American colonial government appointing two former military officers as governor and police chief in 1934. The repression also involved Puerto Ricans who had been increasingly incorporated into the colonial government. As Santiago-Valles (1994) notes, beginning in the 1920s state mechanisms for social control were extended and "privileged Puerto Ricans" were incorporated into the colonial project through employment in federal positions, in Puerto Rico's legislative body (as early as 1917), and in the commissions for social services. As we will see, employment in the colonial government continued to grow as a means of self-promotion in the decades that followed and became a key factor in the rise of the Popular Democratic Party (PPD) in the 1940s. Albizu Campos recognized the political implications of this trend when he made it party policy to reject public employment and favors from the colonial government, deeming them acts of complicity with the colonizers (Tirado 1993).

A key legal aspect of this repression was the enactment in 1948 of Law 53, commonly known as the *ley de la mordaza* (the law of the muzzle). This law made it a grave crime to attempt in any way—whether by violent means or merely through the dissemination of ideas—to overthrow the island's government. The am-

biguity of the law permitted the government to incarcerate not
only members of the Nationalist Party but anyone with dissenting
ideas, purely on the basis of their ideological position and without
any evidence of their involvement in revolutionary activities.[7] This
law proved extremely significant in helping contain social unrest
prior to the electoral process that led to the creation of the
commonwealth in 1952. Specifically, it provided the legal basis
for the arrest and imprisonment of nationalists during the revolt
of 1950, when they occupied several towns on the island in what
still represents one of the most direct challenges to U.S. government in Puerto Rico.

The decline of the Nationalist Party after the 1950s has been
the subject of much research, and it is not my purpose to address
this topic further. I will simply note that its Hispanophile roots,
government repression, and severe economic and social hardships
prevented the Nationalist Party from forging a strong alliance with
Puerto Rico's working classes, a population for whom the discourse of social justice would have been far more effective than
that of national sovereignty. A number of different political programs have since promoted independence for the island, but the
position never received greater support from the electorate than
during the 1952 election.

The Accommodative Option

While the Nationalist Party was being subjected to severe
repression, a new political alternative was becoming consolidated
around the Popular Democratic Party (PPD). Founded in 1938
under the leadership of Luis Muñoz Marín, who had a history
of support for independence, the PPD turned away from the
issue of political status and made the island's economic development a central concern. Muñoz Marín saw economic development as essential if independence was to be a viable option for
the island. This emphasis, in turn, allowed the PPD to form

alliances between disparate groups and successfully constitute itself as a populist party despite its mostly landowning and seigneurial leanings.[8] Worker groups were drawn by the party's promises of land reform and social justice, while nationalists were attracted by its claim to be working for the eventual independence of the island. Meanwhile, intellectuals, bureaucrats, and professionals affiliated with the American governmental institutions on the island found in the PPD an opportunity to increase their local leadership (Quintero-Rivera 1985, Pantojas-García 1990).

These disparate groups were attracted by a populist discourse that presented the PPD as the protector of all Puerto Ricans, who were in differing degrees being exploited by the U.S. sugar corporations. "Pan, tierra, y libertad" (bread, land, and liberty), printed under the bust of a *jíbaro* or peasant, was the populist message of social justice evoking the daily life of the laboring classes (Alvarez-Curbelo 1993). Muñoz Marín also incorporated appeals to justice as "popular-democratic interpellations" (Laclau 1979: 173) to present the Popular Democratic Party as the alternative to the dominant interests of U.S. sugar corporations. Metaphors of Puerto Rico as the "all-embracing family," a recurrent paternalist theme since the nineteenth century, and the message that "all of us are exploited by the corporations," were posited as the alternative to dominant interests. This alternative was embodied in the Popular Democratic Party, which was presented by Muñoz Marín as the "truest and most real and profound unity of the great Puerto Rican family" (Muñoz Marín, November 16, 1940). Meanwhile, the PPD's program in the 1940s aimed to provide land, promote the equitable distribution of wealth, and increase production for the benefit of all the people. As Muñoz Marín stated, "They say our program is too incredible . . . but what is incredible is the exploitative system that has existed in Puerto Rico . . . what is incredible is that in a country that lives off the land, a few corporations have taken most of it, . . . and that children wake up without a piece of bread when millions of dollars are being made and millions leave Puerto Rico, the same millions produced by their own fathers" (Muñoz Marín, Nov. 4, 1940: 13–14).

Muñoz Marín spoke to the working, agricultural, and middle classes while exhorting the powerful to adopt his program of social justice. However, it was the "exploitative capitalist" that the PPD attacked rather than capitalism itself, a strategy that allowed the PPD to take local power within the dominant capitalist system through its control of the colonial state.

Using these populist appeals, the PPD laid the ground for the absorption and neutralization of opposing groups and interests through what Gramsci has referred to as a "transformist hegemony" involving the "gradual but continuous absorption . . . of the active elements produced by allied groups" (Mouffe 1979: 182). These groups included the *hacendados* (landowners), landless peasants, and unemployed workers, who were all, in different ways, affected by the sugar corporations. All these groups contributed to the PPD's landslide victory in 1944, in which it won 34 of the 35 electoral districts and 73 of the 77 municipalities (Quintero-Rivera 1985: 83). However, it was the incorporation of pro-independence advocates into the colonial state apparatus and of nationalist rhetoric into the PPD's program that contributed most to the neutralization of separatist elements. This trend, a precursor of what is today popularly known as *melonismo,* formed the basis for the PPD's "intellectual and moral leadership," almost since the party's inception.[9]

An important tactic leading to the consolidation of PPD's local power was its development of social programs congruent with U.S. strategic interests in the island. The PPD initiated land reforms and laws on minimum wages and labor conditions, most of which were extensions of U.S. congressional measures or of the New Deal program of President Theodore Roosevelt and thus did not threaten American interests on the island (Pantojas-García 1990). However, these measures allowed the PPD to institute a patronage system that generated for it a mass of political support while reinforcing the popular impression that the party could deliver on its promises of social justice. These policies also led to the expansion of the colonial state and the relegitimization of colonialism while providing an infrastructure for semi-autonomous administration that strengthened the colonial government on the island and the PPD bureaucracy.

In turn, Muñoz Marín's focus on economic development soon turned the PPD into a party of accommodation rather than of resistance to colonization. By 1946 the pro-independence faction of the PPD was accused of undermining the PPD government's plan for economic development prior to the resolution of the status issue. That same year the Puerto Rican Independence Party (PIP) was formed; it remains the most popular party advocating independence on the island. By then, however, emphasis on economic development and the enduring repression of the nationalists had strengthened the U.S. hold on Puerto Rico, and independence was seen by the PPD leadership as neither economically or politically feasible. As Luis Muñoz Marín saw it, "The dichotomy [between independence and statehood] could hardly be more unrealistic. The Puerto Rican economy could not withstand, without a tragic collapse, the economic and fiscal conditions of independence, nor the fiscal conditions and the compulsory uniform federal legislation involved in federated statehood" (Muñoz Marín 1959: 5-6).

The historical response to this dilemma was the constitution of the commonwealth in 1952, which turned Puerto Rico into a "free associated state" of the United States, thereby providing political autonomy at the local level while maintaining Puerto Rico in a colonial relationship. Although hailed as a local invention, the commonwealth was both directed and ratified by the U.S. Congress within the constraints of the Federal Relations Act, which stipulated the applicability of all federal laws to the island. The commonwealth has been rightly interpreted as an accommodation on the part of the new elites, descendants of landowners and the new professionals, who required both local governmental autonomy and American capital to constitute themselves as a hegemonic class within the constraints of colonialism (Quintero-Rivera 1985).

With the establishment of the commonwealth, Puerto Rico's colonial situation was institutionalized and cultural nationalism and political accommodation took precedence in the PPD program. By this time, there was a marked decrease in the use of nationalist rhetoric by the PPD (which had initially used it to forge alliances with labor) and the most fervent advocates of independence. Rodríguez-Castro notes that by his later speeches Muñoz had gradually ceased to refer to Puerto Rico as a nation, using instead the word "culture," as the two hegemonic principles of the Puerto Rican elites of the time, nationalism and developmentalism, converged in the PPD program (Rodríguez-Castro 1993). By the late 1950s, the focus was on cultural identity within the colonial status rather than on independence; and the issue of Puerto Rico's nationality was already presented as one of cultural identity. The *patria* (country) was now about "the colors of the landscape, the changes of seasons, the smell of the earth wet with fresh rain. . . . but more than anything, 'patria' is the people, their way-of-life, spirit, folkways, songs, the way of getting along with each other" (Muñoz Marín 1959: 5).

In this way, the PPD deemphasized separatist nationalism, although its appropriation of nationalist symbols such as the flag and the national anthem as official symbols of the Puerto Rican Commonwealth in 1952 attested to the continued importance that nationalist symbols and rhetoric would have in establishing legitimacy within the new colonial arrangement.

To the outside world the newly founded commonwealth was presented as a "breakthrough from nationalism" (Muñoz Marín 1959) that could serve as an international example. Cultural nationalism was a non-nationalism that relied on love of country and cultural identity, not on "petty" attitudes that led to communism, nuclear war, revolutions, and the other "big troubles" of the 1950s: "Some of us confused love of the homeland with a narrow and petty concept of the national state. We felt that love of Puerto Rico had as a necessary corollary the desire for separate independence. We had not yet comprehended that no law, divine or human, demands that countries must be suspicious, vain and hostile, and that they must live separate from other countries whose peoples are a part of the broad equality which the Lord created on earth" (Muñoz Marín 1959: 5).

Thus, the promotion of cultural nationalism by the Popular Democratic Party, along with its adoption of developmental and political policies, contributed to the ongoing neutralization of separatist nationalism on the island and the consolidation of both U.S. and local interests into the commonwealth itself. An examination of the cultural policies of the period will show how after this time culture was integrated into the PPD's modernizing ideology of development to form a rhetoric for effecting social change, development, and progress. The mission given to the Institute of Puerto Rican Culture in the 1950s to "promote cultural development" and the popular perception that "the PPD is the only party that cares for and safeguards Puerto Rican culture" exemplify the confluence of the PPD program with ideas of cultural nationalism and economic development.

Early Cultural Policies and the Consolidation of Cultural Nationalism

During the 1950s, the PPD consolidated its power and laid the economic and political foundations of contemporary Puerto Rican society. The commonwealth, Operation Bootstrap (Puerto Rico's export-led industrialization model), and the cultural policies at work today all originated in this period of social, economic, and political change. Much has been said about Operation Bootstrap, which transformed Puerto Rico's agrarian economy into an industrial one, triggered mass unemployment and migration to the United States, and converted Puerto Rico into an international "showcase of development" (Safa 1974, Bonilla and Campos 1985). Less emphasis is given to "Operation Serenity," Operation Bootstrap's cultural and social counterpart, through which the Institute of Puerto Rican Culture and later its affiliated cultural centers were founded.

Operation Serenity was meant to fulfill the spiritual needs of a people whose political and economic needs were being taken care of by the commonwealth and Operation Bootstrap. The concept was first espoused by Muñoz Marín in the mid-1950s, although allusions to the overall program were already evident in the Division of Community Education (DIVEDCO), a grassroots education program established in 1949. Operation Serenity aimed to provide a sense of spiritual balance to a society threatened by the rapid social change caused by the new economic policies. The idea was to prepare the peasantry for modernity while protecting them from the devastating effects of materialism and consumerism, which were seen as threatening the moral basis on which Puerto Rican nationality was perceived to rest; hence the need to promote more "education than conspicuous consumption, . . . more imagination than acquisitiveness" (Muñoz Marín 1956: 2).

In turn, Operation Serenity marked an important moment in the development of Puerto Rico's cultural nationalism, involving a romanticization and purification of culture by reference to an idealized past. At this time, we see the cultural policies developing an anticapitalist discourse that idealized a precapitalist moral utopia and exalted the very ways of life that were being eradicated by the expansion of capitalist production.[10] Specifically, the new cultural policies were advanced in a context of rapid change. The economic policies of industrialization were affecting the rural economy and spurring migratory flows to urban areas and to the United States.[11] The very rural lifestyle that was being eradicated by the government's own economic policies was now idealized in images of a rural utopia that were said to represent the essence of Puerto Ricanness. In this way, government cultural policies became important channels to reinforce the ideological underpinnings of the PPD populist government: modernity and progress accompanied by the strengthening of cultural pride among the citizenry.

Various cultural programs were instituted in governmental departments at this time,[12] but it was in DIVEDCO and, later, the Institute of Puerto Rican Culture that the culturalist program was most directly forged.[13] Although differing in emphasis, with DIVEDCO focusing on community education and the institute on defining the elements of Puerto Rican nationality, both agencies functioned as important "ideological state apparatus" (Althusser 1971) of the new commonwealth administration. That is, they not only served to convey the ideological underpinnings of the PPD government but also functioned as material representations of the PPD's ideology in institutions that enjoyed relative autonomy from the state yet were key in securing its reproduction. Let us consider the case of DIVEDCO.

DIVEDCO centered around mobile educational and literacy workshops presented mostly in rural communities by regional supervisors allocated to governmental districts and charged with reaching all municipalities. As would be the case later on for the ICP, these supervisors and the majority of DIVEDCO's artists and creative personnel were recruited from the Popular Democratic Party and the Puerto Rican Independence Party (PIP). This helped foster a patronage network among these groups and further bolster PPD's image as the legitimate guardian and leader of the nation despite the colonial implications of the PPD's political program.

DIVEDCO worked mostly through visual materials. Millions of booklets and posters were produced and distributed in rural communities along with hundreds of short films that served as the basis for staff-led community meetings and discussions. These materials covered a vast array of issues but were generally aimed at advising people on how to deal with modernization and adapt to changes in family structure, diet, and other aspects of social life. Through stories, poems, and informational brochures, the program promoted new ways to happiness in modern life such as the self-management of health, nutrition, and family planning as well as self-reliance, education, and a generally modest lifestyle. Thus in the booklet "La Familia" (1967; first published in the 1950s) families were advised to plan and limit the number of their children, to consider children's economic requirements, and to consult with health professionals and educators about family planning. Another booklet, entitled "La Trampa" ("The Trap," 1961), warns readers against the evils of consumerism, which tricks people through special offers, free merchandise, bargains, and lay-a-away plans. People are encouraged to develop modest spending habits, plan their budgets, and, faced with a seemingly unlimited supply of consumer goods, not to confuse the essential and the superfluous. Yet, at the same time, consumerism was promoted through the introduction of imported new foodstuffs, and DIVEDCO recommended that meat, fish, eggs, vegetables, and fruit be added to the traditional diet of rice, coffee, sugar, yams, and beans ("Alimentos" [Food], 1952). Similarly, traditional beliefs, labeled superstitious, were also attacked and dismissed as "the product of ignorance and fear," while science was championed as the "product of research and truth" ("La ciencia contra la superstición" [Science against superstition], 1951).

DIVEDCO, however, did more than ease people's transition to modernity. It also helped to curb social unrest through messages of compliance and self-control that were filled with contradictions. Lauria's (1991) discussion of DIVEDCO films notes the emphasis on modest consumer lifestyles and on discouraging the material aspirations from which poverty excluded most Puerto Ricans. Again, a booklet on emigration counseled potential Puerto Rican migrants to the United States to comply with the U.S. assimilationist policies of the time. They are exhorted to

"integrate harmoniously" into the receiving culture and "to contribute to the betterment and the enlargement of the American
nation." In contrast, those who stayed in Puerto Rico were instructed to affirm and expand their way of being Puerto Rican
("Emigración," 1966; originally published in the 1950s).

DIVEDCO's approach to Puerto Rican culture also contributed to the promotion of cultural nationalism by the local pro-
commonwealth government. It proffered a nonconflictual,
spiritually based view of culture and lifestyle within a context in
which the prerogative of the colonial political powers was taken
for granted. Puerto Rico was presented as "culturally unique,"
often using images that would be developed further by the ICP:
"We are a great family living on this island, which God knew to
situate between Europe and America and which is our *patria*.
What unites us is a past of almost five centuries. Three different
races and cultures gave life and meaning to the Puerto Rican, the
Indian or Taino, the Spaniard, and the black or African race" ("El
Guardarrayas," 1966). Meanwhile, the duty of the Puerto Rican,
to work and contribute to the expansion of Puerto Rican civilization, is an overriding theme in many of the booklets, as is the
strength and continuity of Puerto Rican culture and its legacy.
For instance, the Taino, Puerto Rico's pre-Columbian population,
is presented as "the good heritage which neither the television,
the airplane, [nor] the sport shirt has been able to erase" ("Isla
y pueblo" [Island and People], 1968). The spiritually based definition of culture that characterized discussions at this time was also
reflected in DIVEDCO's written materials: "We understand that
culture refers more to values of the soul, to spiritual values.
Culture, as we understand it here, refers to feelings and attitudes
of the people, to what men [*sic*] are, more than to what they
have" ("Emigración," 1966).

In 1956 the PPD adopted a more overt role in defining Puerto
Rican culture through the creation of the Institute of Puerto Rican
Culture. In the ICP the spiritually based definition of culture

would be further developed by Ricardo Alegría, the anthropologist who directed the institution for eighteen years (1956-79). For Alegría culture served as a synonym for nationality and the spiritual values that he believed characterized Puerto Rican culture. Among these he listed: "Our profound humanitarianism, our commitment to equality, which is manifested in our *mestizaje* and exemplary social livelihood, our love for democracy, liberty, peace and civility, our devotion to culture . . . " (Alegría 1973: 11). Puerto Rico's colonial status is ignored in these spiritual definitions, which emphasize the sovereignty of the nation irrespective of the island's subordinate political situation. In this way, the ICP would help the PPD legitimize Puerto Rican nationality within the new semi-independent yet mostly contingent commonwealth status; at the same time it helped reinforce this status by channeling any separatist goals into art and cultural programs rather than into political action.

Within the ICP, Puerto Rican values would also become operationalized in a program that centered around specific and distinguishable building blocks of nationality. Yet, as will be evident in the next chapter, the modernizing premises of these early cultural policies remained in the ICP's emphasis on education and on promoting local *desarrollo cultural* (cultural development), which entailed embracing Puerto Rican culture as defined by the institute. However, the creation of an institution for the sole purpose of promoting Puerto Rican culture did not come about without resistance.

Defenders and Saboteurs of Culture: The Political Base for the Creation of the ICP

While the government had begun to define Puerto Rican identity in its cultural policy, as exemplified by DIVEDCO, this was never a central priority until the founding of the Institute of Puerto Rican Culture. Thus, more than any other cultural initiative, the ICP faced great opposition from the island intellectuals of the time, who were oriented to a Europeanized "occidentalist" culture and saw little need for an "indigenous" culture. In addition, Puerto Ricans had been subject to policies aiming at converting them into rightful American citizens since soon after U.S. occupation of the island. These policies, which instituted English as the official language of schooling from the early 1900s until 1948, turned the mass education system into a primary medium to teach children about American laws and institutions and to promote American values and the veneration of American symbols (Negrón de Montilla 1990). In this context, the proposal to establish an institute for the sole purpose of advancing Puerto Rican culture met with resistance. Opponents ranged from those who questioned whether Puerto Rico possessed a culture that merited such an enterprise to those who feared open demonstrations of identity and others who were apprehensive that the project would actually limit the scope of Puerto Rican culture.

The debate was long and arduous. Nevertheless, in 1955 Puerto Rico's legislature passed Law 89, which created the Institute of Puerto Rican Culture to "conserve, promote, enrich and disseminate the cultural values of the *pueblo* of Puerto Rico and bring about their broadest and most profound knowledge and appreciation" (Law 89, June 21, 1955, in E. Harvey 1988: 34). Rather than describe Puerto Rico as a "nation," the law used the less charged "pueblo," which designates a distinct community, although its purpose was to create an institution that promoted the island's national culture. This mission was not openly acknowledged until much later, as in the institution's eighteenth-year report, where it was listed as including the "study, conservation, dissemination and enrichment of our national culture" (Alegría 1973: 7).

During the legislative debate, the three ideologically opposed political parties (pro-independence, pro-commonwealth, and pro-statehood) voiced concerns that still frame and permeate contemporary debates about Puerto Rico's cultural policy. A main point of contention was whether the institute would lead to a *dirigismo cultural* (cultural authoritarianism) of the party in power (then the PPD) over the rest of society. Both of the minority political parties (PNP and PIP) feared that the institute would serve as a tool to transmit PPD ideology by selectively emphasizing ideas and historical events that were compatible with party objectives.

These concerns were not ill-founded. The PPD in fact controlled the entire state bureaucracy, from the Education Department to the government radio station (WIPR), through which the writings and thoughts of its leader, Luis Muñoz Marín, were disseminated. Opponents feared that the Institute of Puerto Rican Culture would end up writing the "history of the greatness and the achievements of the immense Popular Party" (Commonwealth of Puerto Rico 1955: 1898). Attempting to limit the risk of *dirigismo cultural,* the pro-independence party representative, Ramírez de Irizarry, proposed to limit the powers of the ICP so that it would not be in the position of formulating an official interpretation of Puerto Rican history: "If enriching or promoting or disseminating [Puerto Rican culture] involves some men having the responsibility for selecting, evaluating and choosing from the range of Puerto Rican values . . . to prefer one interpretation over another and to place all the weight of official backing on one interpretation, then, in my judgment that would be to direct toward specific cultural values. . . . People who do not accept that interpretation would lose their cultural liberty" (ibid., 1894).

PPD representatives challenged their opponents on both technical and ideological grounds. They argued that the proposed institute could not promote or disseminate something that had not first been judged to be significant. Ideologically, they presented themselves as "defenders of the nation," dismissing any criticism of their policy as contrary to the "true essence of the project, against the exaltation of Puerto Rican values" (ibid., 1897). PPD representatives also appealed to the stated aims of

Operation Serenity—to safeguard Puerto Rican culture from the consumerism and excessive materialism that were perceived to be the result of industrialization. As Polanco Abreu put it, "This project aims to create an organism that can identify and give personality and find the soul of the Puerto Rican of today. . . . Should Puerto Ricans today try to find their true personality, or should they continue living day by day not worrying beyond material things?" (ibid., 1906).

PNP representatives also voiced concerns about the institute's local and national outlook, as their party promoted a universalist view of culture that did not conflict with their ideal of U.S. statehood for Puerto Rico. The PNP representative, Luis Ferré, later governor of Puerto Rico (1968-72), argued that

> culture is not static, but rather, culture progresses, and Puerto
> Rican culture today is a culture that came with roots in Spain
> and has already grown roots in the Anglo Saxon culture, and is
> therefore a new culture that is daily growing in strength and
> that aspires for progress and liberty. . . . Any plan to defend the
> culture through static models, through a regression to things of
> the past, is a great danger. . . . As our party wishes that Puerto
> Rico may continue to adapt to the new norms of Western de-
> mocracy and that Puerto Rico may progress in its culture and
> not be directed through governmental mandates that could de-
> stroy liberty, we have to oppose this project. (Ferré 1995: 1906)

The PNP was not alone in appealing to occidentalist concep-tions of culture. Rampant in the debate were appeals to intrinsic artistic values and intellectual freedom, references from Western literature and culture ranging from Aristotle to John Stuart Mill, and definitions of culture drawn from the dictionary of the Span-ish Royal Academy.

Finally, and despite much criticism from both the pro-statehood and the pro-independence minorities, the law was passed and the institute was founded. In turn, as Puerto Rico's heritage became institutionalized in the ICP, it was also appropriated by the PPD, which had won not only the debate but with it the exclusive right to manipulate the symbolic material from which definitions of Puerto Rican culture would be forged. Thereafter, advocates of statehood who had been the project's most vociferous rivals were excluded from participating in the creation of the ICP. In sharp contrast, members of the pro-independence party were sought after and incorporated in its development and operation while the PPD continued to renew itself by incorporating and transforming *independentista* materials and discourses. Indeed, the *independentistas* supplied many of the ICP's administrators, including its first two directors as well as the artistic core of the institution.

The involvement of pro-independence sectors was received with great optimism by those I talked to who had participated in the cultural initiatives of this period, for their acceptance into the cultural sphere countered their persecution in greater Puerto Rican society. However, as the popular epithet for the ICP's projects (*las finquitas de los pips,* or the PIP's farms) attests, their involvement entailed not only the development of the ICP as the PIP's symbolic "private property"[14] but also the strategic enclosure of *independentistas* within the ICP. This served to camouflage the overt and covert political surveillance to which they were continually subjected, even within the ICP itself. This surveillance by the local commonwealth government, which many had suspected, was not fully revealed until the 1990s, when it was disclosed that police dossiers had been compiled on many *independentistas,* including well-known cultural leaders within and outside the ICP structure. Its containment of the pro-independence sector, both under pro-statehood and pro-commonwealth administrations, reveals the ICP's role as another accommodative institution within the colonial government.

The 1955 debate marked a turning point in the consolidation of the PPD's local power and the constitution of a "field of opinion" or "the locus of confrontation of competing discourses" (Bourdieu 1977: 168) in which the PPD emerged as the defender of Puerto Rican culture. Thus, years after the legislative debate over the creation of the ICP, discussions about Puerto Rican culture recycle the same ideas: PNP supporters are criticized as saboteurs of Puerto Rican national culture who favor the dissemination of a universalist, occidentalist view of culture through the state's cultural institutions; the PPD's adherents are still hailed as the true defenders of Puerto Rican culture. These charges ignore the fact that the PPD administration helped to promote the same "occidentalist" high-art forms that have since become popularly associated with the PNP. In fact, four years after the ICP was given a mere $35,000 for its general budget, the PPD administration in 1959 assigned almost six times that amount to the Casals Festival, a classical music festival that was awarded a total of $230,000. Yet the general impression of the PPD as the defender of Puerto Rico's traditional culture, of the ICP as the guardian of Puerto Rican nationality, and the PNP as the major threat to both continues to permeate debates on culture and to frame interpretations of all cultural policy island-wide.

The PPD's victorious claim to culture, however, would have to be constantly defended as discussions about culture continued to be contested and linked to partisan politics. During the 1980s a "cultural war" erupted to which informants within the ICP structure trace the "politicization of Puerto Rican culture," a term commonly used to designate the maneuvering of culture around party lines. It should be remembered, however, that culture was never truly free from politico-partisan manipulations in Puerto Rico.

The Culture Wars

After its establishment in 1956, the ICP remained identified with the PPD and with the *independentistas*. The political composition of the institute's staff remained almost unaltered by changes in government administration (from the PPD to the PNP in 1968), giving the institution an image of permanence and neutrality that contrasted with most government institutions. In 1979, however, the situation changed when the new PNP administration (1976–80) introduced the broadest cultural legislation since the creation of the ICP, directly threatening its position as the government's sole organ for culture.

The PNP measures called for the establishment of an umbrella cultural organization, the Administración para el Fomento de las Artes y la Cultura (the Administration for the Promotion of the Arts and Culture, or AFAC), whose mission was to consolidate all artistic and cultural activity within a single government body. The newly founded fine arts center, the symphonic orchestra, and the theatrical arts were placed under the jurisdiction of the AFAC, giving it an air of high culture contrasting with the more folk-oriented emphasis of the ICP. ICP supporters saw the AFAC as a threat to Puerto Rico's national culture and to the institute's own dominance in cultural matters. The proposal was criticized as an example of *dirigismo cultural*, although this time the charge was leveled against the PNP.

Since the 1960s, when the PNP first came to power, some party officials had promoted the idea of a "creole statehood" in order to enhance the appeal of statehood status. In this conception, Puerto Ricans would retain enough autonomy to defend their language and cultural identity under statehood. Yet PNP cultural policies betrayed such claims in their "high" cultural content, which many interpreted as a strategy to disseminate annexationist ideas and promote a "universal" culture in place of Puerto Rico's autochthonous culture. The threat posed by the PNP's cultural policies was increased by the party's claim that it would bring Puerto Rico to statehood by the next electoral term and by its appointment of a pro-statehood activist and nuclear chemist, Leticia del Rosario, as director of the Institute of Puerto

Rican Culture. Del Rosario was mistrusted almost immediately because of her lack of connections with the arts and intellectual communities on the island. Moreover, her assertion that she would initiate a vigorous fight against the "communists, socialists and *populares* [PPD supporters] who dominated the ICP" made the continuing political persecution of the *independentistas* publicly visible and further heightened fears about the new cultural policies (*Redacción El Mundo* 1983).

Pro-statehood supporters defended their project, asserting that their purpose was not to hinder but to enhance culture through an agency with greater governmental powers. They argued that their proposal would also expand the vision of Puerto Rican culture beyond the "restricted folkloric" perspective that the ICP had always promoted. They now claimed the same right to be *puertorriqueñistas* as any other party. A statement made in 1980 by Carlos Romero Barceló, then governor of Puerto Rico, is a good example of this kind of rhetoric: "What we want is that culture should expand, that Puerto Rican culture should extend its horizons. The culture that remains closed, that does not give way to new currents, wherever they come from, and then choose among those that fit better with our way of being and our personality, that culture dies and becomes petrified" (quoted in Seijo Bruno 1980).

Making democratic claims for culture, the pro-statehood factions denied that only the supporters of the PIP and PPD could claim to be *puertorriqueñistas* and as such solely entitled to speak about culture. The pro-statehood partisans presented the PPD and PIP as "elitists and intellectuals" who were disengaged from the true needs of the people, for whom statehood would mean security, not the abolition of their Puerto Rican identity. These assertions were a reelaboration of a populist PNP campaign motto of the time, "La estadidad es para los pobres" (statehood is for the poor), which presented statehood as the best solution for the Puerto Rican poor (Ramos 1987). The PNP discourse also invoked their love for and loyalty to the nation as proof of their patriotism and their own claim to express such feelings. As Leticia del Rosario, first PNP director of the ICP, put it:

> There is a belief that in order to be a true intellectual or a patriot one has to be an *independentista,* but things are changing. The other Puerto Ricans who are not separatists [identified with the PIP] or autonomists [PPD affiliated] are finally awakening. Everyone has the right to love the fatherland [*patria*] in the way they want, and the right to culture and to develop as intellectuals and to express their Puerto Ricanness in the widest way possible without the narrow limits imposed by the greedy pro-independence elite. (M. Ortiz 1980)

Despite their democratic claims, two problems lay behind the demands of the pro-statehood groups: their ideological commitment to statehood, which required them to explain how Puerto Ricans would be able to legislate autonomously on cultural matters under U.S. statehood; and the fact that their claims were contradicted by their own politically motivated vision of what Puerto Rican culture should be. PNP founder Luis Ferré stated that the party's objective was to promote *una cultura sin apellidos* (a culture without surnames) (*Redacción El Nuevo Día* 1980)—that is, a "universal" culture, one that is not national and that would not constitute an obstacle to the future incorporation of Puerto Rico as an American state.

But in the colonial context of Puerto Rico, this kind of universalist idea has always had dangerous implications because culture remains the most important basis for defining Puerto Rico's national identity. Most Puerto Rican intellectuals saw the ICP as the guardian of Puerto Rican culture and the vehicle for defending it against the threat of Americanization. Any threat to the institute was taken as a threat to Puerto Rican nationality. Even other government cultural agencies founded during PNP administrations

(1968–72, 1976–80), such as the folklife division of Puerto Rico's Economic Development Administration (Fomento), are still regarded within the ICP as appropriating its own legitimate mission.

Moreover, the PNP's charge that the Hispanophile tendencies of the ICP were elitist was undermined by its appeal to a "universal" culture with equally elitist associations. This was evident during the highly publicized public hearings about the proposed cultural policy in the 1980s. At this time the dichotomy between universal and traditional views of culture deepened, and they came to be seen as two irreconcilable and politically opposed poles. Colonial and classist metaphors permeated the discussion. PNP supporters presented their cultural project (AFAC) as an institution that would limit itself to "universal" culture, leaving the "autochthonous" culture to the ICP. The autochthonous was loosely summed up by a proponent of the measure as a "jíbara ñangotá en el campo bebiendo café en una dita" (a female peasant kneeling in the countryside to drink coffee from a coconut cup), whereas universal culture was compared to "un señor sentado en un flamante restaurante, tomando café con toda la expresión de lo que es buen gusto" (a man sitting in a famous restaurant, drinking coffee in an expression of everything that constitutes good taste) (*Redacción Claridad* 1980). In this metaphor, female and male, rural and urban, kneeling and sitting, and even hand-made and manufactured utensils, are opposed to convey the inferior standing of autochthonous culture in relation to the universal.

Despite numerous protests from artists and organized groups, the PNP policies were approved by the PNP-dominated Senate on April 20, 1980. By then it was evident that a culture war had begun. A group of long-time workers at the Institute of Puerto Rican Culture, along with artists and university students who had organized as the "Committee for the Defense of Puerto Rican Culture," became more militant in their mission. They feared the realization of prophecies voiced by many intellectuals, including Ricardo Alegría, that "Puerto Rico was on its way to losing its national culture for a universal culture" (Cabán 1980). Throughout the island, ICP-affiliated cultural centers became the site of battles between the PNP and the PPD as many PNP members entered these traditional PPD strongholds with the support of the PNP-controlled municipal governments.[15]

After three years of cultural strife, the ICP's first PNP-affiliated director, Leticia del Rosario, was forced to resign in June 1983. Her resignation, front-page news in the four national newspapers, was presented as an example of the PNP's inability to legislate on cultural matters and became a campaign issue in the 1984 elections. Then, with culture a major concern, the PPD returned to power with the overt intention of promoting the island's cultural identity. "Much More Puerto Ricanness" (F. Jiménez 1985) was the theme of the new cultural policies instituted by the PPD in 1985. AFAC was abolished and greater power was given to the ICP. Its director was promoted to the rank of government secretary, and the ICP was further decentralized with the establishment of four regional offices charged with supervising the work of ICP-affiliated cultural centers throughout the island.

Through a "Plan to Revitalize the Cultural Centers," legislative grants were conferred on ICP-affiliated cultural centers to buy materials and renovate their physical facilities. A series of traveling programs and conferences were organized at the national level to be carried out at the local centers; and Spanish was instituted as Puerto Rico's sole official language rather than sharing the position with English.[16] Ironically, the move toward more "puertorriqueñidad" was accompanied by a renewed Hispanophile emphasis, in which the "occidentalist" tendencies of Puerto Rican intellectuals surfaced once more. Thus, the culmination of the new pro–Puerto Rican policies was the creation of the Commission for the Celebration of Puerto Rico's Quincentennial, through which the PPD administration emphasized Puerto Rico's ties with the "motherland" through activities, exchanges, and highly publicized official visits to Spain. The celebration also featured a highly publicized regatta to commemorate Columbus's "discovery" of the island, and the opening of a Puerto Rico pavilion in Seville. The official activities were accompanied by free nationwide public celebrations with strong cultural nationalist overtones.

The Rise of the Annexationist Party

Despite the electoral success of the PPD in the 1980s, transformations in Puerto Rican society were making it increasingly difficult for the party to maintain its local dominance. The industrialization strategy had caused unemployment, underemployment, and poverty to increase, especially in urban areas. By 1970, 65.2 percent of the population was living below the poverty line. Unemployment, which had stood at 11.2 percent in 1970, peaked at 22 percent in 1977 (USDC 1979). Local government control of Puerto Rico's economy diminished throughout the 1970s, as the economy shifted from a labor-intensive model to a capital-intensive one that relied mostly on exemptions from federal taxation and thus on the United States rather than on local government prerogatives (Baver 1993). An important aspect of this change was the enactment in 1976 of Section 936 of the Internal Revenue Code, which facilitated the repatriation of profits of U.S. corporations operating on the island to parent companies located on the mainland and provided a variety of tax breaks to manufacturing and export-services activities covering income, property, municipal fees, and manufacturing intangibles. Moreover, federal transfers (such as welfare, social security, and food stamps), which bypassed the commonwealth government, increased the island's economic dependency on the United States and strengthened the appeal of statehood as the only political option that could assure the continuation of these transfers. From 1960 to 1976, transfer payments increased 1,974 percent (from $78.1 million to $1.6 billion) (Pantojas-García 1990: 123).

The rise in poverty and unemployment on the island allowed

the PNP to present itself as an alternative for the poor and to develop a popular base for the statehood option. Previously associated with the local bourgeoisie, beginning in the late 1960s the statehood party began to develop into an intraclass movement in which the discourses of equality and social justice became important bases for political mobilization. "La estadidad es para los pobres" (statehood is for the poor) and the idea of an *estadidad jíbara* (creole statehood) were important concepts through which the PNP aimed to present statehood as an option for the poor and to suggest a way of maintaining enough autonomy to protect the island's linguistic and cultural identity within statehood (Ramos 1987, Meléndez 1993). Indeed, the PNP held power intermittently in the 1970s and early 1980s, and most recently since 1992, on the basis of similar claims that it would promote social renewal and equality and maintain Puerto Rican culture.

The 1970s also saw the strengthening of the left. The base of support for the pro-independence party increased in the 1976 elections, and the PIP and the Socialist Party adopted socialist and Marxist-Leninist platforms respectively. The University of Puerto Rico became an important locus of political action as the site of numerous student revolts and other cultural and political initiatives. The left's resurgence was also evident in the growing number of labor strikes, with an average of eighty-six per year in the 1970s (García and Quintero-Rivera 1986) and in the rise of the environmental and feminist movements. These developments were accompanied in turn by a rise in political repression. (The killing of two *independentistas* in the still-debated Cerro Maravilla case of 1978 is a vivid embodiment of the climate of the times.) This repression, coupled with the PIP's failure to move beyond its strong petit bourgeois component of professionals and intellectuals to attract a populist constituency, diminished the base of support for the PIP following its peak in the 1970s (Carrión 1980).

Conversely, the PNP began to accrue support not only from the marginal economic sectors but also from what has been called

Puerto Rico's new petite bourgeoisie, an economic sector associated with government employment and nonproductive forms of labor created by the government to counter growing unemployment. In Pantojas-García's words, "the PPD had dug its own grave" because the forces behind the PNP were the direct creation of the capital import-export strategy initiated by the PPD (Pantojas-García 1990: 131). These changes were evident in the 1976 election, in which the PNP won almost 50,000 more votes than the PPD.[17] The PPD remained undefeated in some municipalities, including the city of Caone, and it returned to power from 1984 to 1992. Yet the 1976 elections showed that the PNP would continue to be a serious threat to the political dominance of the PPD. Politically, the PNP and the PPD differ only slightly, as is clear from the popular saying, "estadidad a corto o a largo plazo" (statehood in the short term or in installments), which describes the respective political goals of the PNP and PPD. The economic policies of the two dominant parties are also very similar. Both favor the continuation of some kind of political relationship with the United States, and the PNP's economic policies, like those of the PPD, have been responsive to the interests of transnational capital. The most substantial difference between these dominant parties is that, unlike the PNP, the PPD can appeal to the economic advantages provided by commonwealth status, such as the tax incentives of Section 936 and the exemption from federal taxes. These are also the prerogatives of commonwealth status that have been most subject to attack in the U.S. Congress. In 1996, PPD's advantage was further diminished when the Congress voted to discontinue Section 936 at the end of a ten-year phase-out period, ignoring appeals by PPD politicians.

On issues related to culture, however, the PPD remains a resilient contender as the PNP has not been able to answer adequately the question of whether a distinct cultural identity can be preserved under statehood.[18] The party's vision of a creole statehood, under which Puerto Rico would maintain enough autonomy to protect its linguistic and cultural identity, has been limited by the likelihood that the U.S. Congress, rather than the PNP leadership, would ultimately decide these issues. This question was at the center of public debate on the island during the 1993 plebiscite; most people I talked to agreed that the U.S. Congress would have ultimate say on this issue if the island were to become a U.S. state. In fact, the PPD campaign challenged the PNP claim that it could protect Puerto Rican language and culture by quoting U.S. senators advocating that English be made the only official language in the United States. In this context, the cultural wars of the 1980s and PPD policies of "mucha más puertorriqueñidad" can be seen as direct outcomes of the ongoing consolidation of the idiom of culture as the most significant issue of political debate, particularly between what were emerging as two increasingly analogous political parties.[19]

New Players in Puerto Rico's Cultural Politics

With the issue of Puerto Rico's national identity becoming entrenched as the framework for debating politics, it is also through the local culture, not in appeals to universal values or reversals of the cultural nationalistic policies, that different local claims have since been framed. This is evident in the growth of new actors in Puerto Rican cultural politics, such as the many independent groups that sprang up during the 1970s and 1980s.

These new cultural groups and activities have been subject to a variety of interpretations. Some see them as a sign of the autonomous growth of cultural nationalism, or as proof of the intensity of Puerto Rico's commitment to its national culture, or as a "cultural show" conjured up by political parties to strengthen their popular base of support. For their part, Puerto Rican scholars have interpreted this growth as part of a "culture-oriented social movement" (Quintero-Rivera 1991: 97) and as the product of a larger resistance to colonialism in which people emphasize the local food, music, and other cultural aspects that are most threatened by the advance of commercial culture. Local scholars also emphasize the potential of these cultural initiatives to serve as basis for alternative politics (L.-M. González 1990) and their role as a contested terrain between popular and elite sectors of society, where subordinate groups recoup and manipulate dominant views of culture, such as against the growing commercialization of contemporary culture (Sánchez 1991). Also emphasized are the effects of the crisis of economic developmentalism and populism of the 1950s on the growth of cultural initiatives as alternatives at the comunity level. Similar processes have been linked with the growth of social movements in Latin America, which many associate with the inability of state-development strategies to meet the needs of popular classes (Escobar and Alvarez 1992).

However, the growth of cultural initiatives is indicative of more subtle and complex processes than have been recognized in previous research. Contemporary festivals do represent a culture-oriented social movement, but these celebrations do more than vent a nationalist pride; they also serve very specific and local needs of aspiring politicians, activists, and the unemployed and underemployed. These festivals are also a site of struggle and a potential basis for alternative politics but, as we shall see, these struggles are not limited to those between official and popular culture, or traditional versus commercial culture; the "official," "commercial," and "traditional" are also continually contested and manipulated by different segments of society.

This cultural revival has also been directly affected by local-level politics. While local scholars tend to see it as a self-generated reaction to the rise of pro-statehood forces, it is also important to note that, far from self-generated, the growth of cultural activities was directly affected by PPD's cultural policies of *mucha más puertorriqueñidad,* which provided financial assistance and grants for cultural activities at the local level. From the 1980s to the 1990s, the money allocated to these activities grew faster than at any other time in Puerto Rican history, rising from $517,000 in 1980 to a high of $3.78 million in 1989. This is a considerable amount when one considers that prior to the 1980s funding for grassroots cultural groups had generally remained constant, and had actually decreased before the 1980s.[20] This figure does not include the "pork-barrel" contributions of local legislators to their constituencies, which were also channeled to these celebrations. The total amount of these contributions (most of them ranging from one to two thousand dollars) is impossible to ascertain precisely, but the four area senators and representatives I interviewed during my research informed me that sports and cultural activities were the two main recipients of pork-barrel funds. In fact, these activities have become an ideal way for the politicians who vie to sponsor many of these events to present themselves as culturally aware citizens and *verdaderos puertorriqueños* (true Puerto Ricans), an identity that is becoming increasingly important in contemporary cultural politics. A PNP legislator I talked to stressed this point when he noted that while it had been difficult for PNP advocates to be publicly associated with Puerto Rican culture, these festivals were providing added channels to "disassociate culture from politics" (implying from PPD control) and to display PNP dedication to cultural issues through their support of grassroots festivals.

The growth of these activities has also been spurred by Puerto Rico's tourism office—it sponsors and lists as "folkloric festivals" the most "cultural" events (according to government standards) in *Qué Pasa,* its official guide to Puerto Rico—as well as by corporations using promotions and grassroots activities as important marketing tools. These entities provided an additional source of funding for grassroots groups, as will be further discussed.

Another factor behind the spread of these festivals is the emergence of an informal artistic and cultural sector, which includes everyone from food vendors to folk artists, from unemployed university graduates to the long-term unemployed and underemployed who depend upon cultural activities for their livelihood. Folk artists, in particular, play an important role in organizing many of these activities as a way to increase the market for their products.

The rise of the informal sector is a well-known but under-documented aspect of the Puerto Rican economy. The few works that have touched on the subject have recognized this sector's diversity, its extension to the middle classes (L. Ortiz 1992, Pantojas-García 1990), and its economic impact, which in 1984 was estimated to be over $2.5 billion (Auger Marchand 1987 quoted in L. Ortiz 1992). The festival circuit is a vital aspect of Puerto Rico's informal economy.[21] Some people even claimed to make more as vendors than in the formal sector, where salaries for entry-level positions requiring twelve to fourteen years of schooling range from $3.80 to $5.19 an hour.[22] Thus, it is common to find college-educated vendors who claim to be unable to earn enough, or even to find jobs, in the formal sector. One such vendor with a master's degree in criminal justice had worked as a civil servant prior to joining the festival circuit. He claimed to make or lose in a night what he used to earn in a month's work as a civic employee.

Festivals are therefore also a business, and the informal economy is not an "euphemism for poverty" but a vital solution to rising unemployment and underemployment that has developed "under the auspices of government tolerance" (Castells and Portes 1989: 27). Vendors can obtain permits more cheaply and easily for festivals than for other large-scale public events, such as patron saint festivities, which are organized by municipal administrations and where vending permits can cost thousands of dollars. It is also easier for vendors to sell without a permit in grassroots festivals because their reputation as cultural activities shields them from the monitoring that characterizes municipally organized activities.[23]

While the cultural revival is often romanticized as an example of the island's nationalistic fervor, the legitimacy of many cultural groups is the subject of much debate and controversy. Many activities presented as cultural festivals challenge dominant views about Puerto Rican culture; and while registered with the Puerto Rican Department of State in order to qualify for government grants and assignments from local politicians, their organizers are free from direct ICP control. The potential threat that these groups present to the government's cultural policy was evident during my research when, for the first time ever, Awilda Palau, then director of the ICP, questioned the legitimacy of ICP-affiliated cultural centers as the sole representatives of the central institution. Arguing that all local cultural groups should have the same relationship with the Institute of Puerto Rican Culture as ICP-affiliated cultural centers, Palau attempted to discontinue the exclusive relationship between ICP and these centers in terms of grants and programming. Her assertions were controversial on several levels. As the first pro-independence ICP director to be appointed by a PNP governor, she challenged the strict dichotomies of Puerto Rican politics in which *independentistas* are commonly perceived as the exclusive ideological allies of the PPD. She was immediately targeted by the opposition as a traitor for "complying" with the pro-statehood groups because her appointment had undermined the PPD's and the *independentistas'* contention that "PNP supporters do not care about Puerto Rican culture." In addition, her policies were controversial because they were perceived as a threat to the ICP and its exclusive control of cultural activities at the local level.[24]

In challenging the new policies, the ICP-affiliated cultural centers organized as the "Unitary Committee for the Defense of Puerto Rican Culture," a name similar to the one under which ICP staffers protested the PNP's cultural policies in the 1980s. They defended their position as the only legitimate representatives of the ICP by adopting the old argument upholding the ICP as the only legitimate defender of Puerto Rican culture. The argument of the ICP-affiliated centers and the ICP staff, most of whom sided with the centers in asking the governor to dismiss the director, concerned the experience and seniority of the affiliated centers and the inability of the independent centers to portray Puerto Rican national culture accurately. Argued a spokesperson of the committee, "How is it possible that we, who direct ourselves according to the ICP guidelines, and who have a clear image of Puerto Rican culture, should not have financial assistance from the ICP? It is not a matter of thinking small. We want many cultural groups to exist, but they all originate from the example of the affiliated cultural centers." Additionally, the committee emphasized the connections of local cultural centers with the central institution by stressing that their creation was not due to the exclusive will of a group of people but rather that they were "part of the ICP program to embrace the entire national territory in its work of conserving and enriching our culture."

Forced in the end to resign, the director was replaced by a new director who had previously worked with ICP-affiliated centers and was committed to strengthening their ties to the central organization. However, it is important to note that while there were local protests and condemnations of the director, there was no unified protest against the new policies comparable to that of the 1980s.[25] This suggests a certain loss of legitimacy by the Institute of Puerto Rican Culture in relation to the numerous groups that have emerged since the 1980s. By 1994 there was hesitancy to defend an institution that was never able to attain full legitimacy among the greater public, even though it is still regarded by many *independentistas* as the embodiment of nationality and as the "wall of contention" for Puerto Rico's colonial reality.

Perhaps the clearest indicator of this disentangling of Puerto Rico's nationalist ideology from the traditional players was the PNP's recourse (during the administration of 1992–96) to tactics similar to those that the PPD had employed and benefited from for so long. In contrast to the 1980s, the PNP purposely turned away from the concept of universal culture toward "a culture with a last name"—that is, one with a Puerto Rican identity. For instance, although the PNP criticized PPD spending on cultural policies during its last term in office, the PNP administration of 1992-96 avoided direct changes in PPD cultural policies. Instead, it sharply reduced government spending initiated during PPD government, favoring instead the "basic" issues of crime prevention, health, drugs, and education as governmental priorities. This contrasts sharply with the 1980s, when philosophical claims to a universal, more expansive culture were a means of attacking PPD policies.

In addition, during the 1993 plebiscite on the island's status, the PNP affirmed not only the permanence of Puerto Rican culture despite statehood but also the right to maintain Spanish as an official language and to safeguard the island's continued participation in Olympic sports events. Thus, during the plebiscite campaign the PNP pledged to make the state of Puerto Rico the first truly multiethnic "frontier state." PNP focused, for instance, on comparing the Puerto Rican flag and hymn with that of other states along with statistics on population, employment, income, and numbers of senators and representatives. The campaign aimed to stress Puerto Rico's unequal position relative to the states in the union while reminding the public of the diversity that is possible under statehood. PNP's ads featured a caption reading, "Under statehood, we would keep our hymn, flag, language and culture, besides obtaining the economic development that would assure us a better quality of life" (Partido Nuevo Progresista 1993).

The commonwealth option represented by the PPD prevailed in the plebiscite. The PPD countered PNP's claims with public statements by representatives of the English Only movement (such as Republican congressman Toby Roth), stressing that the entire U.S. Congress rather than local officials would ultimately determine the fate of Puerto Rican culture if the island became a federated state. Instead, continuing commonwealth status was presented as the only option that would guarantee both Puerto Rican culture and American citizenship or, as stated in the campaign slogan, "the best of both worlds" (*lo mejor de dos mundos*). Yet, almost indistinguishable claims and assertions for the defense of Puerto Rican culture were made by the three political parties representing different status options for the island. Moreover, the results of the 1993 plebiscite, in which the commonwealth option won over statehood by only 2.2 percent of the vote, showed that the distinctions about who is and who is not a defender of Puerto Rican culture will be increasingly difficult to maintain as other actors become involved in Puerto Rico's cultural politics and as the idiom of culture is no longer limited to specific political interests. Before discussing these dynamics, I will turn to an analysis of the ideas, definitions, and representations of Puerto Rican culture that became authenticated through the government cultural policies. While highly contested, these ideas have since provided a framework of debate and the foundation of government cultural policies.

Chapter II

The Institute of Puerto Rican Culture and the Building Blocks of Nationality

> The absence of an authentic culture is the death of the nation, its restoration, its resurrection. In this sense, nationalist monologism is a dialogical inversion of imperial ideology, caught willy-nilly in the position of a parody, antagonistic but dependent.
>
> —David Lloyd, *Adulteration and the Nation*

Since its inception the Institute of Puerto Rican Culture has been the main governmental agency in charge of shaping and disseminating an official view of what constitutes Puerto Rican culture. Yet, as we have seen, the ICP has historically served as a site of struggle in which social inequalities are manifested. In this chapter I analyze other repercussions of the ICP's project of defining and constituting images of Puerto Rican national identity. As the Introduction discussed, this process entails objectifying and delimiting the national community, however defined, and developing essentialist views of nationhood that are expressed through folklore or the evocation of idyllic pasts. In Puerto Rico these processes are evident in the folklorization of national culture, which constructs the myth of

Puerto Rican identity from the building blocks of the racial triad (Taino, African, Spanish), the idealization of the peasant past, and the "unifying" Hispanic heritage.

This chapter analyzes the processes by which these foundational elements of Puerto Rican culture were established, represented, and disseminated by the government cultural policy. These processes entailed the enhancement of some and the exclusion of other aspects of Puerto Rican culture. Thus, ideas and institutional structures geared at combating colonialism through the enhancement of Puerto Rican culture simultaneously served to reproduce some of the exclusions on which the nation was grounded.

The Initial Program

The ICP was founded as an official "autonomous" institution with a board of nine directors. Of these directors, however, eight would be named by the governor with the Senate's consent, assuring the governor direct links to the institution. Board membership was to be drawn from the principal intellectual organizations of the time, assuring the presence of the island's most prestigious writers, historians, musicians, and intellectuals.

The institution was given thirty mandates including the study and restoration of the historic, architectonic, and cultural patrimony of Puerto Rico, the organization of exhibitions, conferences, fairs, and festivals, and the creation of museums and the establishment of contests and scholarships. It was also made responsible for conducting archaeological, folkloric, and historical research and for coordinating all governmental cultural efforts that were related to the institution's mission in any way (text of law quoted in E. Harvey 1988: 36). All these goals were consistent with the search for a patrimony, a common process in the growth of nationalist projects through which the nation is grounded in a continuous past and its existence is affirmed through patrimony, heritage, and cultural property (Handler 1988, Kaplan 1994).

Most of the artists and intellectuals active in the ICP's early days conceived of the institute as a vehicle for national affirmation and resistance to colonization. They repeatedly described this era to me as one of renewal, regeneration, and overt resistance to U.S. imperialism. In this spirit, museums were built, local artists were promoted, and thousands of posters depicting "Puerto Ricanness" were printed and disseminated at ICP-sponsored activities. In fact, the new cultural policies represented an important reversal of the Americanization campaigns encouraged by the U.S. government after its occupation of the island. An example of the context in which these policies were shaped was provided by Ricardo Alegría, who recalled the replacement of Santa Claus with the Three Kings on government Christmas cards as one of the most important achievements of this period. Alegría said, "People were taught not to laugh at or be fearful of their culture. This is what we fought for." Thus it is no surprise that many of my informants in the ICP saw the origins of the current popularization of culture in these early initiatives. I was even told that "there would not be culture in Puerto Rico" if it were not for the early work of the ICP.

Yet it was not long before the ICP became the repository for the dominant ideas of Puerto Rican culture that had been elaborated by local elites in the nineteenth and early twentieth centuries. Although the organization's stated goals were to embrace all aspects of Puerto Rican culture, its initial program was soon characterized by a reliance on high culture, further illustrating the Hispanophile and occidentalist tendencies prevalent among Puerto Rican intellectuals. Among its first initiatives were the renovation of Spanish military structures and churches, the opening of the National Archives and the Publications Program, which focused on Puerto Rico's history under Spanish colonization, and the publication of poetry and literature elaborating the foundational myths of Puerto Rican culture. Similarly, most of the activities it sponsored centered on Western cultural expressions, such as performances of flamenco and Spanish dances by the Ballet of San Juan; readings of Spanish, Hispano-American, and Puerto Rican literature and poetry; choral, chamber music, and orchestral concerts; and art exhibitions (Instituto de Cultura Puertorriqueña 1960). The Promotions Program, through which ICP-affiliated local cultural centers were founded as "natural and preferred vehicles" for this programming, was also among the first initiatives of this time. Meanwhile, activities dealing with folklore, such as the folk art fairs that dominate so much contemporary programming, were also initiated in the 1960s; but they remained a peripheral rather than central part of the programming until the 1970s.

Many images used by Puerto Rico's literary elite since the nineteenth century as symbols of freedom and resistance became important components of the early ICP program. These included the *jíbaro*, or rural peasant, who had been associated with the creole culture in Manuel Alonso's 1849 *El Gíbaro*, a portrait of customs of the peasant population; and the indigenous population, the Taino, who were an important symbol of resistance in the nineteenth-century novels of Daniel Rivera and Eugenio María de Hostos.[1] While these elements had been associated with Puerto Rican culture since the nineteenth century, they had never been standardized or publicly embraced as part of Puerto Rico's national identity. Indeed, the racial syncretism of the island population had often been associated with the "weakening" and "disorganization" of the Puerto Rican character. This is evident in Antonio Pedreira's *Insularismo* (1985), the most influential essay of national interpretation in the 1930s, in which the superiority of the white Spanish race is contrasted to the "inherent inferiority" of the indigenous and African components of Puerto Rican nationality (Flores 1979). In the productions of the ICP, however, the racial mixing of the population and other ideas that had been associated with Puerto Ricanness were rid of their overtly racist implications as they become folklorized into images of harmonious integration. The institute's official seal came to represent this new relationship in its depiction of the three racial and ethnic strands—Taino, Spaniard, African—next to each other as equal foundational elements of Puerto Rican culture.

Especially in its initial stages, the ICP also served as a venue for the legitimation of the Popular Democratic Party through the exaltation of historical figures associated with the PPD's formation. Thus, one of the most important programs organized by the ICP during its first five years was a traveling exhibition on the life and works of Luis Muñoz Rivera, who was the father of the then governor, Luis Muñoz Marín, and the leader of the landowner-dominated Liberal Party, which was an important precursor to the PPD. This exhibit traveled to almost every town on the island.[2] In addition, Luis Muñoz Rivera's house and a mausoleum in his honor were among the first twelve structures to be constructed or restored during the first years of the ICP.

Perhaps the clearest example of how ICP-sponsored activities became permeated with strong politico-partisan overtones is the National Folk Arts Fair of Barranquitas. Founded in 1961 in Muñoz Rivera's hometown, this fair still provides an annual occasion for the PPD leadership to gather for speeches and to invoke the memory and legacy of Luis Muñoz Rivera.

The Turn to Folklore

Folklore was part of the ICP program from its inception, but it was only in the 1970s that the institution developed the central focus on folklore that persists to the present day. Peasant music, folk dances, and folk arts, conceived as ethnic markers of Puerto Rican identity, became the backbone of ICP programming. This change was accompanied by a decrease in ballet and classical music performances, which remained part of the programming in the 1960s but were almost entirely removed from the ICP program within a decade.

With the folklorization of Puerto Rican culture, its ethnic building blocks became articulated in all aspects of the ICP's program, from the musical genres and instruments to the folk arts that were deemed authentically Puerto Rican. Thus, typical instruments such as the *cuatro* (double five-string guitar), the *güiro* (gourd scraper), and the *bomba* drums are deemed to represent respectively the Spanish, Indian, and African influence upon Puerto Rican music. In the folk arts, the Afro-Caribbean *vejigante* masks, the Hispano-Christian wood saints, and the indigenous hammocks are continually presented as representatives of the same triad, which is also promoted in the traveling conference program. Conferences with such titles as "The Indian in Puerto Rican Poetry," "African Footsteps in Puerto Rico's Oral Storytelling," "Hispanic Influences in Puerto Rico's Oral Tradition," and "Indigenous, African, and Hispanic Influences in Puerto Rican Music" have been prevalent in the ICP's programming since the 1970s. The founding of the national folk-art dance troupe Areyto in 1970, which featured Europeanized "salon" dances along with peasant and Afro-Caribbean rhythms in its repertoire, is yet another example of the consolidation of the building blocks of Puerto Rican culture.

In turn, this emphasis on folklore by Puerto Rican intellectuals in the 1970s is not unique to Puerto Rico. The search for and emphasis on ethnic and local identities at this time was part of a concurrent worldwide trend that some have linked to the reconfiguration of hegemonic centers and to global economic changes since the 1970s (Friedman 1994). Similar movements toward rediscovering ethnic pasts and folklore were documented throughout Europe, Quebec, Brittany, and in many postcolonial contexts throughout the Caribbean (Badone 1992, Friedman 1994). Indeed, Puerto Rico saw great transformations in the 1970s, as the 1950s development strategies culminated in economic crisis, and the PPD's hegemonic aspirations were curtailed by the rise of the pro-statehood party.

These developments opened up spaces for local grassroots activism and the strengthening of the Puerto Rican left. Many of these movements developed cultural initiatives as a way of expressing their demands for social change, thus contributing to a renewed interest in Puerto Rico's folk heritage. In particular, cultural and folk-music groups influenced by the Cuban-derived rhythms of Nueva Trova and "countersong"[3] in Latin America became widespread and important mediums of the Puerto Rican left. Nueva Trova, a musical hybrid that combines modern and traditional instruments with patriotic and oppositional lyrics drawn from Puerto Rican and Hispano-American literature, was extremely important in popularizing Puerto Rican folk rhythms and instruments. Its most important local exponent in the 1970s, a group called Haciendo Punto en Otro Son, was the first to gain broad exposure for folk music on the radio.

Not surprisingly, this emphasis on local culture was accompanied by a heightened preoccupation with the popularity of imported cultural products. Thus, my informants recalled their concern over the encroachment of commercial genres as a major motivation for the ICP's folk-oriented cultural policies of the 1970s. Among other issues, they pointed to the pervasiveness of rock and other American styles and to the continued relegation of folk music to the Christmas season, giving it a popular reputation as "Christmas music." They also recalled divisions between supporters of the new rhythms of rock and Afro-Caribbean popular music, such as those between the fans of *a go-go* and *conserva*,[4] as a consequence of the bombardment of imported cultural products at this time. As one ICP officer remembered: "Then you had a commercial bombardment of merengue and American music bands, whereas before foreign artists would come to Puerto Rico, but the radio and the television were still Puerto Rican. Our intention was to place the Puerto Rican artists involved in folklore at the same level as any other."

Puerto Ricans have been historically unable to control the importation of cultural products, as all mass media are under U.S.

regulatory jurisdiction (Subervi Vélez and Hernández López 1990). Thus, Puerto Rican radio and television were not all "Puerto Rican," as the informant suggests. The local media had been dominated by Cuban immigrants, who developed a niche in Puerto Rico's entertainment industry after the Cuban revolution, and local rhythms had been affected by and in direct negotiation with American commercial rhythms since the onset of American colonization (Glasser 1995). Thus, more than as a cause of debate over whether there was more or less space for "showcasing Puerto Rican culture" prior to the 1970s, I view the comments above as further evidence of the context and concerns leading to the search for and emphasis on folklore at this time. Interestingly enough, this search would lead intellectuals to Puerto Rican radio and television, which were, and still are, key components in the dissemination of Puerto Rican music. Specifically, variety shows, an important genre in the earliest TV and radio programs, were significant catalysts for the popularization of Puerto Rican popular music, Afro-Caribbean rhythms, and Latin romantic songs throughout the island. Early TV programs such as "Borinquen Canta," "Rambler Rendezvous," and "Conociendo Puerto Rico" featured Puerto Rican popular performers and were important in popularizing and giving mass recognition to many musical genres that were bypassed or ignored by the ICP but were now being reassessed in its program as folklore.[5]

This was the case with *bomba,* an Afro-Caribbean rhythm, and *plena,* a rhythm associated with the Puerto Rican working class at the turn of the century. These rhythms were originally popularized and valued through the music of Manuel Jiménez (Canario), who was a popular radio performer since the 1930s, and in the 1950s by Rafael Cortijo. The ICP was initially ambivalent about including these rhythms in its programming because, according to a member of a contemporary *bomba* group, they were perceived as "too black and primitive." In an interview, this performer recalled the racism that delayed the inclusion of his music in the ICP program: "How would anyone be interested in this music when these rhythms began to be referred to by the experts as the music of black people, made of jumps and contortions, or as erotic and grotesque black music?[6] What is worse, these studies were done by people who never dared to go and mix with the musicians. To study peasant music was no problem, they went and talked to them, but to come here to the urban communities to study the composers and interpreters of *plena* was difficult for them." Instead this same performer added that *plena* and *bomba* groups were recruited by the ICP whenever it needed to show something "African." He explained that it was not until the mid-1970s that his group was approached by the ICP: "They called us and told us that we should be affiliated, and since we were already famous, it was very easy to become affiliated with the ICP. No audition or anything. They knew us from TV."

In this context, the ICP's emphasis on folklore in the 1970s should be considered more as a response to changes in greater Puerto Rican society than as its own innovation. As we have seen, although folklore had been part of the ICP program from the beginning, it was broadly promoted only after the popularization of folklore in the media and among the Puerto Rican left. By then, even commercial sponsors were turning to folklore in their advertising campaigns, taking advantage of the popularity of folk elements and nationalist imagery in the popular culture.

Thus, the ICP's emphasis on folklore could be also interpreted as part of a greater containment of oppositional genres through their incorporation and redirection in the cultural program. Specifically, in ICP hands, many of the rhythms originally associated with opposition or resistance would became "peasantized," as in the case of Nueva Trova, which originally was directly oppositional and was even accused of being subversive or *música de comunista*. As a contemporary performer of the style recalled: "The Nueva Trova is supposed to be music to open one's social and political conscience. Here the concept was transformed. They thought that Nueva Trova was about mixing old and new instruments and singing about the *jibarita* [peasant girl] or the *bohio* [shack]. Those groups that became part of the ICP and were called Nueva Trova were not really Nueva Trova because they did not include a message of opposition. We, however, received a lot of resistance from the ICP." In its present manifestation Nueva Trova has become "peasantized" and "folklorized," and once again peasant life, the mountains, land, and nature have become the major themes.

The Building Blocks and the Blending Myth in Puerto Rico

Since its inception, the Institute of Puerto Rican Culture served as the main disseminator of the blending myth in Puerto Rico, or the idea that Puerto Ricans are made up of three ancestrally distinct cultures that, long extinct as separate populations, have merged into a unique whole: the Puerto Rican culture. Yet as in other colonial and postcolonial contexts, the idea of *mestizaje* and racial syncretism has amounted to an "inclusive ideology of exclusion" that hides the unequal valorization of its racial components under the trope of racial mixture (Stutzman 1981). Accordingly, national unity is equated with racial miscegenation, hiding the ideology of "blanqueamiento" (whitening) while unequally associating contributions and moral characteristics with the different components. A look at how this myth is portrayed by the ICP exposes the fallacy of the presumed harmonious integration of its constituent components.[7]

In the ICP program, Spanish culture is associated with language and religiosity. The ICP's seal, for instance, portrays the Spaniards' role through the image of a conquistador flanked by Spanish vessels with Christian crosses, signifying the Spanish "discovery" and Christianization of the island. The Spaniard, centrally placed between the African and the Taino, is shown holding a book of Spanish grammar. Shown to his side is the Taino, surrounded by indigenous plants and holding a carved stone god or *cemí,* evoking the imagery of Taino art and spirituality. The African holds a drum and a machete, evoking a frozen image of the work relations of the colonial period (Buitrago Ortiz 1982).

The Spanish heritage, deemed the most distinctive element of Puerto Rican culture, is associated with the most prestigious crafts such as *santos* (wooden saints) and *mundillo* (Spanish lace), as well as with the most valued folk-music genre, the peasant *trova,* and with a whole architectural legacy. Meanwhile the Taino is one of the most important figures in the triad because of its symbolic malleability. Since their last documentation as a distinct group in the 1700s (Brau 1978) the Taino have been officially treated as an extinct heritage, of which only traces remain. As such, the Taino add temporal depth to the national myth by representing the nation's roots in the past while supplying a continuity with the present that is essential for establishing the legitimacy of a nationalist ideology. It is the indigenous component of the national myth that provides the authentic link to the territory upon which the nation is established. The Taino has been promoted as an important figure by the ICP through its sponsorship since 1969 of the National Indigenous Festival, the Museo del Indio, and various archaeological excavations throughout the island.

Puerto Rico's African heritage, also known as the "third root" (*la tercera raíz*), is seen as the last to arrive and as having the least to contribute. This legacy is acknowledged in the music and dance genres of *bomba* and *plena* and in the carnival masks that are characteristic of the coastal towns of Loíza and Ponce. Strongholds of the slave-based sugar economy during Spanish colonization, the coastal regions are associated with much of the island's African-based cultural expressions. Yet the folklore of these regions has evolved into the embodiment of what is "African" for the rest of the island, erasing the Afro-Caribbean aspects of popular culture and everyday life. Thus, *bomba* and *plena* are always included in cultural activities (although to a lesser extent than peasant music styles), but the African contribution to other aspects of Puerto Rican culture—such as to the food, folk and contemporary music, and even the racial make-up of the Puerto Rican—is "Tainoized." Traits that are not identifiably Spanish are attributed to the Taino rather than the African, with the result that everything and everyone can trace a mythical descent from the Taino.

Thus it is common for organizers of cultural events to evoke the Taino, rather than the other figures of the Puerto Rican triad, to legitimize their festivals as authentic. The organizers of the Festival of the Burén in Loíza, for instance, associated the *burén* (an iron cooking sheet) and recipes using coconut milk, cassava, and yucca with the Taino, while in the Festival of the Lechón (roast pig) and the Festival of the Flat-Bottomed Boat, the roast pig and the flat-bottomed boat were attributed to the Taino. Taino images are most popular among the artists who adorn the folk crafts, T-shirts, and other paraphernalia sold at the island's numerous cultural festivals. None of the festivals I visited, with the exception of *bomba y plena* festivals, emphasized the African component directly, except while appealing to the "triad." Conceived as an intermediate tradition distinct from the dominant Spanish or enslaved African, the Taino constitutes the most easily evoked symbol of a legendary past that is mystified and permeated with nationalist overtones. Thus, the Taino image serves to conceal the socioracial tensions of contemporary Puerto Rican society. For while African and Taino elements are overtly proclaimed as constituent elements of Puerto Rican culture, their respective contributions are ultimately subverted vis-à-vis those of the Spanish.

The overt bias in favor of the Spanish heritage as the most salient influence on Puerto Rican culture is most evident in the interpretation of the origins of Puerto Rico's peasant culture. The rural peasant (*jíbaro*) is represented as the embodiment of all three ancestral heritages in a single Puerto Rican culture. Yet the *jíbaro* is usually portrayed as a white male whose main influence comes from his Spanish predecessors although he has a tinge of Indian

heritage. An African contribution to the *jíbaro* is never acknowledged or emphasized, as neither is a female gender identity (M.
Alonso 1968, Laguerre 1968).

In part, this whitened view of the *jíbaro* responds to notions
of race on the island that are constructed around geography and
economic history and associate the interior mountainous areas,
strongholds of the hacienda economy, with "whiteness," in contrast to the "blackness" of the slave-based sugar plantations of the
coast. Ironically, however, the dominant presentation of the *jíbaro*
as a white peasant belies the historical reality of racial intermingling
on the island—that is, the same foundational principle for the
blending myth of nationality. It conceals that the Puerto Rican
peasantry was characterized by racial intermingling from the earliest period of Spanish colonization, and that peasant adaptations
were never limited to rural, more "whitened" areas but rather
developed alongside the plantation system itself (Mintz 1989,
Scarano 1993). Similarly veiled is the fact, documented by Puerto
Rican ethnomusicologists, that "jíbaro" music and culture never
developed independently of African influences (Alvarez 1992).
Yet, while based on the principle of miscegenation, signs of cultural merging and creolization between the ethnic components
are strategically erased in dominant definitions of Puerto Rico's
peasant past. The result is the "cultural and racial apartheid" of
the individual building blocks of nationality (Dufrasne 1996: 25).
So constituted—as white, male, rural based, and devoid of recog-
nizable African and Taino components—the *jíbaro* comprises the
most important building block of nationality. It is the *jíbaro*—associated with the countryside and with freedom and rebellion, in
contrast to what is modern, Western, urban, and foreign—that
provides continuity with an agrarian past.[8] It is also this
"whitened" legacy that provides the model for the traditional folk
costume as well as the core repertoire of Puerto Rico's many folk
dance groups. It is peasant music, mostly genres associated with
the Spanish legacy such as the *seis* and the *aguinaldo*, rather than

Afro-Caribbean rhythms, that are deemed the purest representatives of Puerto Rico's peasant culture. The fact that the *trova* is not unique to Puerto Rico, but is also found in other Latin American countries, strengthens its appeal because it links Puerto Rican culture to a greater Hispano-American tradition, to which performers of this genre often point proudly. In this way, the peasant culture, the rural landscape, nature, agriculture, and the soil are recurrent images that are idyllically portrayed by folk singers affiliated with the ICP. Many groups have peasant-influenced names such as "Song of the Mountain" or "Peasant Heritage," or "Essence of the Mountain," or else Taino-influenced names such as Guayciba.

Analyzing the relationship between race, class, and nation in Guyana, Brackette Williams (1991) found that the claims of different ethnic groups to rights and civil entitlements were contested in terms of each group's relative contribution to the nation. Accordingly, economic and political dominance was justified through an ideological rationale that claimed a greater contribution of some groups over others. Similarly, ICP's emphasis on the contributions of each of the three building blocks of Puerto Rican culture continues to provide an ideological justification for the superiority of Puerto Rico's Hispanic legacy, based on the "greater" and more significant contribution it made to the peasant and thus to the nation. The dominant explanation of Puerto Rican culture, which reduces the African contribution in relation to that of the two other components, coincides with a persistent racism and the continuous idealization of the Spanish heritage, part and parcel of the presentation of Puerto Rican society as undifferentiated.

The Building Blocks at Play: The Case of Folk Music in the Reproduction of Cultural Hierarchies

The unequal appraisal of the different constituent elements of Puerto Rican culture come to the forefront in the ICP's evaluation program. Evaluation of the authenticity of artists, artisans, and lecturers that can rightfully represent Puerto Rican culture has been part of the ICP program since its outset. Some of the first musical groups added to the program were even announced in the national newspapers, illustrating the prestige that accompanies the affiliation of artists to the ICP. However, since the 1970s and with the growing number of folk artists, evaluations became increasingly standardized according to a more defined set of criteria. Now those deemed worthy of representing Puerto Rican culture are incorporated into the ICP as affiliated artists, and they gain prestige and legitimacy thereby. Their names are included on a list from which institutions, businesses, and tourist hotels draw whenever they need "authentic" Puerto Rican artists and performers.

To learn about the evaluation process and how "authenticity" is safeguarded by the Institute of Puerto Rican Culture, I interviewed ten groups who had passed these evaluations and are active in the ICP-sponsored festival circuit. These included three peasant folk-music groups, two Nueva Trova groups, three *bomba y plena* groups, one *bomba* dance group, and one group specializing in *música de ayer* (popular music of the forties and fifties). The performers ranged widely in their backgrounds, but many were college-educated civil servants and professionals with full- or part-time jobs who wished to supplement their earnings. All the groups were led by men, although some had woman vocalists or dancers. They represent the higher echelons of folk art, and (in sharp contrast with other artists, artisans, and vendors whom I will discuss later) none relied solely on music for a livelihood.

Those I interviewed regarded the screening evaluations with ambivalence. While they considered them a good method for distinguishing their own group from others who "do not know about Puerto Rican culture and are not authentic representatives of it," most admitted having engaged in some kind of manipulation of the ICP guidelines in order to pass the evaluation, thus acknowledging their own lack of authenticity or the ICP's.

According to these musicians, ICP standards for measuring authenticity in folk music include adherence to the rhyme and rhythmic specifications for particular genres and the group's use of at least the most typical instruments for the genre (thereby maintaining the strict separation of "peasant" and "African" instruments with their respective genres). The themes of the songs—especially patriotic or peasant-related themes about the mountains, nature, or farming—and the presentation of the musicians themselves in either folk attire (a straw hat and white trousers) or clean and attractive standard dress were also listed as important criteria. Yet it soon became evident that the "purity" they represent as "authentic" artists is more illusory than real and that most artists were constantly pushing the limits of the formal boundaries to make their productions more appealing to the public. In the process these musicians were simultaneously engaged in stretching the official definition of culturally relevant music. One example of this is the tendency among musicians to use the canon to question the canon itself. The racial triad, for example, was often used by artists to legitimize the inclusion of percussion instruments like the *bomba* and the conga in typical peasant music groups, which traditionally include only the *cuatro* guitar and the *güiro*. Strict adherence to ICP guidelines, however, would mean only the Indian and Spanish traditions were represented, leaving the African out. As I was told by one performer: "In my shows, I always play two or three pieces with the three typical instruments [*güiro, cuatro,* and guitar] so that no one tells me that I do not play typical music. But the public watching you wants more, so I add the percussion." Appealing to the racial triad is always a good tactic, as this performer discovered:

We always wanted to belong to the ICP but we were never able to until we entered a contest of Christmas music, and we competed with a song I wrote entitled "The Three Kings Are My Three Races," which went: "Melchior was the African, the

Taino was Gaspar, the Spanish, Baltasar, and the child was
Borincano [Puerto Rican]," as if Jesus would have been born in
Puerto Rico. We won the first national prize. . . . The song was
a typical [folk] song, not the Nueva Trova that we now play.
That was a trick I used to be able to enter, and after that we
went back to our old music.

The issue of instrumentation is a difficult one, and the purist
view of the ICP is constantly at variance with the many groups
who increasingly employ all types of modern and foreign instruments. Yet to manage these restrictions, groups who perform
with "non-Puerto Rican" instruments do not use them when
they are being evaluated and add them to their performances
only later. One musician who did this commented, "They criticized me for having an instrument of Cuban origin, a *tres* [a type
of guitar], in the group. Yet this instrument was once popular
here and even substituted for the *cuatro* at a given time. Nobody
would have criticized me if I had added an accordion to the
plena, but the *treses* are manufactured here, and the accordions
are imported from Germany. That is a case of purism that I do
not swallow."

By mixing elements from other genres, or adding instruments
and other features commonly used to attract youth and the general
public, performers are bringing about great changes in what is
officially deemed to be Puerto Rican music. In fact, contemporary
folk music is increasingly influenced by the very commercial
rhythms the ICP so adamantly wants to exclude.[9] Even Edwin
Colón Zayas, a renowned ICP-affiliated folk artist who has traveled as far as Japan to represent Puerto Rican music and is
considered by many to be among the purest performers of folk
music, added percussion instruments (such as the conga and the
bongo) as well as a flute to his group. He had this to say about
his music: "There are some people who criticize my use of the
flute, but I tell them that I am not losing the folkloric element;

on the contrary, I am going to show the public that with another instrumentation I can also make typical music, and that I can even *criollizar* [creolize] any international number. They keep hiring me so I know that people are OK with my views."

Besides adding instruments, many musicians have also introduced innovations into the lyrics of their songs. The incorporation of environmental themes and lyrics in contemporary folk music is a recent trend. Yet while musicians continually innovate, the identification of their music as a folk genre and thus as a marker of identity places limits on their innovations, which never go as far as to challenge their status as folk artists or their music as folkloric. Thus, some standards represent the quintessential boundaries of authenticity and are carefully maintained by the ICP and those who aim for the status of "authentic" performers. In this way, the permanence of elements that distinguish the "folk" is directly related to the state promotion of folk arts as national icons and objects for tourist consumption. This supports García-Canclini's (1993) findings in Mexico, where he argues that it is through the maintenance of a standard of authenticity that the value and profitability of the folk genre is ensured. In Puerto Rico adherence to rhyme and rhythms, the use of at least the most representative instruments, and, most importantly, the presentation of the group as cultural and educational, rather than purely for entertainment, are carefully guarded by musicians.

Another way in which folk artists differentiated themselves from other musicians was by describing themselves as *luchadores* (fighters for the nation), or *trabajadores de la cultura* (cultural workers), or as educators, but never just as entertainers. In this way they conform to government cultural policy, which prioritizes a didactic purpose for such groups, as well as to the ICP view of folklore as an intrinsic aspect of cultural resistance. The director of another musical group affiliated with the ICP explained: "All folkloric groups should seek to reaffirm some roots. They are in charge of representing Puerto Rico and educating Puerto Ricans about our cultural heritage. We are in folklore because of our love for Puerto Rico, but there are other groups that only have commercial purposes and are doing this because it is fashionable or because they want to get *guisos* [gigs]." Like this musician, many ICP-affiliated artists emphasized the distinction between education and entertainment. For them only patriotic reasons for performing folk music were regarded as authentic; economic motives would disqualify musicians from claiming authenticity. In this way, education and patriotism were used as synonyms for authenticity, whereas playing for entertainment or profit was considered unpatriotic and illegitimate. These issues will be more evident in later chapters. What I want to emphasize here is how folklore is always placed by the ICP standards in an elevated cultural category relative to popular music, which is devalued as inauthentic and commercial.

Thus, despite some innovations, groups continue to recycle the peasant-centered material that forms the core of the ICP's programming. Moreover, many innovations on rhythms that are deemed to represent Puerto Rican culture are nonetheless subject to the ICP's constraints, which tend to "peasantize" new forms and genres, as is the case of Nueva Trova. *Bomba y plena* groups, for instance, complain that they are given fewer referrals and invitations for activities than peasant folk groups and that these groups are encroaching on their rhythms, playing a "whitened" version of *plena* with string and wind rather than percussion instruments. As the leader of a *bomba y plena* group put it, "There is not a lot of respect for *bomba y plena*. There are some groups that the ICP likes more, but you have to ask yourself whether they sound black or white. Do they sound like Nueva Trova or do they sound European?"

As a result, although there has been some diversification in the categories of folk art employed by the ICP since its inception, the constituent elements of the overall program have remained unchanged. The ICP's program still draws on the peasant past and the racial triad, and innovations to the program are judged irrelevant or authentic according to how closely they keep to these themes.

These ideological ceilings reinforce the folkloric emphasis of the ICP's cultural policy, and the ICP's insistence on purity and authenticity translates into the exclusion and devaluation of other aspects of Puerto Rican culture. Thus, true innovation remains a difficult feat within the context of these parameters. The conceptualization of Puerto Rican culture through the building blocks of Puerto Rican nationality not only dismisses aspects of popular culture that are seen as polluting and damaging to the purity of folklore but also serves to encourage the unequal valorization of the "building blocks" themselves.

The Institute and Its Cultural Centers

The unequal valorization of Puerto Rican culture is not only evident in the expressive forms deemed representative of Puerto Rican culture. It is also reproduced in the institutional organization of the ICP and its affiliated centers. As early as 1957, cultural centers were founded throughout the island to replicate the ICP's mission at the local level. For the most part, they were top-down creations established by the central office in San Juan, whose staff and director were important catalysts in their creation. Director Ricardo Alegría periodically visited towns throughout the island to explain his vision of the centers' role.

The centers were conceived as autonomous entities that would elect their own directors and organize their own activities while serving as the legitimate representatives of the ICP; they were the "preferred and natural organ" for carrying out its mission at the local level. With some exceptions, only one ICP-affiliated cultural center was founded in each municipality, where it acted as a miniature version of the ICP. In this way, centers served as direct channels for financial resources, technical assistance, and programming from the ICP, and as aids to nonaffiliated cultural groups in their communities.

The cultural centers soon became an important component of the ICP program by providing both symbolic and direct connections between the central office in San Juan and towns throughout the island. The ICP still uses them today to counter criticism of its political and elitist underpinnings, presenting the centers as evidence of its involvement with local communities. As a former director described it, "The ICP was never an elitist institution, because the *espina dorsal* [backbone] of the institution was composed of its cultural centers. They were its institutional heart because they were the ones who made the mission of the ICP transcend from the center to the people."

Additional evidence of the cultural centers' "popular" nature was seen by the ICP staff in the composition of their membership, which was and still is free and open to any community resident willing to work for the continuation of Puerto Rican culture. Yet, as "mini ICPs," the cultural centers have reproduced, from their inception, the general characteristics of the ICP in San Juan, a fact that has greatly undermined their democratic pretenses. During my conversations with leaders and members of affiliated centers, I found that their membership is mostly composed of teachers, civil servants, and local civic, religious, and political leaders, depending on the historical, political, and economic characteristics of the area. This membership makeup was partly the result of the urban character of the centers, which are always located in the urban heart of their respective communities, and by the class, educational, and political background of the ICP staff in charge of recruiting members and supervising their work. The leadership was most exclusive in centers located in Puerto Rico's largest cities, which were often dominated by doctors, professionals, and small businessmen. Centers whose physical facilities were subsidized by the ICP or by their municipalities were particularly liable to attract a select membership because these facilities endowed them with more visible prestige.

In turn, local centers have exerted a certain amount of influence on their respective communities, especially at the time of their origins in the late 1950s and 1960s. A former member recalled the great influence of his area's cultural center as follows: "Around that time, the Cultural Center and the Department of Education were the same thing. The membership was drawn mostly from the teachers, and the director was the school superintendent. Then every teacher had to help out in the cultural center's annual festival. Even if they did not want to, they had to provide time from their classes for everything related to the festival. Working in the festival became a moral obligation."

Politically, the cultural centers served as a refuge for pro-independence advocates, who were persecuted in the workplace and their communities but were able to air their views through cultural work. In turn, the bringing together of the middle classes, educated professionals, and *independentistas* in the cultural centers contributed to the common perception that they were dominated by intellectuals. This perception has been strengthened by the concentration of *independentistas* among university-educated professionals and intellectuals.

All these factors have contributed to a widespread perception that one needs a formal education in order to be part of the leadership of a cultural center. This has made leadership a means of attaining status because those active at the centers are esteemed as "culturally aware citizens." The centers often serve as springboards for political advancement to the extent that, in some towns, the centers are even directed by the local mayor, and many political leaders have been directors of their town's cultural centers. Youth have traditionally been excluded from the cultural centers, both by the traditional programming, which appeals mostly to the older sectors of society, and by a regulation that prevents persons younger than eighteen from voting in ICP elections.

The relationship between the ICP office in San Juan and the affiliated cultural centers has always been hierarchical. Regional cultural promoters (ranging from five to eight, depending on how a region is organized) are hired as full-time paid staff by the ICP office to orient and supervise the work of the centers and to mediate all communications between the local and national centers. This organizational structure was strengthened in the 1970s when most of the promoters now affiliated with the program were first hired.

During the course of my research I interviewed eleven individuals who were former or current promoters within the ICP structure. Of these, nine were male and most were *independentista* artists, teachers, community workers, or political activists. They were selected from within the ICP structure itself, where they had workers as administrators or had been affiliated as folk performers, although some came in as political appointments or were drawn from the cultural elite of their respective region in order to tap its social and political resources. They all described their recruitment process as informal. One cultural promoter described his recruitment of another promoter as follows: "He was kicked out of his job after the teachers' strike, and I knew him and wanted to help him, so I explained to him what we were about, that we go against the current, about our commitment." Other promoters, especially those hired in recent years, are screened in interviews in which their knowledge of Puerto Rican folklore, music, and so forth is examined by a committee. Overall, the position of cultural promoter is one of considerable prestige, as are many positions in the ICP regardless of the tasks involved. As I was told by a recently recruited promoter:

For me the ICP was the greatest there was in terms of culture. Anything that had the seal of the ICP was like a Mecca for the Muslims or the church for the Christians. That is where the greatest thing is. That is where God is, what I adore, what I do not know, and if I get there, then that means that I am great myself because I arrive at the end. And I saw the ICP as that

place, because it is a place of intellectuals, because here in
Puerto Rico they do not award an academic degree for folklore
or culture, but there is the ICP which serves as the equivalent.

This aura of prestige, along with its politicized image and the
purist conception of culture, are intrinsically bound up with each
other and mutually reinforce the ICP-affiliated institutions' distance from the general public.

Women, who were not appointed as cultural promoters until
recent years, have not attained the prominence or the length of
employment of male promoters, some of whom have remained
in their posts for over twenty years. As a result, they have not
been able to establish the same authority in their respective regions
nor the personal relations that their male counterparts have established with local directors, who have also traditionally been
male members of the local elite or political activists.[10] Of eighty-
one ICP-affiliated cultural centers in 1994, only twenty-eight were
led by women compared with fifty-three led by men.

While the gender imbalance among the centers' leadership was
commonly acknowledged by the groups I interviewed, their racial
homogeneity was not. Approaching this issue was a complicated
task. Despite the importance of race as a variable for the attainment
of status, race and racism are not generalized discursive categories
on the island. There is even a lack of racial classifications in census
statistics on the island, precluding anyone's identification as anything other than a "Puerto Rican." Moreover, the ideas of racial
syncretism promoted by Puerto Rico's nationalist ideology have
historically circumvented discussions about race, and most of the
people I interviewed within the context of the ICP groups denied
that there is racism on the island. In fact, the "lack of racism" has
served as an important element for the construction of the
"moral" Puerto Rican in the nationalist ideology, in which only
"immoral" Americans are branded as racists.

Meanwhile, racial conflict and difference are ignored, for they are believed to hinder political unity and to perpetuate American colonialism. As one contemporary scholar put it, "Are we going to substitute the integrationist myths for the dividing counter-myths of racial tension? We would then be like the Americans with their ethnic and racial divisions. It would mean adopting a view that ultimately serves assimilation" (Carrión 1993: 11). Puerto Rico's racial classification system, characterized by a racial continuum (rather than the bipolar racial categories of the United States), does indeed differ from the American system. Yet, this difference does not reside in the absence of racism but in the nature of racism on the island, where it is buffered by a dominant ideology that denies its existence and subverts it to the common identity that "we are all Puerto Rican" (Jiménez 1996).[11]

When the issue of race is brought up, it is either dismissed as the imposition of American racial categories and problems on the island, or it is regarded as entirely irrelevant to Puerto Rico's situation. This latter attitude was the most commonly expressed by my respondents. People in the cultural centers would acknowledge, to differing degrees, the gender gap or the similarity in the political or class background of those involved in these organizations, without touching race as another element producing their homogeneity. Yet on the outside, the cultural centers were often described as being composed of *blanquitos* ("little whites," a colloquialism for white and rich), which attests to the close correlation of race and class on the island.

For their part, cultural promoters refused to acknowledge any racial homogeneity among the cultural centers because this would challenge their democratic image. In a patronizing tone that denoted his higher status vis-à-vis these local groups, one cultural promoter voiced this view when he maintained that these groups are made up of *gente de pueblo* (the common people), which was a common response to any questions about issues of race or class in the cultural centers. This attitude is encouraged by the cultural promoters and is most evident when they are confronted with questionnaires from American funding sources, which the ICP has been tapping in recent years. These questionnaires always inquire about the racial composition of these groups; such questions challenge local understanding of race and are therefore seen as an American imposition. As one promoter explained:

> I hate those questionnaires handed out by the federal government that inquire about race. I always tell my centers to answer like I do, to mark that we are all a "minority" or Puerto Rican. Look, I am one of the darkest people in this town. The problem is that here no one speaks of race, we are all of the same three races. I know that I have an Indian ancestor and I should have a black one somewhere too, but I do not know.

The same advice was given by another promoter while distributing one of these surveys to a cultural center under his care. After briefly reviewing the cultural center's membership, the promoter instructed the people to ignore that question because it "did not apply to our case, or to anyone here." This was the only question that was edited out by the promoter.

Toward the "Cultural Development" of the Chosen Children

Individual promoters have different styles of interacting with the cultural centers, although certain commonalities surfaced during my discussions with them. Among the most salient of these were the use of paternalistic and developmental metaphors to refer to the cultural centers and the ICP's supervisory role, and a defensive preoccupation with the purity of culture.

I often heard the centers' membership described with such paternalistic metaphors as "the sons of the institute" or "children who need to be raised and molded." Their dependency on the ICP for activities, resources, and guidance was seen as the behavior of "spoiled little children who are used to getting everything and now cannot do anything for themselves." These children, I was told, needed to be constantly "taught and guided" by the ICP. One promoter reiterated this view as follows: "The cultural centers are *criaturas* (offspring) of the ICP who need to be constantly guided and educated. In the past we stimulated them by giving them half of the activities, so that they would feel as if they were part of the program, but now with shrinking budgets it has become more difficult to encourage them and some of them are still in their infancy."

For their part, the "children" have a variety of different relationships with the promoters. Those who have been able to acquire more financial help from the ICP tend to follow the promoters' advice. As the president of one cultural center told me, "All you have to do is let yourself be guided by him. We never say no to any of the activities he wants to bring to this center." Often, however, the "children" are "mischievous," and promoters often complained of their being lazy and stale and having authoritarian and inactive leaders. The promoters felt unable to change the situation, however, because the cultural centers are voluntary "autonomous" entities led by unpaid volunteers who cannot be forced to work. In the resulting stalemate trying to induce them to work was likened by one ICP staffer to "giving breath to a dead person."

Paternalism and excessive dependency are manifest in the over-reliance of local centers on the ICP for most of their activities, funding, and technical support. There is a sense of entitlement among the centers, who see themselves as legitimate representatives of and workers for the ICP, rather than as self-generating entities. Consequently, whereas ICP promoters would like local centers to raise their own funds and be more self-sufficient, local centers see themselves as entitled to funds and support and even monetary remuneration from the central institution in return for their work and time commitment. Thus, if their work is not being done, it is because they are not given either the funding or the contacts they need. An organizer of the National Folk Arts Fair in Barranquitas dismissed the ICP's claim that it had no money for the fair by arguing that "this is *their* fair and it is their responsibility to give us the money" (emphasis mine).

This same local organizer, whose role appeared to be more of a mediator, also complained that he had not yet received the names of the folk artists who would participate in the fair, who had been selected by the San Juan office. However, funds and resources are hard to get from San Juan. The bulk of the ICP budget has always consisted of allocations by the local government, and thus it is always affected by changes in the political administration at the national level between the pro-statehood and pro-commonwealth parties, which affect the amount of government funding allocated along political lines. The agencies' dependency on the local government is evident when one considers that out of the institution's 1995 total consolidated budget of $15,216,863 (including government grants and self-generated income), only 3.6 percent derived from federal funds and less than 3.5 percent was self-generated income.[12] Most of these funds were allocated to operational costs, leaving little for the cultural centers, which rarely receive contributions surpassing five thousand dollars for their yearly activities. Yet years of ICP-directed work have led many to believe that they are not allowed to do fund-raising. As a result, a sense of helplessness grips both the leaders of cultural centers and the promoters who hopelessly try to motivate them to engage in a project that they fail to embrace as fully theirs.

While most ICP-affiliated cultural centers draw primarily from the ICP's list of affiliated artists (especially because half their cost is paid by the ICP), the promoters have had a more difficult time with independent cultural groups throughout the island. These independent groups frequently make requests for subsidized ICP-affiliated artists, but they are often rejected for refusing to follow ICP guidelines. As another ICP promoter said, "I told these groups that I would help them but that they have to let me be part of their planning meetings. In this way I can monitor them and make sure they do a good job. But they don't want me to do this. They want to do things by themselves and they just see the ICP as a barrel of money, not as a place from which they can get technical help about how to conduct their activity." Often, requests from independent cultural centers were sidetracked by the promoter through referrals to the ICP-affiliated center in their community, which lacked the funds to help the group.

However, there is also a trend among promoters toward establishing connections with the most active independent groups, especially those whose activities and programs are more compatible with the ICP's cultural guidelines. For instance, I found cases where the cultural promoter had formed alliances with independent groups as a means of restoring the ICP's presence in certain communities. This was the case with a cultural group led by environmental activists in a town in the center of the island; they were particularly interesting to the ICP because of their environmental concerns, a current and important issue for the Puerto Rican left. When I first met the group in 1992, they emphasized their independence and openly criticized government cultural groups for their lack of involvement in social and community problems. Yet when I saw them in 1994, this group had been approached by the ICP to manage the area's cultural center, which they have been doing ever since. However, while the promoters have tried to incorporate the most "cultural" and socially active leftist groups, they showed a marked reticence about working with independent groups whose activities were not perceived as cultural according to ICP guidelines. In turn, this reticence has created a sharp distinction between ICP-backed activities channeled through the ICP-affiliated centers and other popular activities, which are normally categorized as purely commercial. This again has limited the ability of the ICP to reach out to different groups. A sound and lighting technician who has worked at popular festivals for over twelve years commented, "It is the ICP's fault that people are not more interested in *jíbaro* music because they do not send musical groups to our *fiestas de pueblo* [grassroots festivals].[13] I myself like *jíbaro* music but I never get to see the groups because they [the ICP] never send this music to these festivals."

Due to the cultural centers' conformity to ICP guidelines and their restraint in mixing musical genres, the programming of many of these centers was described to me as boring and repetitious by audience members. Most of the organizers of the local ICP-affiliated cultural centers I interviewed also complained about this issue, but they simply shrugged when I asked them what could be done to revive the programming. "The problem is that nobody cares," argued a local member. "It is difficult to motivate people, and people do not know how to innovate activities. They think that bringing a musical group from the ICP list is all they have to do to have a cultural activity." In this way, the traditionalism permeating the official view of culture is itself a major obstacle to its popularization and dissemination. Those charged with "selling" the authenticated view of Puerto Rico's national identity find this difficult to do without breaching the standards of authenticity.

Although a certain indifference characterizes the work of the local groups and their relationships with the San Juan ICP office, some issues were actively debated. A common cause of conflict between local centers and the central promoters stemmed from the preference of the former for regional artists and culture. This emphasis often clashed with the ICP's policy of promoting nationally recognized groups that have been legitimated as "authentic" representatives of Puerto Rican culture through the ICP's evaluation process. For instance, one group wanted to organize an exhibit featuring local painters rather than hold a folk art exhibition. In another case, in Aibonito in the mid-1980s, organizers daringly invited a local rock group to the Festival of the Mountain: "We used to draw only from ICP-affiliated activities, but in the third and fourth year of the festival we included a local rock group. We received so much criticism! There were so many dogmatists, especially the *independentistas*, who thought it was an intrusion. The ICP could not do anything because we had a tense relationship with them. We were struggling for control of our activities. We were real anarchists."

Cultural centers also complained about the legislation regulating their work and their responsibilities as affiliated centers. Although supposedly "autonomous," ICP-affiliated centers are expected to comply with the fifteen-page "Regulations for Cultural Centers," which govern everything from the names given to the centers to the order to be followed in their meetings to the need to ratify elected boards.[14]

A large part of a promoter's job is to interpret these regulations and to assure the centers' compliance with them by examining reports, summaries of activities, and financial statements and monitoring meetings and elections. This degree of central control has, in turn, reinforced the local centers' dependency on the ICP bureaucracy. In addition, any resistance to complying with the promoters' expectations was seen as evidence of *subdesarrollo cultural* (cultural underdevelopment) or lack of cultural awareness, which needed to be corrected with discipline and "education." These interpretations replicate the development ethic that pervaded the PPD's cultural policies in the 1950s, when cultural development became associated with the cultural policies of the PPD government.

To further the cultural "development" of their respective areas, promoters consider themselves entitled to intervene in most aspects of the work of the cultural centers, ranging from administrative work to the organization of the membership. There are cases in which promoters have taken it into their own hands, in their words, to "accommodate" and "activate" a membership they deem inactive or ineffective. This involves making value judgments about which groups should be represented at the center, making contacts, and mobilizing groups. Although this practice is quite common, as I learned from group members who traced their involvement to recruitment by individual promoters, no promoter I spoke with admitted to actually managing a center because this would contradict the official position that the centers are autonomous and self-generated entities.

Many of these issues relating to the implementation of national cultural policy and the ICP's unequal valorization of different aspects of Puerto Rican culture surfaced during my study of the cultural center of Caone, which is discussed at length in the next chapter. Here I briefly address how this area was perceived by the ICP central office.

Caone: The Gray City

Caone, a city of about fifty-seven thousand people located in the eastern part of the island, is often called the "gray city." This bleak name, referring to its cloudy weather and the smoke that once rose from thriving sugar plantations to fill the skies, also captures the area's economic and political stagnation since the 1960s. Similarly, the region in which Caone is located is generally regarded by the ICP staff as a zone of "enormous cultural deterioration." According to a 1993 report by one of the regional promoters, four of the eight ICP-affiliated centers in the area are inactive, and two towns have never had such a center. The lack of ICP-affiliated folk artisans in the area (only two among hundreds of government-registered artisans come from Caone itself) was considered another indicator of its "cultural deterioration." Not surprisingly, this appraisal did not acknowledge the region's many nonaffiliated groups that organize cultural activities.

Psychological explanations of people's low motivation to work and meet the standard expected by the ICP were also common. Cultural promoters working in other areas said of Caone: "There has historically been less cultural activity in the eastern zone because people here have a closed attitude and are always more distrustful compared with people in the central zone, who are warmer and more willing to establish trusting relationships." Or, "This region is too Americanized. They also have a different style. Here the attitude is that *somos poquito* [we are little], and people are less progressive than in the North. The eastern personality is more provincial. Also, they have an apathetic personality, they do not show much warmth to you ever. That is their style." The perception that the eastern zone is too Americanized was explained by its proximity to the capital, compared with the more "traditional" rural interior, and by the existence of two military bases in the eastern town of Ceiba and on the island of Vieques. However, more than the area's Americanization I found that its perceived lack of cultural vitality was based on the unequal attention that the ICP has bestowed on it due to preconceptions about its contribution to national culture.

In contrast to the central area, which has been sanctioned as the stronghold of the Taino heritage, or the western and southern parts of the island, which are associated with Puerto Rico's colonial Spanish legacy, the eastern zone's cultural contribution remains indeterminate. One of the least populated regions of the island until the mid-nineteenth century, the East did not attract significant population growth or experience a full peasant adaptation until after the mid-eighteenth century, when it became one of the first regions to undergo the transformation of cattle-grazing *hatos* (ranges) into titled farmlands (Scarano 1993). Moreover, the area's attention was for years directed eastward toward its neighbors in the Virgin and Leeward Islands, with whom area residents engaged in open contraband, migration, and cultural exchanges.[15] These factors have contributed to an overall lack of knowledge about this region and its contribution to national history.

Moreover, the East lacks the architectural monuments found in the West, the Spanish military structures of the capital, and the Taino archaeological sites of the central region, or any other remnants of "culture" that would attract the attention and monetary resources of the ICP. Only the northeastern town of Loíza and the island town of Vieques have received attention from the ICP. Loíza is regarded as the embodiment of Puerto Rico's African tradition in its most folkloric version. Thus, while African Caribbean cultural elements are predominant throughout the eastern area, especially the coastal rim, it is only in Loíza that they are officially recognized (through the folklorization of the patron-saint festival, which has become a carnival-like tourist attraction for Puerto Rico). Meanwhile, the ICP has channeled resources to Vieques, as I was told, to "build culture in the area and counter its ongoing militarization and Americanization." Of course, Vieques is also attractive to the ICP because of its Spanish fortress, rated as "the best example of Spanish defense architecture outside of San Juan" (Instituto de Cultura Puertorriqueña 1993: 42).

Moreover, the East is considered to be "too close to San Juan" and too urban to be of any cultural interest to the central office, for which the rural inland areas are the quintessential guardians of national culture. The virtual oblivion into which the East has fallen is worsened by the lack of continuity among cultural promoters in the area: there have been six since the 1970s, in contrast with regions that have had the same promoters for over ten years at a time. Considering the top-down character of ICP cultural promotion, it is no wonder that the East remains "culturally underdeveloped" according to government-sanctioned standards of culture.

Nevertheless, the East is not untouched by the popularization of culture as a basis for contending and advancing different interests. There, too, the idiom of culture and Puerto Ricanness is being borrowed, transformed, and put to service by local groups and activists as they struggle to advance different interests and gain greater justice and representation through their work. The many independent cultural groups that celebrate activities and work in the area are evidence of that.

As in the rest of the island, the 1980s saw a rapid increase in community groups that celebrate cultural activities as part of their program. Most of these groups were founded in the 1980s, although some of their members had previous experience of cultural organizing within their communities. At present there are about seven independent community groups that celebrate a major cultural festival as part of their activities in Caone, whereas there are countless others throughout the island. In the next chapters, the micropolitical dynamics within and across different kinds of cultural groups in Caone will be more closely explored in order to elaborate on the local uses of and challenges to the government cultural policy.

DIVEDCO poster, "La buena herencia" by Eduardo Vera Cortés, 1973. The poster is for a film of the same name. *Courtesy of El Museo del Barrio, New York.*

"Our Heritage," museum exhibit at Puerto Rico's Museum of the Americas, Old San Juan. The exhibit shows a Taino weaving a basket, a Spaniard carving a wood saint, and an African drumming. *Photo by Arlene Dávila.*

The building blocks of nationality shown in a poster depicting "our heritage" during Caone's bicentennial celebrations in 1993. *Photo by Arlene Dávila.*

Cultural Center of Jayuya. Some of the most important ICP-affiliated cultural centers are housed in historic structures similar to this one and are centrally located in their respective municipalities. *Photo by Arlene Dávila.*

View of Barranquitas Folk Arts Fair. Note that artisans are given a common tablecloth to standardize their presentation. *Photo by Arlene Dávila.*

Festival stage sign showing the racial triad leading to the Puerto Rican man on the far right. *Photo by Arlene Dávila.*

Chapter III

From the Center to the *Centros*

Cultural Politics from Below

I t is easy to locate the ICP-affiliated Centro Cultural de Caone. It occupies a prominent place on the town square, right across from the Catholic church in a historical building that was once a prison and later the city hall. Formerly its social and political heart, the plaza is still Caone's administrative center but no longer its core, as new shopping malls and housing developments have redirected public life to the outskirts of town. Yet despite its relatively prominent location, Caone's cultural center is not well known in the immediate community; the same is true for many ICP-affiliated cultural centers throughout the island. If it were not for the fact that the eastern regional office of the Institute of Puerto Rican Culture occupies two offices in the building, there would be little activity on the premises, aside from the public car drivers waiting for passengers in the center's doorsteps.

Nevertheless, as was evident from the many local struggles over its management and control, the cultural center continues to be an important institution for some sectors in Caone. This chapter analyzes these struggles as an expression of the microdynamics at play in Puerto Rico's cultural politics. The chapter focuses on the case of Caone, although it incorporates information about other

ICP-affiliated groups. As representatives of national cultural policy at the local level, these groups are caught up in similar struggles.

Organized in 1957, Caone's was one of the first local centers founded after the establishment of the Institute of Puerto Rican Culture in San Juan. Metropolitan areas, PPD political strongholds, and areas with nationally recognized intellectual figures were preferred for these first centers, which were established through contacts with local intellectuals and political figures.[1] In Caone the contact was Aguedo Mojica, a local independence advocate, noted intellectual, and university professor from a black working-class background who was directly involved in shaping the idea of cultural centers in San Juan. Mojica had been active in a cultural group in Caone that had caught Muñoz Marín's attention as an example to follow in shaping his cultural policies of grassroots decentralization in the 1950s. This makes Mojica a key agent in the development of the cultural centers, a role overshadowed by the emphasis given to the anthropologist Ricardo Alegría at the national level.

The group that caught Muñoz Marín's attention was Club Ariel, an intellectual and artistic center founded in Caone in 1917 by a group of teachers, poets, and other local intellectuals. Conceived as a center of social and cultural renewal, the club aimed to provide children with free education and workers with an "environment of relaxation, of cultural creativity and solidarity against injustice" (Mojica 1983: 38). Club Ariel is a fine example of the cultural initiatives put forth by the island's intellectual elites in response to U.S. occupation. Even its name evokes the intellectual climate of the times. Specifically, the club was named after the free-spirited Shakespearean character Ariel, popularized by the Uruguayan writer José Enrique Rodó in a 1900 essay of the same name. In it Ariel symbolized the nobility and spiritual nature of Latin culture as distinguished from the materialism and imperialism of Caliban (representing the United States). As Flores (1979) has noted, Rodó's essay was highly influential among Puerto Rican thinkers who saw Hispanidad as the embodiment of civilization in contrast to the paganism and lack of culture of the American invader.[2]

Thus, like other cultural initiatives that took shape during this time, Club Ariel emerged in a context of social change. The U.S. occupation was rapidly transforming the island's political economy, and American sugar monopolies directly threatened Caone's sugar-based landowning elite, who dominated the town's economy and politics through their control of administrative posts in the municipal government (Ortiz Cuadra 1986).[3] The production of sugar, spurred by the building of a port in 1815, had contributed to Caone's economic and demographic growth in the nineteenth century and led to its designation as a bureaucratic and administrative center in 1881. With the advent of American sugar monopolies, sugar production in the area increased from 900 *bocoyes* (large barrels) in 1899 to 16,657 tons in 1920; but the number of small, individually owned farms (between four and nine acres) declined from 2,484 in 1899 to only 380 in 1910, reducing the number of individual landowners and the land available for subsistence farming (Ortiz Cuadra 1993).[4]

It was also in a context of social and economic change that the ICP-affiliated center was founded in Caone. By 1957, following the new commonwealth government's policies of export-led industrialization, civil administration and manufacturing had replaced sugar as the mainstay of the town's economy. When both the port and the sugar mills closed in the late 1950s, thousands were left unemployed and the city's dramatic economic decline dominated the pages of the national newspapers (Rojas Daporta 1958a, 1958b, 1958c). Thousands left for the mainland in the largest emigration in Caone's history.[5] Today, 30 percent of the population is employed in services, 23 percent in manufacturing (with thirty-seven factories in the area), and 20 percent in civil administration (Commonwealth of Puerto Rico 1992). Unemployment stands at 19.76 percent, and about 59 percent of the population lives below the poverty line. These figures are quite similar to those for the island as a whole (58.9 percent in poverty and 20.4 percent unemployed) (Negociado del Censo 1990); but given Caone's formerly strong economic and political status in the area, many believe that it has been abandoned and that its progress has been slower than that of nearby towns.

In this context, the ICP cultural center, like its predecessor, the Club Ariel, became a site for cultural regeneration. The center quickly developed into a forum for the development of a proud history for the city, but one that predictably omitted some important pieces.

Selective History and the "True Caoeños"

Verdaderos caoeños (True Caoeños) is the term used by one member of Caone's cultural center to describe the center's membership. In her words, these are people who were born and raised—and currently work and live—in Caone, and who have built a "respectable" reputation at the local level and are perceived as having contributed to Caone's growth and development. As we shall see, the label serves as a selective screen for Caone's middle classes, who are whiter and more educated that most Caoeños. It also refers to PPD supporters, who are more likely to constitute Caone's *buenas familias* (good families) in a town that was a PPD political stronghold from 1945 until the last mayoral election in 1992, and in which political clientelism and patronage are indispensable in securing jobs and resources. Partisan politics was the most important influence on all ICP-affiliated cultural centers included in my research, yet in Caone the importance of partisan politics is heightened further by the town's role as the metropolitan and political center of the eastern area. This assures Caone an important role in civic government and makes politico-partisanship an important source of employment, status, and resources.

However, the relatively privileged background of Caone's cultural center's membership was, as in other ICP-affiliated cultural centers, veiled behind the popular notion that the centers are composed of *gente de pueblo* (the common people). This is the key to understanding the position of the center's membership and leadership—their politically motivated need to "connect" symbolically to the popular classes whom they actually shun in practice.

In Caone, members of the center claimed humble origins by contrasting their own social status with that of the "big names"—that is, the landowners and families involved in sugar production, an association that evokes the paternalistic class relations within the sugar industry prior to the advent of large-scale capitalist production. For instance, members often asserted their *gente de pueblo* status by comparing themselves to the higher-status elite who attend the Casa Roig's activities. Casa Roig is the residence of one of Caone's former seigneurial families (one that is still economically successful) and a metaphor for wealth and power in Caone. It was converted into an art gallery in the 1980s. The exclusiveness of this gallery, frequented only by the area's wealthy and by affluent visitors from San Juan, gave members of the cultural center a measuring stick to represent themselves as ordinary residents of Caone.

The prevalence of *verdaderos caoeños* in the cultural center dates back to its early years, when the membership consisted of medical doctors, schoolteachers, merchants, intellectuals, and government workers, who collectively enhanced the center's social status and set it apart from the immediate community. A schoolteacher recently invited to join the center explained: "I remember that all the people involved in the center were selected people. I do not remember if they were known because of their names or their political affiliation, but I heard them mentioned a lot. You knew they were respectable people because of their social values and their good families. You know, in all towns there are some important names you hear a lot."

The most prominent members had political connections with the PPD, as did the first president, Aguedo Mojica, who from 1956 to 1968 was incorporated into the PPD political program as a consultant and representative at large for the eastern area. Today a mostly middle-class membership, drawn from the urban residential areas of Caone and from the *verdaderos caoeños,* continues to constitute the bulk of the center's leadership, although regulations stipulate that any city resident who wishes may join the cultural center. Many members saw this homogeneity as a problem yet continued to reproduce it through their practices and activities.

Initially, the center's elitist character was reinforced by its lack of a public location. Meetings were held in private houses, and participation in its activities was mostly solicited by written invitation. However, the center's seclusion continued after it obtained a public location in the 1970s. Nor did a short-lived radio show and a newsletter initiated in the late 1960s change the common assumption that one needed an invitation to its activities. The cultural center's concern with social status is still evident in the formality of its meetings, which follow the parliamentary method laid out in the "Rules and Regulations for Cultural Centers" passed in 1986 and disseminated by the ICP. The center's leadership (during my study) even increased the formality of the meetings by instituting formal seating arrangements for the leadership.

Politically, the cultural center's leadership has traditionally been composed of pro-independence and pro-commonwealth supporters. It provides a good example of the ideological synthesis of the two sectors within the context of ICP-affiliated cultural centers I have been discussing.

Until the 1980s, when a group of PNP supporters joined the cultural center, precipitating a struggle within the organization, the center had a relatively good relationship with Caone's municipal government, which remained a PPD stronghold until 1992. This positive relationship was assured by the PPD's need to document its commitment to culture, a key component of the party's policies. As Alberto Jiménez, a former director and pro-independence member of the center, explained, "The PPD municipal government almost always helped the cultural center but only because they had to. You had to know who to talk to and what to say. However, the mayor would always come through because he had to prove that he cared about culture, even when we know that the PPDs do not dare to speak about the *patria*."

Another member gave evidence of the way in which pro-independence party members working in the cultural center would be "ideologically transformed" into potential PPD members, an example of the *melonismo* tendencies of Puerto Rican intellectuals and a result of the 1950s transformist processes. "I have always been a PIP member, in favor of independence, but I remember that while I was working at the center I got to be good friends with the PPD mayor and other PPDs, and I was even offered a post in the PPD government, which I refused." This same person later learned that he had been subject to political persecution; local intelligence officials had covertly maintained dossiers on him, just as they had on thousands of pro-independence activists, until these operations came to light in the 1990s. Meanwhile, the cordial relationship between the municipal government and the cultural center and the political homogeneity of its membership contributed to the common perception that culture and politics never mixed at the cultural centers, at least until the PNP's political offensive in the 1980s.

In its programming Caone's cultural center has drawn primarily on the offerings of the Institute of Puerto Rican Culture in San Juan. Similarly, the members often consulted with the ICP regional promoter to prepare their programs in accordance with formal guidelines. The local center's adherence to national ICP priorities is evident in its revival in the late 1950s and early 1960s of the Festival of Saint Cecilia, which was founded in the late 1800s but had been discontinued for many years. This project corresponded to those of other ICP-affiliated cultural centers throughout the island, which revived or initiated regional celebrations soon after their founding. This was part of a national policy instituted by the ICP's director to develop distinctive festivals in each town on the island as a way of reinvigorating local culture. Such were the origins of the most important contemporary festivals, such as the National Folk Arts Fair in Barranquitas and the National Indigenous Festival in Jayuya, founded in the early 1960s.

Initially the activities of the Caone cultural center consisted primarily of conferences on Puerto Rican history, along with concerts by quartets and big bands performing boleros and *danzas*—or "popular yet refined music," as it was described by a member who was active at this time. As with the ICP in San Juan, there was a turn in the 1970s toward folklore along with the institutionalization of activities that are now traditional in Caone and that form the backbone of the center's programming. These include the annual Festival of Saint Cecilia and the Fiestas de Cruz, two Catholic-derived celebrations that also demonstrate the cultural center's religious homogeneity.

The Festival of Saint Cecilia is among the few activities organized by the cultural center that have traditionally been oriented to the general public; it is always celebrated in the town's public plaza. In the past ten years, however, the festival has consistently failed to draw a broad public, and it is openly criticized for not being a "real" festival. This is because the festival genre is now associated with the many celebrations organized since the 1980s by independent groups in the area. These feature popular music, dancing, entertainment, fried-food stands (*kioskos*), and folk arts. In contrast, the Saint Cecilia festival, which has remained almost unchanged since its inception, is a quiet, quasi-religious celebration of the patron saint of music. It features large bands that play in the middle of the plaza during the early evening hours. There are few food kiosks and no popular dancing to attract the public, as there are at other festivals, and its religious aspects deter many who are nonreligious or non-Catholic.

The cultural center's activities and publications are a vehicle for disseminating the dominant version of Caone's history, which exemplifies the Hispanophile tendencies in standard interpretations of Puerto Rican history. The few written accounts of the town's history were compiled by a founding member of the cultural center, who is commonly known as the town historian, and another member, who was formerly in charge of cultural activities for city hall. This history is also elaborated in the publications of the Absent Caoeños, an organization made up of former residents of Caone,[6] many of whom were also members of the cultural center.

Caone's founding is traced to a group of Canary Islanders who arrived in 1721 to settle and colonize the area, and who are seen as responsible for the growth that culminated in its designation as a city in 1793. No other immigrant group is so well remembered as the Canary Islanders, despite the continuous influx of slaves, "libertos" (freed slaves), and workers from the Anglophone and Francophone Caribbean who arrived at Caone's port and settled the area after the onset of Spanish colonization. The only attempt at analyzing this influx and its effects on Caone's history is Ortiz-Cuadra's (1991) discussion of the English, French, and Danish surnames that are common in *la costa* or the waterfront areas of the city. Caone's slave history is not recorded anywhere or remembered, even though, like the rest of the island, the sugar industry in Caone was maintained by slave labor, and there is evidence that slaves entered the port of Caone even after the slave trade was prohibited for Spanish subjects in 1829 (de la Rosa 1986).

The town's official history also draws heavily on the cacique Caone, a Taino chief who ruled the area before the Spanish colonization and is credited with being the last Taino leader to surrender to the Spaniards. Official regard for the cacique Caone was evident in the celebrations of the city's bicentennial in 1993: an official hymn was written for the cacique, and his picture decorated the celebration's print and commemorative T-shirt. A statue and a sanctuary park were created in his honor at the same time.

Besides these foundational elements, Caone also prides itself on its musical past, which is perceived to be the city's greatest contribution to Puerto Rican culture. Caone has produced nationally recognized composers and musicians, and the municipal band and its *cuatro* string orchestra have represented Puerto Rico at international events. Both the band and the string orchestra are almost always featured in the cultural center's activities.

The continuity of programming and approach within the local cultural center is secured through the limits imposed by the San Juan office and by the ICP's regional promoter, who only sponsors ICP-affiliated artists. Continuity in programming is also secured by the cultural center's role as the local guardian of Puerto Rican nationality, which means presenting Puerto Rican culture as it is defined by the official cultural policy. It is a role that prompts much tension when people who are not officially recognized as defenders of Puerto Rican culture enter the ICP's domain.

Microwars for Political Representation

In the 1980s there was a struggle for political representation in Caone's cultural center that mirrored the national cultural wars of the time. As Chapter I discussed, this struggle pointed to a decline in the PPD's political dominance and a questioning of its control of culture, which had been an important basis for its political power. Similar struggles occurred in different towns on the island, where PNP supporters backed by PNP-led municipalities turned their attention to the ICP cultural centers. Similarly, for the first time in the history of Caone's cultural center, PNP supporters purposely set out to dominate its leadership and membership through the active recruitment and mobilization of PNP party members.

This episode is highly significant for the center's history. It still provides moral legitimacy for the current leadership, again composed of PPD and PIP supporters, who present themselves as the rightful guardians of the cultural center, which they had to rescue from the PNP, who are regarded as *vende patrias* (sellers of the nation). It also reveals the tensions that emerge when those not entitled to speak about culture and who lack the "cultural capital" (Bourdieu 1993), or the knowledge and disposition to expound on Puerto Rican culture according to the dominant frameworks, enter ICP-affiliated cultural centers.

The new group shared certain similarities with, but also had important differences from, the group that had traditionally dominated the cultural center. Like the latter, the group that entered the center in the 1980s was mostly drawn from the middle sectors of society; but unlike its predecessors, who were more representative of the traditional petite bourgeoisie (merchants and professionals), the new group represented what Pantojas-García (1990) and Carrión (1980) have called Puerto Rico's new petite bourgeoisie. This sector is associated with civil administration, the service sector, and nonproductive forms of labor. These were the groups that emerged from the capital-intensive, export-processing strategy instituted in the commonwealth in the 1950s, along with the expansion of the public and service sectors.

Moreover, the new group had less education than the older leadership, who had attended the best local and foreign universities. They were thus perceived to differ from the older, more intellectual leadership, who pointed to their lack of qualifications to lead the cultural center. As a longstanding member of the cultural center put it, "The new people were just a political committee of illiterates who did not even know how to write their own name and who never went to the university. Before, the cultural center was a serious institution, and only educated people would dare to speak of culture."

Besides these similarities, there were also new actors behind the changes in the cultural center, mostly women who were emerging as a key force in the organization. They had previously been involved in the cultural center, but only as assistants helping to organize activities and preparing food for receptions, never in important leadership positions. Yet it was women, also middle class and from the group of *verdaderos caoeños,* who planned what is known as the first "takeover" of the center in 1978. A woman who was active at this time but has since detached herself from the center explained, "We saw that this town was so dominated by the same people that no one could go against it. We thought that by becoming involved in the cultural center and by giving it a different orientation . . . we could solve this. As pro-statehood women, we wanted to do something . . . because everywhere we went there was always the PPD inviting the same people, and the PNP inviting their own people."

Despite their pivotal role in seeking PNP representation in the cultural center, none of the women ran for the presidency. Their husbands' disapproval of their involvement, lack of time for such responsibility, or the difficulty of attending evening meetings were among the reasons they gave for turning down their own candidacies. Nevertheless, some of the women who told me that they could not join the cultural center's leadership were active in other local organizations, such as the church or female-centered groups like the "Mothers of Caone." This suggested a preference for other types of organizations rather than the cultural center, which many perceived as a limited domain for women. This was articulated by a church leader in her community, who contrasted her work in the church with her previous work in the cultural center: "God has given women a great capacity, and if we go to the home of the sick we get involved in everything, and we cook and we read for them, and the sky is the limit. . . . In the cultural center I felt limited in my capacities, but not in the church, where women are the *voz cantante* [the leading voice]." This woman's observation about being "limited" in the cultural center is corroborated by the fact that while many women hold important positions in many cultural centers, they are less likely to be elected as directors or move up in the ICP structure to become regional promoters.

The new leadership's political identification with the PNP caused them to be subjected to political and intellectual attacks and to charges of ignorance and inexperience. Examples of these views were provided by a current member of the cultural center: "Only the PIP and the PPD care about culture. Everyone knows that even if the PNP cares for Puerto Rican culture, it's because of hypocritical motivations and because they ultimately want Puerto Rico to become a state. You can never believe that a pro-statehooder wants to defend Puerto Rican culture."

For their part, the PNP members involved in the "takeover" of the cultural center denied these charges of fraudulent motivations. Such views were exposed by the first PNP president of the cultural center, Víctor, elected in 1978. Respected in the community, he was recruited by the women to represent them, given that none of them ran for the presidency. He is a lab technician and composer of popular songs (boleros) who has a history of civic involvement. Víctor looked back at his presidency with nostalgia and is still convinced that there is a need to rescue the center from the "*independentistas* and communists" that presently dominate it. This is a recurrent perception among PNP and, to a lesser degree, PPD supporters of the older generations, who see the ICP-affiliated centers as *independentista* or communist strongholds. Víctor is openly pro-American, and at my slightest hesitation in Spanish, he would insert an English word or phrase into the conversation. This contrasted with the attitude of other cultural centers leaders, most of whom spoke English because they had learned it in the States but who always refrained from mixing languages to the point of apologizing for any anglicism they used. Yet, despite his pro-American attitude, Víctor repeatedly asserted that he was pro-Puerto Rico. "We [the PNP] came to prove that we are *puertorriqueñistas,* that we can work for our culture," he said, echoing PNP claims for participation in Puerto Rico's cultural policy being voiced at the national level during the 1980s.

Comparing the activities of the cultural center under his leadership to previous programming, Víctor gave evidence of continuity. He claimed not to disagree over the kind of programming that should be presented in the cultural center but rather was critical of the use of culture for political manipulation. As he claimed: "It is not that I have different ideas of what is Puerto Rican culture, but I do denounce the use of culture for political manipulation. Today we do not know what 'true' culture is because the ICP has always politicized culture." Víctor was outspoken in his denunciation of the ICP cultural policies as political manipulations rather than "true" representations of Puerto Rican culture. For instance, he criticized the ICP's designation of Nueva Trova as Puerto Rican music: "That music is from Cuba and the ICP wanted to introduce it here, but it is not really Puerto Rican music. There is a great difference between the legacy of our peasant *trova* and the Nueva Trova, which is from Cuba and is played by militants." His questioning of Nueva Trova's legitimacy concerned the ICP's endorsement of what he saw as a foreign genre for what he considered political reasons. His criticism exemplifies the close association of the ICP programming with the PPD and the PIP, which has only recently begun to be curtailed. This association has historically prevented PNP supporters from drawing upon sanctioned cultural symbols (and thus from asserting their Puerto Ricanness, according to the dominant ideology) because these are symbols that have been politically appropriated by the PPD at the national level.

Some examples of these dynamics are provided by the second PNP president of the center, who was described to me as the most controversial ever. Although he had a reputation as an expert in Puerto Rican popular music, Carmelo was the first president with no formal higher education. Similarly, he was the first from a working-class background, having spent over two decades in the

United States after migrating in the 1950s to seek work on one of the New England farms hiring Puerto Rican laborers. His background raised doubts in the cultural center, where people questioned not only his education but, because of his long absence, his actual knowledge of Puerto Rican culture. What is more, during his term as president he appeared on a radio program during a political campaign, speaking in favor of PNP candidates. This also made him an easy target for PPD and PIP groups, who accused him of politicking and united to force him to resign.

When I met him, Carmelo appeared nervous and was defensive in talking about his term as president of Caone's cultural center. He made constant references to *la guerra* (the war) to denote the opposition to his tenure and said he had felt politically persecuted during his administration. He complained that the PPD-controlled municipal administration withdrew the center's secretarial and cleaning staff as well as the financial aid that it traditionally awarded the center. The ICP also "made our lives impossible," he said, by refusing to affiliate the local folk artists he referred to them, merely on the basis of "personalism," which he thought was based upon his political affiliation.

Carmelo called himself a regionalist because he considers regional culture, rather than the views of culture promoted by national government cultural policy and institutions, to be the legitimate culture. Like Víctor, he questioned the validity of many governmental ideas about culture, regarding them as arbitrary judgments of what is original to Puerto Rico. For instance, he questioned the ICP's promotion of the *danza* and the *bomba* as autochthonous Puerto Rican rhythms, arguing that they had really originated in Europe and Africa and thus could never be truly representative of Puerto Rico. What he did not question, however, was the permanence of peasant music and peasant-derived styles (*aguinaldo, seis*); he agreed with the ICP that these represented the essence of Puerto Rican culture.

He also was critical of the annual homage to one local musical legend, Juan Peña Reyes, whose descendants are still important musical figures in Caone, when other local musicians are never recognized. "What culture are we promoting when nobody knows anything? When everything is the same and no one knows anything about local history?" More daringly, he questioned the veracity of the cacique Caone, whom the cultural center had been honoring as part of the bicentennial celebration of the founding of Caone. For him this celebration was part of a current trend to revive Taino chiefs mentioned in fictional and legendary accounts for political purposes, and therefore an example of an ICP-inspired fabrication of history.

Apart from Víctor's disapproval of the participation of Nueva Trova groups, and Carmelo's emphasis on the local musicians, there were no major differences in the center's programming during their tenure. Recall that the San Juan office, rather than the local groups, largely determines the programming, and that it was dominated by ICP-affiliated musicians and performers. In the case of Caone, programming continuity has been assured since the mid-1980s by the presence of a regional promoter on the center's premises. Moreover, by the time the new group was in office in the 1980s, the cultural center's work had been consolidated around the aforementioned "traditional" activities, which formed the backbone of its work.

However, it was seen that statehood supporters were more likely to denounce the ICP view of culture as politico-partisan manipulations because their political ideology has not been historically tied to these official definitions of Puerto Rican culture. Thus their views of Puerto Rican culture and their open identification with the PNP made this group a threat to the ICP-affiliated cultural center and its predominantly PPD- and PIP-affiliated membership. This "threat" was evident in the comment of a PIP schoolteacher active in the cultural center during recent years: "PNPs do not know anything about culture. They want to destroy anything that smells of Puerto Ricanness. If we had cultural centers directed by PNPs they would feature plays in English, or celebrate American holidays of Halloween or Saint Valentine, or sell folk arts with Mickey Mouse designs."[7]

Even though "American programming" in the centers was the greatest fear of people involved in ICP-affiliated groups, I found no examples of it in Caone or in any of the other ICP-affiliated cultural centers I visited. Continuity in the programming is mostly assured by the ICP limits on sponsoring anything that departs from the lists of ICP-affiliated artists. Fears of American programming, however, a by-product of colonialism in which the American dominant culture has been the historical "other" against which Puerto Rican culture is defined, were behind the PPD's "rescue" of the cultural center in the late 1980s.

The Rescue

As I have noted, the cultural center underwent few changes during the PNP administration in terms of programming and the composition of its membership. The new administration's open ideological identification with the pro-statehood party remained problematic, however, especially after Carmelo's involvement in the PNP political campaign and the political radio show. At this time, opposition to the leadership peaked and there was a swift mobilization to overthrow it.

The opposition was organized from within the cultural center itself by an *independentista* high school teacher who was part of the center's leadership. Luisa had friendly personal relationships with two of the *independentista*-led, unaffiliated cultural groups that had been established in Caone in the 1980s and from which she drew support for this endeavor. They included the Asociación Recreativa, Educativa, y Cultural del Barrio Mariana (ARECMA), a community-based group whose work will be discussed shortly, and a group of students and young musicians (now dissolved) that had organized to celebrate a festival of *bomba y plena* music.

As the PNP's supporters had done in the 1980s, Luisa and others affiliated with the Caone cultural center recruited as many new members as possible to vote in the general elections. This practice, known as the *plancha* (or ironing, for "ironing" or arranging the board), became a common way of covertly manipulating the cultural centers after the 1980s, when PNP partisans first staked claim on the cultural centers and these became most contested by the island's dominant parties. Often *planchas* were carried out with the knowledge and assistance of regional promoters of the ICP, as was the case in Caone. On election day, the PNP's candidates were greatly outnumbered, and a new, mostly PIP- and PPD-identified leadership was elected. The militancy of this event is evoked by some present members, who referred to it as their "mission, their duty, to rescue" the center.

The new leadership of the cultural center was much younger than its predecessors and had little knowledge of the center prior to the election. Luisa had recruited them because of their political affiliation and their expressed commitment to "changing the center" and reinvigorating it to make it more representative of the greater community. To do this, they had branched out of the urban areas to seek support among the new independent cultural groups, and selected Luisa as the first female president of the cultural center.

Behind these changes, however, lay the same ideas that the previous leadership had embraced and that constitute part of the historical legacy of ICP-affiliated centers throughout the island. These are the beliefs that the center should be directed by "educated people" and that it should be the venue for conserving Puerto Rican culture in its highest forms of folk expression. The new leaders also perceived the cultural center as both a political battleground and a source of political prestige in Caone. Thus, two years after the "takeover," the current leadership (that is, the group active during my research) was composed of college-educated high school teachers and civil workers; and the new director, although not a "true Caoeña" (she was born outside Caone), was a well-respected woman and a university professor at a local branch of the University of Puerto Rico. The membership of the cultural center continued to be drawn mainly from schoolteachers, civil workers, and the urban residential areas of Caone. The new leadership also exhibited the preoccupations with pure culture that characterized the older leadership, and reenacted their predecessors' role as authorities on culture in Caone.

The new leadership's concern for pure culture was most evident in their revival of a long campaign to evict the downstairs tenants—merchants operating drinking, dancing, and gambling establishments—from the cultural center's premises. These businesses, some of which had been in the same location for over thirty years, were seen by members of the cultural center as obstacles to enlarging its space and housing more of the regional offices of the ICP, which would be a source of added prestige for Caone. While most cultural centers have some type of government-subsidized facility, not all are housed in historical buildings. Moreover, only the most strategically located centers share space with regional offices of the Institute of Puerto Rican Culture, as is the case in Caone. Housing one of the regional offices of the Institute of Puerto Rican Culture is a source of great prestige for the center; it serves to strengthen its identification with the ICP and makes it more of a locus of political power than other ICP-affiliated centers. Thus the merchants were accused of promoting prostitution, alcohol abuse, and gambling; and when they denied this, they were said to be clashing and "disharmonizing" with the goals of the center. It was seen as "a matter of culture versus the *bolita de azar*" (gambling), or culture as defined by the cultural center versus the "decadent" life.

This issue has a history dating to the late 1960s, when the Caone cultural center first moved into the building, already partly occupied by some of these tenants. The center's intentions were therefore sure to stir controversy in Caone. Some of the merchants are well known and have personal and political connections in the area. Each business also supports a network of families. Thus not even the previous mayors had dared to evict them, fearing public opinion and reprisals. As early as 1974, when a national newspaper featured the problem, the mayor at the time had recommended that the issue be handled by the ICP in San Juan, or by an outside office with no local interests in the issue. The mayor argued that while he was in favor of cultural activities, "as a politician, as a mayor, and as a human being" it was impossible for him to remove the tenants (Giuscafre 1974). After a short hearing process, the case was suspended, unresolved. Later I learned that with the help of a local legislator, the Caone cultural center had secured a law that, pending the governor's signature, would allow the building to be transferred to them.

The merchants' defense, however, exemplifies the widespread appeal to culture as a basis for contention. Their defense evoked their roots in the town and the fact that their long presence has given them status as a *tradición de pueblo*. This, they argued, made them just as "cultural" as the center next door and entitled them to remain in place. One barber who claimed to have been in the locale for over thirty years commented: "This town does not have traditions. We are the traditions, the barber, the merchant, the shoe-shiner, all who gather here. I was going to bring these old scissors to the trial to show them what culture is." The merchants' defense was further legitimized by their hiring of *independentista* lawyers ready to present their clients' case as one of popular culture versus the "high" culture of the ICP.

The merchants' defense illustrates what is at the core of contemporary cultural politics in Puerto Rico: the idea that there are ways of locating and identifying culture other than those sponsored by the official guardians of Puerto Rican culture. The existence of different ways of identifying Puerto Rican culture interferes with the cultural center's aim to reach out into a community that already perceives itself as Puerto Rican.

While the members of the cultural center readily acknowledged their inability to attract popular support and reach wider publics, they were puzzled about this situation, especially because of their self-perception as *gente de pueblo* and not as elites. Clues to understanding these issues lie in Caone's history of class and regional stratification as well as in politico-partisan issues. These issues became evident in the relationship of the ICP-affiliated cultural center with other groups in Caone.

Toward the True Keepers of Puerto Rican Culture

As local representatives of the ICP, its affiliated cultural centers are charged with advising local cultural groups and serving as conduits for communication between them and the central office in San Juan. Yet for the most part, the ICP-affiliated center in Caone has remained independent from other cultural activities, which are perceived to be too regionalist, commercial, or devoid of authentic cultural content.

Similarly, with one exception, none of the members of the other community groups I encountered in Caone, two of which will be discussed in the next chapter, had either visited the ICP-affiliated cultural center or participated in its activities. For many, the center was seen as a "secluded group of people," and there was a generalized impression that one needed to be "properly invited" to its activities. This reinforced people's impression of the center as a "civic, by-invitation-only" kind of association.

The most important aspect mediating these perceptions of the ICP-affiliated cultural center was its urban identity, which stemmed from its predominantly urban membership and its urban location, alongside other civic clubs, associations, and the regional Catholic church of Caone. This urban identity confers a prestigious image upon the cultural center, even though the status of civic organizations has dwindled considerably since the 1960s. Specifically, changes in the urban landscape and a steady growth of suburban developments, with their accompanying shopping centers, have redirected social, economic, and political life away from the urban center in most towns of the island. Consider that out of the twenty-nine suburban residential developments built in Caone by 1984, twenty-five had been opened after 1960 (Abreu-Vega 1984). These changes have lessened the role of the urban center as the site of public activity, although Caone's cultural center is still perceived by many as a prestigious organization. Contributing to this prestige is the preponderance of male intellectuals among the leadership, as noted by a woman who was once very active in the center: "One had to be from a respectable family to be part of the center. You would see a lot of men, not the typical men but the man of the university, a humanist, or a sociologist. . . . The idea is that one had to be a prepared [educated] person. I think I was only invited back then because I was a teacher. I tried to recruit other teachers, but many were intimidated."

The potential of ICP-affiliated centers to become caught up in politico-partisan debates was another factor that mediated the cultural center's relationships with other groups in Caone. ICP-affiliated centers, much more than independent groups, are seen as highly politicized entities. They are either dominated by PPD and PIP groups, or they are extensions of whatever political party is in power at the municipal level. For instance, a PPD leader of another community group in Caone mistakenly thought that the cultural center was dominated by the PNP, which had won, for the first time, Caone's mayoral elections. Discussing the relationship of his group to Caone's cultural center, he said: "No, we never have contact with them. I do not know what kinds of activities they have. It is not that it does not interest me, but I say that I do not like to go where I am not invited. I think it is difficult to go there, especially now [referring to the PNP in the municipal government], because we are PPD and politics are everywhere. Everything is involved with politics."

Of all the cultural groups in Caone, the ICP-affiliated cultural center had the strongest links with ARECMA, a community group that has had the reputation of being an *independentista* stronghold. This relationship is partly explained by the political affiliation of the leadership of both these groups with the pro-independence party, which led to the recruitment of some ARECMA members in the "take-over" of the PNP leadership in the 1980s.

The center's image as the keeper of Puerto Rican culture, which limited its program to ICP-affiliated artists and activities, also shaped its relationship with other groups, who were perceived to be more or less "cultural" according to their choice of programming. For instance, ARECMA's programs draw more closely on "authentic" Puerto Rican culture, as defined by the ICP's cultural policy, in its choice of folk artists, music, and entertainment. This earned ARECMA a higher estimation by the ICP-affiliated center relative to other independent groups. Comparing a coastal-based celebration known for presenting salsa music and other popular music and entertainment, a member explained, "You can tell that ARECMA's festival has some thinking behind it. It is not just a salsa band and a stage, but there is typical music and Andrés Jiménez [a singer known for his nationalist lyrics]. That is why it is more cultural while the others are just a show."

However, compatibility of programming between ICP-affiliated and independent groups does not always ensure amicable relations between the two. Many independent groups, even while they include musicians and artisans who fit ICP's standards of authenticity, have had poor relations with the ICP and its regional representatives. The latter assessed these activities based on the regional, political, religious, or personal identity of their organizers. One notable example of this is provided by the Festival of the Tomato, which is celebrated by a Protestant religious group in a rural community in a central municipality of the island. This event is one of the most "traditional" festivals I visited. It features folkloric and nationalistic musicians like Andrés Jiménez and Roy Brown, whose music advocates independence for the island; it even prohibits the sale of alcohol (mainly for religious reasons). Yet, the local ICP-affiliated cultural center refused to help the festival, dismissing their celebration as a "religious fund-raising activity" rather than a cultural event, even though Catholic masses are often part of ICP-backed cultural events such as the Festival del Acabe.

The location of different communities in relation to Caone's urban center also mediated the relationships of Caone's cultural center with other groups. As I noted in Chapter II, different locations on the island are accorded more or less cultural status according to Puerto Rico's urban-rural dichotomy. Rural communities are regarded as the purest bearers of Puerto Rican culture; they are seen as being both whiter and more evocative of Puerto Rico's peasant past than urban and coastal regions of the island. Caone, while a city, is subdivided like most municipalities on the island into barrios (or neighborhoods), some of which are considered more rural or urban according to their location vis-à-vis the urban center (or the plaza). As a general rule, barrios located toward the interior, in mountainous and residential areas that have undergone little commercial development, are considered "rural." Those located by the waterfront are regarded as "coastal," while the urban areas are defined as the barrios that have undergone the most development. Thus, the activities of ARECMA, a group located in the rural areas of Caone, were more positively regarded by the cultural center. Their festival was considered to be more "cultural" because it is a "country event," and because "it is easier for them to present certain things with their country background."

Moreover, rural parts of Caone are perceived as the stronghold of whiter Caoeños, vis-à-vis the coastal areas, all of which are positioned in a subordinate position against Caone's urban areas. The distance between the ICP-affiliated cultural center and other communities in Caone was evident during the celebration of the city's bicentennial, which the center was involved in organizing.

With the exception of two renowned intellectuals from the rural town of Mariana, most committee members were drawn from the urban center. Most of the people working in other community groups whom I talked to claimed not to have been fully informed of these activities, which were not widely publicized. The activities were only announced in the local newspaper, which is freely distributed in Caone, and broadcast on the local radio station. These, however, are limited media because they are perceived as being politicized (with a PIP/PPD bias) and as having an "aged" outlook—especially the radio station, which plays a lot of *música de ayer* ("oldies"). Most people, especially the younger generation, regard the local media (the local newspaper and radio station) as a *cosa de viejos* (something for old people), which they never read or listen to. The center's insistence on relying just on these two media, and on written invitations, and on avoiding other forms of public information (car speakers, street signs, or announcements) continually undermines their intention of reaching a diverse public in Caone.

Nevertheless, the center's image as "the keeper of Puerto Rican culture" serves to limit internal criticism of its work and of its elitism. I saw critics of the ICP-affiliated cultural center actively defend it against government initiatives that, as Chapter I explained, aimed to discontinue the designation of the cultural centers as the only legitimate representatives of the ICP. One informant in particular, a musician, had been critical of the new leadership, but for him the ICP was ultimately the *muro de contención* (the wall of contention for Puerto Rican nationality) that must be defended regardless of his own opinion of its work. This sanctioning of the ICP as the guardian of Puerto Rican culture has not only dissipated attacks against the cultural center but has also created great tension when those who are not considered to be proper defenders of Puerto Rican culture enter its domain.

Finally, the cultural center's preoccupation with protecting the integrity of Puerto Rican culture against its commercialization and deterioration has further isolated the ICP-affiliated cultural centers from other groups organizing cultural activities in the area. For it is through this issue that the members of the cultural center in Caone, and those in other ICP-affiliated cultural centers throughout the island, most often distinguish themselves from the many newcomers. As previously described, those involved in the ICP structure tend to emphasize their cultural and educational status to claim their authority over cultural issues. Thus members of the cultural center defined their cultural mission by emphasizing their educational mission and distancing themselves from the commercialism they attribute to the newcomers. Comments voiced by several members of the leadership reveal these tendencies:

> We are different in our approach to the activities. We try to bring activities that are more cultural, to keep alive certain things that you will not see in other festivities, but because those are more commercial those activities draw larger crowds.
>
> People compare our Saint Cecilia Festival with other festivals. People do not understand that a festival of Saint Cecilia is different from these other festivals, where the music is different and is very commercial, whereas in Saint Cecilia, the music is very cultural. A lot of people tell me that they do not like the music that we bring, but if it is a cultural festival, you cannot bring music other than cultural music.
>
> What happens is that everyone uses the word "festival" for anything, and this devalues the idea of a festival, and people think that there will be a merengue orchestra playing in the festival. We have remained at one stage, and they [the other groups] have gone beyond to a more commercial stage.

The leadership and most of my informants in ICP-affiliated cultural centers used the word "commercial" to designate a variety of situations, but always with the connotation of being "less cultural" and of inferior quality. For instance, in the comments above, the "commercial" is associated with entertainment, with popular dance music, and with the involvement of commercial sponsors, all of which place these activities in a lower category relative to "real" folk culture. Most important, any activity that is motivated by economic rather than patriotic purposes is berated as commercial.

The preoccupation with appearing too commercial was a constant concern of the cultural center's leadership, and one that often undermined their goal of reaching a wider public. For instance, street signs and loudspeakers, which are popular forms of communication in Caone, and would help the group branch out into different communities, were never employed by the center because they would make it appear too commercial. This concern also guided their choices for the entertainment portion of their activities. As one member explained, "There should not be Coca Cola but rather maví [a local fermented drink] and Puerto Rican fruit drinks, some sausage, guava, and beer accompanied by *música de aquí*" (Puerto Rican music).

While they maintain strict guidelines for their own activities, I saw many members of these cultural centers attending the different cultural festivals that they criticized so much for being too commercial. They acknowledged the appeal that these activities have among the public, including themselves, yet they are unable to act to popularize their own activities because they are restricted by authenticated conceptions of Puerto Rican music and culture, against which popular music is considered low class and *chabacano* (cheap). In a sense they are reproducing the negative criticisms that are levied against them as elaborators of *cultura de viejos* (culture of the aged). For instance, when trying to explain to me why their Festival of Saint Cecilia should continue to be celebrated in the early hours of the evening (approximately from 7:00 to 9:00 P.M., another member of the leadership said: "Yes, you can have an activity until 1:00 A.M., but that will attract the kind of public that you do not want, the *muchachería* (a pejorative term for youth) or the people that do not work outside their homes. Instead, from 7:00 to 9:00 you will have families, adults, and even the elderly." A member of the center explained the low turnout for their activities, compared to the independent festivals, as a natural by-product of their more mature image: "It is true that what is fashionable is merengue and a beach festival, but only youth go there. Everything has its time, and they will become interested in culture."

Until audiences do become "interested in culture," however, new grassroots cultural groups stand as a vehicle for promoting competing positions on Puerto Rican culture. The next chapter discusses two of these groups.

Chapter IV

Just One More Festival

New Actors in Caone's Cultural Politics

> This activity, awaited by all, is faithful testimony of a people
> who wish to be recognized for their values and for the efforts
> of those who, preceding us in history, marked our identity as a
> people.

> —José Rivera Rodríguez, Fiesta Jíbara del Tomate, Jayuya,
> Puerto Rico, 1992

> Welcome all who love our traditions and wish to pay homage
> to our culture in a sound and enjoyable environment. We wish
> you to enjoy this festivity with enthusiasm while supporting
> our traditions and ensuring their permanence and continuity.

> —Welcoming remarks by the organizing committee of
> the Festival of the Pineapple Worker, Vega Alta, 1993

Nothing demonstrates the dynamics of contemporary cultural politics more clearly than the lively proliferation of festivals that are celebrated annually in Puerto Rico. They encapsulate the variety of interests that are currently promoted in cultural terms and the ensuing struggles involved in forging definitions of Puerto Rican culture. While most festivals are popularly referred to as "cultural," not all are deemed significant by politicians, intellectuals, and the public at

127

large; instead they are rated as more or less "cultural" or valuable. Festivals of all kinds, however, have attained great popularity in Puerto Rican society, becoming in the process important vehicles for the promotion of competing views of Puerto Rican culture and for enlarging the range of interests that can voice concerns in cultural terms. The popularity of these events is such that posters connected to cultural festivals are common decorations in municipal offices, corporate quarters, people's homes, and restaurants (from McDonald's to the local tavern), where they are an easy way of identifying oneself and one's party, business, or product with Puerto Rican culture.

As a performance genre, festivals are events that "occur at calendrically regulated intervals and are public in nature, participatory in ethos, complex in structure, and multiple in voice, scene and purpose" (Stoeltje 1992: 261). In her discussion Stoeltje argues that while many events can fit this description, those that purposely present themselves as festivals are often "contemporary modern creations" following a festival format but serving as mediums for wider commercial, ideological, and political interests. Festivals are also key elements for the construction and communication of identities at the local, regional, or national level, by which they attain political dimensions and become involved in greater political movements (A. Cohen 1993, Manning 1983). Throughout the United States, community festivals are held to celebrate aspects of regional food and culture (Humphrey and Humphrey 1988), and governments throughout the world use festivals as tools for disseminating and affirming whatever symbolic materials are deemed to represent a given national identity (LiPuma and Meltzoff 1990). In the case of Puerto Rico, however, the ambiguity of the island's political status heightens the stakes of any activity involving the public display of "culture," which is imbued with meaning and nationalistic overtones in ways that go beyond the objectives of their organizers. It is this context that makes Puerto Rican festivals subject to constant scrutiny and debate about what is and is not a "proper" event and that makes them so revealing of contemporary cultural politics. Thus, my focus is the ongoing contentions over issues of legitimacy and representation that surround these events, in order to emphasize the distinctions to which they help give voice and expression.

Although there are many different kinds of festivals, they share similar components. All are *fiestas de pueblo* (people's festivities) in the sense that, although they are organized by a specific, identifiable group, they are free and open to all members of the immediate community as well as to all Puerto Ricans. They are fashioned after a theme linked with the community that organized the festival, and they generally last between three and four days. They all emphasize a musical component, which consists of a day and a night program presented on a central stage, around which are placed *kioskos* (kiosks, or food-vending stands). Besides the music, there are activities oriented to a wide variety of people, from cooking contests to marathons. Festivals are also important components of Puerto Rico's informal economy, serving as a key venue for the sale of food, drinks, and cultural products.

Although contemporary festivals are fashioned after, and are not much different from, the patron-saint festivities that have been celebrated on the island since Spanish colonization, these contemporary festivals represent a new development in Puerto Rico's cultural politics. For example, they are organized by grassroots groups rather than by local governments, and they are distinguished by having a cultural theme that is chosen and highlighted by the organizing groups as a means of self-identification. Moreover, as local scholars have documented (Quintero Rivera 1989, Sánchez 1991), and as will become evident in our discussion, many organizers struggle to distinguish their work from the patron-saint festivities and other types of municipally organized activities.

The distinctions people draw to highlight the uniqueness of

their cultural activities is important in understanding the constraints and motivations that have led people to organize them. They occur in a politically charged and a commercially inundated environment, which makes them primary targets for political and corporate agendas. They also represent one of the few spaces for open public interaction and entertainment in a society where everyday public life is perceived as crime ridden, dangerous, and even life threatening. The cultural content of festivals is often a source of legitimating activities that are used to voice wider concerns about social space, quality of life, or the economic development of a given community. These concerns have introduced many people to the struggle over definitions of culture, as they seek to legitimize their activities to a larger community through materials that bridge regional, class, and political divisions.

In this chapter, I highlight two independent grassroots groups located in Caone in order to explore contemporary issues shaping Puerto Rico's cultural politics and to analyze how these groups affect and are affected by these dynamics. In particular, I examine the groups' role in fostering more encompassing views of Puerto Rican culture and emphasizing nationally unrecognized features of Puerto Rican history. In this way, they can be seen as part of an evolving public culture, an arena of cultural debate where "types, forms and domains of culture are encountering, interrogating and contesting each other in new and unexpected ways" (Appadurai and Breckenridge 1988: 6).

The concluding part of the chapter also considers how these groups help to reconstitute communality by claiming public space through their festivals and how these events cut across the societal dichotomies created by Puerto Rico's colonial context. Important dichotomies that these groups struggle to supersede include politico-partisan divisions, stereotypes that claim that the adherents of one political ideology are more "Puerto Rican" than others, and the distinction between "authentic" expressions of culture and commercial culture.

Composing Culture with Breadfruit Lasagna

In 1982 a group of residents of the Mariana community, in a rural section of Caone, came together to found the Asociación Recreativa, Educativa, y Cultural del Barrio Mariana (ARECMA), one of the first independent community groups in Caone.[1] The purpose of the organization was described as follows: "ARECMA is a not-for-profit organization founded to obtain services to assure the well-being of the community, develop recreational facilities, solve social problems that affect community life, and contribute to the social, educational and cultural well-being of our sector" (mission statement in "¿Qué es ARECMA?" undated leaflet).

While the educational and cultural components of ARECMA's mission were important, the need to organize and mobilize the Mariana community was the primary motivation for creating the group. This organization was particularly needed to lobby for the extension of municipal water to the neighborhood, the construction of roads, the installation of telephone lines, and the development of much-needed recreational facilities in the area. These needs had been neglected by the municipal government due to the community's geographical distance from the urban center of Caone (in the rural highlands, which lacked accessible roads until the 1960s) and its history of political opposition to PPD-dominated Caone. Once a stronghold for the Socialist Party, even known as "Mariana, the Republic," Mariana continues to be a bastion of political dissent, although today the political majority in Mariana is no longer socialist but pro-statehood and pro-commonwealth.[2]

ARECMA's members are mostly drawn from three or four large families, to which a large percentage of the Mariana highland population are related, either through kinship or marriage. They are descendants of peasants who worked small farms on the steep, mountainous lands that were of no interest to the sugar landowners; this allowed Mariana a degree of economic security not present in the coastal area. While many Mariaeños, like most Caoeños, grew sugar cane during the 1920s, and some even lost their lands to the *centrales* (sugar mills), their farming of tobacco, rice, corn, beans, yams, breadfruit, and other crops sustained the community during the harshest economic times. ARECMA's familial composition has allowed the organization to bridge political and religious differences among its members, who represent all political and religious denominations as well as all age groups in the community.

There is no formal criterion for membership other than a commitment to work in the planning and organization of activities, and the size of the organization varies throughout the year, peaking during the annual festival, when most members are mobilized to work. Most members work in civil service and manufacturing, which provide 37.5 percent of the jobs in the community. Women, who represent almost three-quarters of the population in Mariana, compose the majority of ARECMA's members and of its leadership, which includes up to fifteen members. Nevertheless, the most important leaders of ARECMA have traditionally been among the most educated members of the community, and they are mostly pro-independence supporters related through kinship to those who originally founded the organization. Two of its most important leaders are a university professor of social work, commonly known as the "only Ph.D." in the area, and her husband, a former Catholic priest who is now a high school teacher.

Such leadership has given the organization a reputation of being composed of *independentistas* and intellectuals. This reputation has also been strengthened by ARECMA's mobilizations to demand basic resources like sanitation and water supply for the community, which were regarded as "subversive" and "troublesome." These attitudes are part and parcel of the colonial context of Puerto Rican society, where social compliance and submission, rather than social activism, have been promoted as the social rule.

The organization's reputation as an *independentista* bastion led to its persecution both within and outside the community. For instance, ARECMA's inclusion of overtly nationalistic folk singers in its annual festival was initially regarded as subversive. Even a walk against drugs organized by the group took on political overtones when the drug dealers were identified as PNP supporters; thus ARECMA's mobilization was believed to be motivated by politico-partisan concerns. ARECMA members complained of having been accused of storing firearms in a member's basement and of sending money to Nicaragua in the organization's early days. Its meetings were infiltrated by local agents and police informants, who kept files on its activities. All the most important leaders of ARECMA learned in the 1990s that they had police dossiers listing their political activities and their meetings with the organization.

ARECMA was also subject to criticism from the local Catholic and Protestant churches, powerful organizations in a community that is almost equally divided between these two religious affiliations. Because some of ARECMA's first activities took place next to the Catholic church premises, where one of its leaders had functioned as priest, Protestants initially saw the organization as a Catholic group. The inclusion of dance music and the sale of alcohol in ARECMA's festival also turned away the most conservative Protestants from the group. Meanwhile, the Catholic church condemned the ecumenical nature of ARECMA's initial activities, which were open to the entire upper Mariana community irrespective of their faith. At stake was the very definition of community. Whereas the Catholic church limited the concept to its own members, ARECMA aimed to mobilize every community resident without reference to their faith.

Another cause of criticism from the Catholic church was the community activism that the group had encouraged. Whereas ARECMA began as a community movement, some of its leaders had been developing from within the Catholic church itself, where a pro–Puerto Rican stance was being generated through the introduction of typical instruments and Puerto Rican music. As Carlos explained, in commenting on how his police dossier had omitted his religious activities: "How silly of them! They included all of my most mundane political activities, but there is no word here about my work in the church. How could they have been so stupid to have missed it? It is in the church that this community learned to love our Puerto Rican things."

While ARECMA's experience of persecution and mistrust was common to many groups I interviewed, this situation was more frequent among groups that began their work in the 1970s and early 1980s, when social mobilization around culture was becoming commonplace among the Puerto Rican left and these initiatives were perceived as openly oppositional. Repression was greatest for groups, like ARECMA, that voiced specific social, economic, and political demands. ICP-affiliated cultural centers, although some have also experienced persecution (due to the concentration of pro-independence advocates among their membership), have generally been more tolerated than the newcomers because, for the most part, they have refrained from expressing social and political concerns and their cultural work is sanctioned by the government.

Even today, when ARECMA's membership is mostly drawn from the majority parties (PNP and PPD), the organization's reputation as an *independentista* organization of intellectuals still lingers. However, the group has earned a favorable reputation in the community, where people I talked to described ARECMA's members as "good workers" and as people who "care about the community." ARECMA's activities, which ranged from lobbying for services in city hall, to walks against drugs, to organizing a children's summer camp, have won the organization greater popularity. The group has also made itself visible beyond the immediate community by participating in events sponsored by other organizations in and out of Caone. In 1992 their festival was even dedicated to Caone on behalf of the city's bicentennial, an act that members pointed to as a sign of the growth and capacity of their small group and community to give a "gift" to larger Caone and momentarily transform their subordinate position in relation to it. In turn, these transformations have imbued the group with a sense of moral pride, as evidenced by the statements of a long-time member: "We have overcome so many barriers in this community. This is a very closed community, and we have overcome many obstacles. At first people were fearful and no one wanted to protest in city hall, or work in the community, but we have achieved great intellectual, spiritual, and moral development in our community through the work of ARECMA."

An important element contributing to ARECMA's popularity was the "Festival de la Pana" (Breadfruit Festival), which ARECMA initiated in 1984. The festival, which grew out of a cooking workshop in 1984, was originally conceived as a small community celebration. Yet, much to the group's surprise, it soon became one of the most important celebrations for the whole of Caone and the rest of the island. At present, the Breadfruit Festival is ARECMA's single most important activity and the one that members credit with enhancing the group's standing and respect in Caone, with forging a name for the organization, and enabling it to reach out into the community. The event is now attended by thousands of visitors from inside and outside Caone, which has lessened its early identification as a politico-partisan event. These changes have not come without a price, however, for ARECMA has had to face challenges and engage in many compromises.

Like many other grassroots festivals, ARECMA's drew on a symbol that is particularly important in the community. Puerto Rico's public festivals embrace a diversity of themes, but most acknowledge the ICP's official regard for the peasant past by selecting fruits, vegetables, and other agricultural staples for thematic inspiration. Generally, however, most groups reject an idyllic, romanticized image of the past by honoring the most mundane and ordinary subsistence crops that are associated with specific regional histories in very particular ways.

ARECMA's selection of the breadfruit, for instance, honors the historical role of this fruit as a subsistence staple in times of scarcity. Introduced to the island as food for slaves and animals, the breadfruit became the main subsistence staple in Mariana, as well as the rest of the island, because it yielded nourishment during the sugar industry's *tiempo muerto* (dead time), when the area was most dependent on its own products. People came from all over Caone to pick wild breadfruit in Mariana, from which Maria-eños coined the pejorative name of *paneros* or *come pana* (breadfruit eaters). By selecting the breadfruit as their symbol, ARECMA intended to transform the *pana* from a symbol of poverty, backwardness, and inferiority to one of community identity and pride.

During the festival, the breadfruit is featured in the stage decorations, in fried foods and "gourmet" dishes (flan, pies, lasagna, donuts), and even in the *trova* (folk music) played in honor of the breadfruit. As ARECMA's current director explained, "What we wanted to do was exalt the breadfruit through its 'gourmetisación' because the breadfruit was important for the survival of this community, where people had to eat breadfruit for lunch and dinner. The breadfruit contributed to Mariana's lower status because it was believed to be only for pigs. Peeling and boiling a breadfruit were seen as low status." The festival has indeed contributed to transforming the breadfruit into a symbol of community pride. As one long-time member noted, "At first, the young people complained about the name of the festival and were embarrassed by it, but now everyone is proud and they are the first ones to wear the T-shirts of the festival."

In 1994 even the national newspaper, the *San Juan Star*, featured some of the festival recipes and noted the changed image of the breadfruit, pointing to an 81 percent growth in its cultivation since the 1970s and to new recipes using the fruit (Zehr 1994a:

25-27). This is a good example of the national recognition many independent cultural festivals have attained in Puerto Rican society. Today, pride in the festival is evident among ARECMA members throughout the year. Discussions about the festival dominate many conversations in the area and festival T-shirts are worn year-round by the members and throughout Caone. Moreover, the festival has become one of the primary means through which ARECMA reaches out to different segments of the Mariana community. In previous years, the festival has been dedicated to the youth and to Mariaeños *ausentes* (former residents of Mariana, many of whom live in the United States, mainly in Delaware, where many Maria-eños migrated to seek agricultural work in the 1940s).

The Breadfruit Festival was initially very similar to an ICP-defined cultural event. Although they had no ties to the ICP, organizers drew mostly from the ICP's list of affiliated artists to find "authentic" representatives of Puerto Rican culture. Festivals similar to ARECMA's are more often organized by *independentistas* and intellectuals (schoolteachers and college professors), like the leaders of ARECMA, who purposely seek out musicians who are overtly nationalistic. Folkloric artists were also selected because they were considered to be the most representative of the community's rural history, which is the festival's identifying theme. In addition, nationalist artists who have attained great popularity nationwide were a common feature of ARECMA's festival from the start, even prior to its recent popularization.

Events like the Breadfruit Festival are thought to be more cultural than commercial, judged by ICP standards, and are often (although not always) looked favorably upon by the ICP. The latter attempts to identify with and show its approval of these types of festivals by awarding small contributions to their music program (usually no more than five hundred dollars to pay an ICP-affiliated artist). Their folkloric style also provides the basis for the common scholarly interpretation of these festivals as expressions of colonial resistance (Quintero-Rivera 1989).

Nevertheless, like most locally organized festivals, ARECMA's program has always mixed ICP-affiliated artists with local musicians and entertainment. Included in ARECMA's mostly folkloric program, for instance, was a Menudo-like pop group[3] and a karate demonstration. "Esto también es cultura" (this too is culture), I was told, after I noted that these groups appeared to depart from the stated goal of a more "traditional" program.

The development of the festival as ARECMA's primary activity did not occur without internal resistance. In keeping with the dominant view of culture as educational and not for entertainment, some members believed that the popularization of the festival would detract from the organization's cultural objectives. The growth of the festival, for example, made the organization more dependent on support from the wider Mariana community, which in turn required the organization to "popularize" itself by reaching out to PNP sectors of the community to diversify the mostly PIP leadership. This involved taking more flexible positions on issues affecting the community in order to safeguard social consensus, which had the effect of softening ARECMA's reputation as a "subversive" group. One member who distanced himself at this time was a local leader of the Socialist Party. He now recalls: "We realized that some of the positions we were taking were perceived to be too radical in this community. Some people thought that we were jaded [quemados, literally "burnt"]. At that moment we shifted toward reconciling with the community."

In addition, the growth of the festival required the organization to seek corporate sponsors, as well as support from local politicians. ARECMA had initially eschewed these sources of funding; now it needed a way of defraying the higher costs for folk artists and salsa groups, whose prices had sharply increased with the growing popularity of cultural festivals throughout the island. The same artists whom ARECMA booked for between six and eight hundred dollars for the first festivals in the mid- and late 1980s were charging over two thousand dollars in 1994.

Despite the festival's great impact inside and outside Caone, some felt that it was distracting the organization from other priorities, given its demands on members' time and its cost to organize. Operating funds are raised through the sale of vending stands and products like drinks and food in the festivals, and through donations from politicians and corporate sponsors; yet because the activities are free to the public, festivals often do no better than break even. Profits, if there are any, commonly range from two to five thousand dollars, but many festivals end up losing money. Disagreements about the role of the festival led to the resignation of some key members of ARECMA. Its family-based structure, which had been a source of its strength, ended up hurting the organization at this time because these members left accompanied by their relatives.

The result of these tensions has been the transformation of the group and the reorganization of the festival. PNP members began to outnumber the socialist core of the group, and the group began to yield to popular demands. For instance, ARECMA has begun to showcase popular music over the last years, adding a salsa or merengue band each night in addition to the traditional folkloric programming, something it had once resisted doing. At the same time, however, the nationalistic genres that initially provoked criticism of ARECMA began to attain greater acceptance and have now become an intrinsic part of its annual program.

However, ARECMA's popularity has made it susceptible to greater political and economic constraints, making the "gourmetization" of the breadfruit a costly task. For instance, because ARECMA's work has gained national recognition, it is a likely candidate for ICP's attempts at incorporating the more "cultural" expressions to strengthen itself through the appropriation of alternative cultural productions. In fact, after contributing $250 toward a musical group, the local ICP-affiliated cultural center listed the Breadfruit Festival among its sponsored activities in its 1994 application for the annual "Winston Medal for Culture."

This caused tensions with ARECMA when the center won the $5,000 prize and national recognition. ARECMA had previously applied for this prize, unsuccessfully, but Caone's ICP-affiliated center won on its first application. It is generally easier for such centers to win this prize, given that R. J. Reynolds grants at least two awards per year to ICP-affiliated cultural groups as a means of involving the ICP in the promotion of the award and selection of the winners. (I was told that when the prize was first instituted in 1983, all awards went to ICP-affiliated centers.) The major cause of offense to ARECMA was that its own festival was publicly linked to the cultural center, when they saw that the latter's contribution to their festival had been minimal, and threatened ARECMA's exclusive identification with the festival.

ARECMA's leaders have also had to defend the autonomy of their festival against the municipal administration, which always requests that some kiosks be reserved for city hall in exchange for technical support (trash collection, lighting, and permits). These kiosks have been used for political fundraising activities. The group felt particularly persecuted by the first PNP administration of Caone (1992–present), which they perceived as suspicious and uncooperative. In turn, more conservative PNP members tended to regard ARECMA as a communist stronghold. This mutual suspicion, which permeated ARECMA's relationship with the local PNP administration, peaked when the group began to borrow a municipally owned space to celebrate the festival, which had outgrown the original site within the Mariana community. This has made it increasingly difficult for ARECMA to defend its autonomy from the municipal administration. During my research, ARECMA had to organize a public demonstration in front of city hall before the administration bestowed permits to celebrate the festival in municipally owned facilities. ARECMA also monitors the exposure politicians receive onstage during the festival's inaugural activities (which always include welcoming remarks from the mayor or key area politicians who have contributed to the activities) in order to limit their use of the festival for self-promotion.

The group has also had to defend its autonomy vis-à-vis corporate sponsors. After they hired a promoter to help boost corporate sponsorship, ARECMA saw their association with their own festival compromised when the promoter allowed more concessions to the corporations than were originally authorized by ARECMA. In previous years, ARECMA had permitted advertising in the drink kiosks, along with flags and promotional banners around the festival's perimeter. Without consulting the group, however, the promoter promised the corporations far greater exposure, including placing by the stage a giant balloon that touted one sponsor's product. ARECMA members were extremely upset about the concessions, which gave the companies too much credit for what was really the community's effort.

Despite these difficulties in preserving the festival as a financially self-sustaining community event, discussions about the festival always stressed its importance to the community and concluded that it should continue. As one person put it: "This is our gift to this community. We are making history with this event." Like other groups who have had to make similar compromises in their festivals, they perceived the changes as a "need" that would not compromise the cultural nature of the festival. Instead, the group emphasized continued control of the activity, and measures were taken to limit the involvement of politicians and advertising in areas considered "most cultural." In the next chapter I elaborate on how ARECMA and other groups negotiated corporate sponsorship to safeguard the cultural content of their activity. Suffice it to say here that trying to defend their festival's autonomy has been a difficult task.

By the time I left Mariana, ARECMA was on the verge of accomplishing its long-time goal of establishing its own multi-activity community center. It had made a down payment on some land with money earned from the festival and donated by the local senator, and it had called community meetings to plan the project. In one such meeting, held to discuss proposals for the newly acquired space, a cultural center was one idea most community residents supported. Their dream facility would include, among other things, an all-purpose activity and recreational area, a child-care center, and even a pool, features that point to their concern over issues of recreation and quality of life. They also envisioned that the Breadfruit Festival would no longer be celebrated on municipal property but would be "brought back to the community," which organizers felt would lessen the risk of crime, provide a more familylike setting, and enhance the group's control over the activity. These objectives point to their continuing search for greater autonomy and independence, even when these goals may become more elusive for the group.

The Flat-Bottomed Boat: Whose Boat?

Another well-known group in Caone is the Committee of the Lancha Planúa Festival, founded in 1988 purely for the celebration of a festival. There are many groups throughout the island, especially those founded in the late 1980s, that were inspired by already existing festivals. This festival originated in city hall, where the main organizer—a long-time resident of the La Playa coastal community in Caone, a PPD activist, and a physical education instructor—was working at the time. As he explained, "The idea was to organize something to highlight La Playa because most of the nearby communities had their own regional celebration and nothing was happening in La Playa." The group was registered with the following mission statement: "The festival is founded to provide La Playa with a recreational, cultural and sport activity and to promote internal tourism to contribute to the socioeconomic development of the eastern area" (Comité Organizador del Festival de la Lancha Planúa 1994).

The festival soon became the primary venue for the expression of a regional identity in an area that had been heavily dominated by the sugar industry. Unlike the residents of the Mariana neighborhood, coastal residents had been unable to rely on farming since most flat coastal land was in the hands of the sugar mills. A port, the most important in the eastern area, served as the lifeline of the community until its closing in 1958 (Ortiz Cuadra 1991).[4] During the most active days of the port (between 1910 and the 1950s), a public infrastructure grew up—a school, police department, and mail station—along with a booming commerce, allowing La Playa a degree of independence from Caone's municipal government. As a result, people in La Playa fostered a local identity that glorifies the richness brought by the port while deemphasizing the region's history of active trade unions and its dependence on the sugar-based economy.

Now the days of the port are presented as the real cause for Caone's growth, rather than the achievements of the urban center itself, and many area residents define themselves as *playeros* rather than as Caoeños. The most utopian of all even talk about turning La Playa into a separate municipality, a goal achieved by other coastal communities in Puerto Rico that have developed independently of their respective municipal towns.[5] It is this regional pride that the festival committee drew upon to organize a setting where the "greatness" of the area could be re-created.

This re-creation is particularly important today, thirty years after the port's closing, when poverty and unemployment are common in the area. A post office is the only administrative enclave left in the region where 26 percent of the civilian workforce is unemployed and only 10 percent of the residents work within the locality (Programa de Educación Comunal de Entrega y Servicio 1994).

Like ARECMA, the festival committee of La Playa mirrors the regional history of the area. For example, its membership evidences the continued class and race segregation of the residents, a legacy of the area's sugar history. This segregation is apparent even in the layout of the neighborhood, which is divided into the waterfront area and the less-desirable Las Parcelas. The waterfront properties are presently occupied by descendants of the wealthy merchants who once dominated the town's economy. Some of them still run small stores, but most work outside the community in service occupations. They are lighter skinned than the rest of the community, and many are linked to one another by kinship. Las Parcelas, on the other hand, are mostly inhabited by descendants of workers in the port and the sugar industry. The section is named after the *parcelas* (parcels) program, one of the early populist measures of the PPD government that led to the distribution of small plots of land to landless workers in the 1940s. Today Las Parcelas residents are currently unemployed or make a living through fishing, part-time construction work, or welfare subsidies.

The festival's organizing committee is composed mainly of merchants, mostly restaurant or grocery-store owners, with the addition of representatives of community groups whose help, connections, and consent are indispensable for the celebration. Thus the committee also includes the president of the Fishermen's Organization, a woman with connections at the Lands Authority Administration (which helps arrange for the loan of municipally owned space for the festival), a woman with experience organizing pageants, and a man who is a known community leader. Membership, which is mostly by invitation, confers prestige, and once in the group members generally attend most meetings. These meetings are organized informally in a member's home and begin seven to eight months prior to the festival's celebration. Only members and friends or visitors who want to be involved in the festival attend the meetings, which deal primarily with its organization.

The festival is presently organized by a committee of La Playa residents, but the association of its leader with the municipal PPD administration has given the group a pro-PPD image. Despite this, and like ARECMA, the group's present constitution is more politically diverse than its image. This diversity of political representation, more common among independent groups than among the members of ICP-affiliated centers, is assured by the dependence of these groups upon the resources, skills, and contacts of community members, irrespective of their political affiliations. What has remained constant, however, is the autocratic leadership of the organization, whose founder wields disproportionate influence.

Although the committee is not open to the broader public, the popularity of the event is assured by the group's symbolic appeal to the flat-bottomed fishing boat, the *lancha planúa,* which endows the activity with great popularity among the area's fishermen. This boat, while similar to craft made in various coastal areas of Puerto Rico, is believed by La Playa residents to be unique because of its flat-bottomed design and method of construction. The flat-bottomed boat is useless for fishing today because pollution has made it impossible to fish near the coast. Instead it is used for short trips along the coast or to ferry passengers to larger fishing boats anchored offshore. Moreover, the flat-bottomed boat has become a sports and tourist attraction, which has led to transformations in its design. Now the boats are designed to be faster in order to compete in a race during the festival.

Descendants of the originator of the *lancha* are known residents of Las Parcelas community in La Playa. However, they trace the origins of the *lancha* not to their own family but to the Taino, who (as a local *lancha*-builder claimed) "were the first ones to navigate with a *lancha planúa.*" As previously noted, finding a Taino origin for the object or event around which a festival is celebrated is a common way of legitimizing festivals that do not draw directly on Puerto Rico's peasant past, and that are more likely to be targeted by local intellectuals and politicians as "fads" for the celebration of one more festival.

Most people, however, traced the lancha to La Playa, as something "original to Puerto Rico," without seeking any other legitimation to celebrate a festival in its honor. The festival has been embraced by the community, which constantly compares it to the famous festivities that were common during the days when the port was in use, La Playa's glory days. Local enthusiasm for the festival even overrides divisions and contradictions, such as the fact that local merchants do not buy local fishermen's fish because frozen imported fish is cheaper, even though the fishermen are the greatest supporters of the festival. Fishermen provide financial support, and they help with construction and maintenance and the organization of the Lancha Regatta or boat race. It is they who construct the *lanchas*, which can cost up to five hundred dollars apiece, and which may or may not be bought by a participant in the regatta. But the regatta is never publicized as much as the fishermen would like. One fisherman acknowledged that the *lancha planúa* was just a good excuse for the celebration of a festival: "They just have the *lancha* because of the name. You can see that because they even schedule three main activities at the same time as the *lancha* regatta."

The committee's version of La Playa's history, briefly summarized in the festival's program, and its account of the origins of the fishermen's village, read on stage during an homage to the fishermen, also revealed the fishermen's subordinate position. The committee had begun by taping interviews with the oldest residents of the population, which it used to develop the first written account of La Playa's history. The history emphasizes the best-known merchant and landowning families of La Playa (additionally revealing the permanence of class and status hierarchies in the area) as well as the "innovations" (factories, farms, barbershops, cars, festivities) and achievements (best workers in different areas, war heroes, musicians) that various individuals contributed to La Playa. The tribute, however, ended up focusing on the merchants' role in La Playa and deemphasizing that of the fishermen and port workers. Most of all, the text provoked questions about relatives, forebears, and others who were not mentioned. Some fishermen, like Juan, who identified himself as a lifelong fisherman, disowned the village history read on stage during the homage to the fishermen: "What was read was Jorge's version. He is a descendant of the merchants, and his father used to steal the workers' salary through his canteen. He enriched himself at the cost of keeping his workers poor and their children hungry. What was read was a lie. We recognized it but no one said anything because we were already on stage."

Despite this controversy and the stinting attention accorded to the *lancha*, notwithstanding its status as the festival theme, I was surprised that most residents of La Playa with whom I discussed it defended both the festival and its organizers. (I found similar views voiced by the participants of other festivals whose theme was not given a lot of attention.) Instead, other aspects of the festival were regarded by the participants as being part of La Playa community. For instance, the competition over the *palo ensebao* (greased post), a discontinued popular game that was a centerpiece of previous celebrations of the area, and the beauty pageant, in which a young woman is selected to represent the region in other activities throughout the island, were elements of the festival that people identified as "traditions" of La Playa.

The beauty contest was not originally part of the program but was added on the initiative of one of the women in the group. Its organizer, a single mother whose daughter was later selected as queen, took the idea from the annual patron-saint festivities, in which a queen is chosen to represent Caone. Believing that Caone's queen could not adequately represent La Playa as well, the organizer aimed to create a local pageant that would also serve to involve young women like her daughter in the festival. The pageant has since become one of the most important and well-attended activities in the festival, as well as a way for La Playa to gain visibility at the national level. Pageant winners are given the option of becoming part of the festival committee, where they constitute its youngest members.

In order to understand the popularity of this pageant it is important to note that Puerto Rican beauty contests and sports competitions are highly charged with nationalistic overtones. At the international level, beauty and sports competitions have historically enabled Puerto Rico to shed its colonial identity momentarily and to participate as a "sovereign" nation (Mac Aloon 1984, Torres 1994). These pageants are similarly charged with regional pride. The queen of the Lancha Festival, for instance, is expected to attend most festivals throughout the island to represent the community of La Playa. The success of her tenure is judged according to the number of queens from other towns whom she is able to gather and bring to La Playa for her outgoing ceremony. One teary outgoing queen, an eighteen-year-old in her first year at the university, was considered a very successful queen because she attended almost forty festivals throughout the island during her tenure and invited fifty queens from other towns to her outgoing ceremony. She expressed her regional pride in a monologue that is evocative of the emotionally charged language used by queens all over the island:

> My dear Playeros, it has been an honor to represent La Playa and exalt the name of the community, and represent our Playero traditions, which are the pride of La Playa and all of Puerto Rico. I am a Playera at heart, and the trophies I have won, everything, is all for La Playa. . . . everywhere I went my pride was telling people about this community, and when people asked me which town I came from, I always proudly said La Playa. Some had heard about this festival, and others had even visited, but others learned for the first time that Caone had two queens, not only the one of Caone, but also a queen of La Playa.

Local residents also pointed to the festival's role in attracting commerce and visitors to the area, projecting an image of the community to the outside, and providing a safe, carefree setting (*un ambiente tranquilo*) for social interaction. Unlike ARECMA's Breadfruit Festival, the Lancha Festival involved corporate sponsors from the beginning. The number of sponsors that have become interested in the activity is one measure of its success and popularity, and members are not ambivalent about this funding. Their attitude is related to the festival's role in attracting commerce and tourism to La Playa, which provide sources of income to La Playa's residents. Thus the number of people from other towns attending the festival, the volume of cars in the parking lot, the number of absent Playeros returning to La Playa during the festival, and the increase of sales and commerce, were all cited to me as important in making this festival the "best in the area."

While the Lancha Festival has evolved into the most popular activity in the community, the organizing committee has not been free of internal and external criticism. Women members have voiced dissatisfaction with the autocratic attitude of the group's founder. But interestingly, while some accused this man of "childish" behavior, they blamed the vice president, another woman, for failing to "handle" him and induce him to control his temper, reflecting their belief that women should not lead themselves but rather be of assistance to the leader. One woman quit the organization and another was thinking of quitting by the time I left Caone.

Within the community a local environmental group, founded in the mid-1980s to challenge a plan to build a primary wastewater treatment plant in the area, publicly criticized the failure of the Lancha Committee to oppose this plan, which would have worsened the area's pollution problem. Although some members of the Lancha Committee belong to the environmental group that organized protests against the project, the committee itself, as well as the majority of fishermen and merchants in the community, remained apart from the environmental struggle. It, like ARECMA's early mobilization for improved community resources, was feared and targeted as revolutionary. Besides these fears, which are commonly directed toward groups organizing protests in their communities, it was believed that the Lancha Committee's lack of participation was due to its links with the PPD municipal government, which backed the plant and discouraged local mobilization. The environmental group publicly attacked the Lancha Committee for not joining in their struggles and for not being truly representative of the community, inasmuch as they are not elected by it but are appointed by existing committee members.

The Lancha Committee has also been criticized for being unresponsive to the needs of the larger community of La Playa. One member of a neighborhood committee noted: "They are planning to build a *glorieta* [small shrine-like niche] in the cemetery, but if they really were in touch with the community they would know that what we really need is a basketball court and recreational areas to give the youth things to do that will keep them off drugs." Accordingly, it was believed that the Lancha Committee's more "superfluous priorities" were related to the fact that they are mostly decided by festival organizers without consulting with other sectors of the population. Thus it is the merchant-dominated leadership who set the group's priorities, emphasizing initiatives that might boost tourism and economic development rather than addressing the more basic needs of the community.

The environmental group, in turn, has organized around a neighborhood committee and, like ARECMA in Mariana, is planning to establish a cultural center in its community and possibly a coconut festival in La Playa. I was told that the proposed new festival was the group's response to the failure of the Lancha Committee to include the full community in its own festival's organization. The neighborhood committee hopes to involve more of the community by adding a voting process to make decisions about the scope and content of the festival. The new festival is in its earliest stages; yet the reasons given by one committee member for its creation accurately describe the rationale behind other local initiatives: "We want something that is organized by us, and that represents us, where we could bring the things we like, and that is something that unites the community, that is organized and directed by the community."

The plan for a new festival in La Playa exemplifies the value ascribed to these celebrations for increasing the public recognition and representation of particular communities. The plan also indicates the importance placed on a festival's community orientation as a means of popular legitimization. And, while the new celebration will probably not be free of internal contradictions, it is likely to broaden the discussion of what and who should represent La Playa.

"Haciendo Patria": For Space and Representation

So far I have emphasized how ARECMA and the Lancha Committee differ in origin, scope, and content. ARECMA was born out of community work, whereas the Lancha Committee was originally the creation of a city-hall worker and is now mostly composed of merchants from the community. Membership in the former is also more open than the latter, where it is mostly by invitation. ARECMA is more cautious about commercial and governmental involvement in the festival than are the Lancha Festival's organizers. As merchants themselves, the latter are firm believers that commercial involvement is a mark of the festival's success. Lastly, ARECMA draws on activities that more closely represent the institutionalized views of Puerto Rican culture than does the Lancha Festival, in which most activities revolve around beach games, sports, and music rather than folk art and nationalist artists. Beyond these differences, however, ARECMA and the Lancha Committee share many similarities with other community groups I interviewed throughout the island.

Most significantly, these groups are working at the level of civil and political society (J. Cohen and Arato 1992); they are opening new venues for public discussion while exerting political pressure on behalf of their particular communities for expanded resources and representation in greater Caone. Their work is similar to that of grassroots groups active in other contexts, where issues of social reproduction, space, resources, and identity take precedence over class struggle, and where the construction of collective identities becomes the site of struggles over meaning and representation and resources (Castells 1983, D. Harvey 1989).

During the period of my research, ARECMA members had secured from their district senator[6] a three-year allocation of $10,000 per year toward their community center. This grant bypassed the PNP municipal government, which had not contributed to its work (for what members saw as politico-partisan reasons). In addition, through the successful organization of their festival, which has grown in complexity since its origin, the group's members have secured a reputation as competent organizers, thereby increasing their leverage with the municipality. The Lancha Festival, for its part, is regarded by people in La Playa as the most important medium for attracting commerce, visitors, and tourism and attaining greater standing in Caone. However, these advantages affect La Playa residents unequally since it is the merchants, some of whom have beachfront establishments, who benefit most by attracting tourism through the festival. Other groups have been even more successful in obtaining resources for the community through their work. The most successful group I met had received $250,000 from their local municipality toward the sum they needed to open a facility that will incorporate environmental, recreational, drug-prevention, and cultural goals.[7]

As a way of attracting public attention to community needs, the celebration of a cultural festival was a common priority for most of the groups I encountered in my research. Indeed, most of the independent groups I interviewed have organized, as the Lancha Committee has, solely around the celebration of a festival. The public character of the festival, which local residents see as a tool for attaining social recognition and drawing attention to their community within and outside their respective municipalities, contributes in important ways to its appeal. The popularity of being involved in a festival was even described to me as *la fiebre de festivales* (festival fever). This in itself is significant because it entails an expansion in the number of individuals, groups, and interests that can actively participate in the public representation of Puerto Rican culture. Many individuals are thus transformed from consumers of cultural representations into active producers and participants through the organization of public events.

In this process, these groups both validate and challenge the standards of the government cultural policy for defining authentic Puerto Rican culture. They sometimes draw from official definitions of Puerto Rican culture in selecting the content of their activities, thereby contributing to the reproduction of the government's standards for defining culture. For instance, many groups seek legitimacy by including at least some folk music in their programming (although it is usually showcased in the morning or early afternoon rather than during prime nighttime hours); by requesting ICP assistance, even if it is often declined; or by presenting the artisans participating in their events as ICP-affiliated, even if this is not always true. Most often, however, these groups promote elements of regional and popular culture and thereby serve as important venues for expressing aspects of Puerto Rican culture that go beyond what is recognized by official cultural policy. In the context of the festival, different aspects of contemporary life, including food, music, and contemporary folk arts, were presented as expressions of Puerto Ricanness. Similarly, contributing to the festivals, such as by preparing cod fritters to sell or simply by attending them, was referred to as *haciendo patria*, or helping to forge and strengthen the nation.

It should be mentioned here that, due to political and economic constraints, organizers are rarely able to highlight their identifying theme fully. Sánchez's (1991) study of eight Puerto Rican agricultural festivals also noted the inability of organizers to emphasize the agricultural product celebrated in the event. For instance, consider the case of the 1993 Festival of the Pineapple Cutter, organized by a committee of residents of Vega Alta and led by a former local assemblyman and self-identified community worker. In this festival the only allusion to the pineapple was a stand selling piña coladas and a cardboard cutout of a pineapple on stage. Once an important pineapple-growing region, Vega Alta is now primarily an urban area and not one single person still works as a pineapple cutter there. Yet, while the pineapple was lacking, the festival was still considered a significant cultural event and was presented by its organizers as a "traditional festival honoring the legacy of Puerto Rican culture, of our people and of the cane worker" (Comité Organizador del Festival del Trabajador de la Piña 1993).

Even activities organized by government-affiliated cultural groups fail to comply with standards of authenticity. In the Festival of the Chipe, organized by the members of the ICP-affiliated cultural center of the town of Añasco, chipe fish are only found in the turnovers sold in one of the kiosks, and these were bought frozen from large chain supermarkets rather than fished by locals. Similarly, in the numerous fishermen's festivals organized by members of fishing cooperatives, most of the fish used in *pinchos* (shish kebab) consists of imported imitation-fish products. Among other reasons for this, the local fishing industry is affected by saltwater pollution and the lack of markets for local fish. Often more expensive than imports, local fish are not bought by small vendors who sell at these festivals.

Yet, despite the lack of elements that clearly associate them with specific themes, most of the festivals I visited were presented as "cultural." Even activities that had only been celebrated for two or three years were presented in this manner—as traditions that should be safeguarded and continued by the community. This characterization was associated with their being "organized by our communities," which made them expressions of Puerto Rican values and traditions. When I asked what those values were, people pointed to the history of the region, the fried food that is sold in the festival, or the familiar setting that characterizes the event. Thus, far from being seen as a contradiction, the absence of objects or features representing the themes in the cultural festivals did not lessen their appeal or identification with culture for their communities. This has also been noted by Quintero-Rivera (1991), who observed a preponderance of sensory stimulus in these festivals, where food, music, and enjoyment were always at the center of the activities. Thus, the meaningfulness of a particular spectacle is not circumscribed by specific "proofs" of representativity or "the degree to which the elements displayed to the public seem to represent key elements in the public's cultural and emotional life" (Beeman 1993: 380) but is derived from the experiences generated within the context of the festival.

Moreover, through their showcasing of diverse genres, rhythms, and forms of entertainment, these festivals attract diverse sectors of society that are perceived by public opinion as distinct and isolated. In order to understand this issue, it is important to note that music has been an important element around which identities are constructed in Puerto Rican society. As discussed by Ana María García's 1993 film *Cocolos y rockeros,* the categories of *conserva* and *a go go* or *cocolos* and *rockeros* (to denominate fans of Afro-Caribbean music and rock in the 1960s and 1980s) have served to identify distinct class and race groupings on the island. While these social groups are not self-contained, *cocolos* are perceived as darker, lower-class Puerto Ricans in contrast to *rockeros,* which refers to whiter, middle- and upper-class Puerto Ricans. In most cultural festivals, these categories are crosscut through the showcasing of popular, oppositional, folkloric, or dance music, forms that have served as an important basis for expressing societal differences yet are now jointly presented in the same setting. (Not surprisingly, many ICP promoters strongly disliked this cross-fertilization of rhythms, as Chapter II notes.)

Of course, involvement in the actual production of these events was not the only way by which people actively participated in or affected the constitution of the program. This becomes evident when one analyzes the disjunctures between a group's objectives and the ensuing events.[8] ARECMA's original intention to organize a more "cultural" and "community-based" event was transformed as the Breadfruit Festival attained great popularity among a regional and national constituency. Achieving this level of success required ARECMA to negotiate greater acceptance in the local community, which spurred internal transformations and moderation of its political identity that made it possible to work with other groups in the community. Similarly, the Lancha Committee's original aim was to develop an activity that represents La Playa and to attract business and tourism, but the Festival of the Flat-Bottomed Boat evolved into an important catalyst for other groups in the nearby community. These have either reacted to a perceived lack of interest and responsiveness by the Lancha Committee to the greater problems affecting the community or become inspired by its festival's popularity, which has led other groups to consider organizing similar events in the area.

Many groups I interviewed had similar experiences, especially because these festivals often constitute the forum in which a community's internal differences, conflicts, and contradictions are worked out. Thus while organizers recognized the great appeal of these festivals and their ability to draw attention to the group and help "give a name" to their community, they were also aware that these events often take on a life of their own.

In light of these issues, I became convinced that, beyond the particular program or content of the activity, the importance of these festivals also stems from the events themselves, and from their role as a venue for social interactions that would otherwise not occur. In a local context where everyday public life is deemed dangerous, the work of these groups speaks to a common preoccupation with the lack of space for public expression and encounters in contemporary Puerto Rican society. Indeed, Puerto Rico's crime rates have continued to increase in the last years, reaching levels that are far above the average for most cities in the United States (which serves as the major reference for local statistics).[9] It cannot be ignored, however, that the local media contribute to this heightened fear of crime, which is encroaching on public space and serving to maintain class distinctions on the island. Fear of crime, for instance, is being used to mark class through space by justifying the segregation of middle- and upper-class residential areas. These areas are increasingly being converted into exclusive security havens by the addition of security gates and the closing of residential streets except to residents.[10] Consider that a survey conducted in 1994 showed that 64 percent of the population was afraid to venture alone a mile away from home and 67 percent felt that the level of crime was worse than ever (Redacción *El Nuevo Día* 1994).

In this context, attendance at a festival can also be seen as an act of defiance, and the proliferation of these festivals as a means to create and expand public spheres. That is, these festivals help reconstitute communality by allowing for exchange and communication to occur around the public events and outdoor public spaces that have been encroached upon. I refer to "public spheres" in the plural to go beyond Habermas's conception of the bourgeois public sphere as an idyllic and unattainable, inclusive public space centered on "rational critical discourse" (Habermas 1992). Instead, I draw from some reelaborations of Habermas's term that emphasize the variety of public spaces and venues that are used to create parallel and alternative models of community (Calhoun 1992, Urla 1995). For instance, these festivals and cultural groups are enlarging common grounds and spaces by shattering the strict politico-partisan dichotomies that dominate much of everyday interactions in Puerto Rico. This is evident in the emphasis that people give to superseding individual political and religious identities for the sake of communal goals. This aspect is especially important in contemporary Puerto Rico, where the sharp political dichotomies between the dominant pro-commonwealth and pro-statehood parties, to the exclusion of the separatist option, have helped to perpetuate the colonial situation and to further dependency on the United States. A self-identified political "fanatic" recounted how his attitudes about politics changed through his involvement in one of these local groups:

> Initially these people from an opposing political party entered the group, and I was suspicious until I realized that their involvement did not affect the work of the community, but that they had the same preoccupations as I did. I began to wonder whether it is positive to identify with different political parties. Today, I consider myself an "apolitical" person. I decided that it is not worth it to be identified with partisan politics, but that what is important is that people are identified with the community. Now I hold the vision that whoever is concerned with the community will have my friendship and support.

This common preoccupation to appear nonpartisan is also revealing of the island-wide reconfiguration of politics since the 1970s that I described in Chapter I. Specifically, since the PNP first challenged the PPD's power, people have seen enough evidence to conclude that, as I was told, "civic work and politics don't mix." Many cultural groups have been adversely affected by having a close identification with a particular political party; their funding support is jeopardized whenever there is a change of administration. Most ICP-affiliated centers have been equally affected, and have also sought to shed their identification with given political parties, although for them this goal has been most difficult to achieve given their historical legacy of domination by the PPD and PIP. Thus, the concern to forge intraparty community groups could be signaling a growing obsolescence of the older party patronage system and a growing disenchantment with formal politics in favor of civic activism.

The common concern among these groups with opening new venues of public interaction is also evident in their plans to establish and administer a physical space, just like the groups in Mariana and La Playa. In fact, many groups originally came together around a project to reclaim a physical space within their immediate community—either unused lands, old houses, or historical sites—and share similar goals of establishing multipurpose activity centers. Organizers often distinguished these proposed centers from their towns' existing ICP-affiliated cultural centers by stressing the community and social-service orientation that will characterize their independent projects. A cultural group planning to open a physical space in its community explained this difference as follows: "The cultural center is for all of Vega Alta [the municipality], but our organization is for the community, and it is not restricted to culture." Instead, their group was about "serving the elderly and youth, and about increasing spaces for recreation and leisure."

In order to safeguard their reputation as community organizations, people often stressed the familiar community setting of their activities and contrasted them to the municipally organized patron-saint activities that are celebrated annually by each town. Even though the community festivals often shared many similarities in content and programming with the patron-saint festivities, and many have even been modeled after them, organizers avoided identifying their activities with the latter because they have developed a reputation for being overcommercialized as well as crime- and drug-ridden. Most importantly, because they are organized by city hall, patron-saint celebrations are commonly seen as being linked to the political party that dominates in the particular municipality.

Even the most boisterous festivals were presented by their organizers as cultural, family oriented, and "community based."

One reason to protect the family image of these festivals is that most criticisms directed at them have questioned their community value, raised doubts about their safety, and pointed to their excesses. This view was voiced by a member of the cultural commission in Puerto Rico's legislature, who expressed his wish to minimize the number of these festivals as follows: "It is not that I am against these festivals, but why do we have to have so many? Why not concentrate them into four or five and do them the right way, and spend the money for these festivals on other things? You make more *patria* that way. I do not understand how you make *patria* and culture standing up on a stage and yelling insanities while a [Catholic] mass is going on in the plaza. If that is culture, then let God come down and say so!"

In order to protect the festivals' reputations, there is a marked tendency to downplay any violence that occurs there. Dismissing an incident that happened during one festival, an organizer told me, "Yes, there was a stabbing, but that had nothing to do with the festival. That was a lover's quarrel that was cooking before and was going to happen at any moment, and the woman did not get hurt. That was not about the festival." Similar comments separating this incident from the festival itself were made by various community people, who defended the family-oriented nature of their celebration and denied that it was dangerous. This effort also speaks to people's defense of public space by attempting to prevent the spread of fear even when crime and violence cannot be so easily curbed.

Another important aspect of the public spaces created by the work of the cultural groups is their emergent transnational character. Many groups have borrowed from the patron-saint festivities the celebration of "absentee days" (that is, festival days dedicated to community members who are now living elsewhere, often in the United States). It is also common for people living in the States to schedule their visits to the island during a festival.[11] These visits are facilitated by the many travel agencies that are geared to the

Puerto Rican community; they will often keep a register of festivals so visitors may avoid the *tiempo muerto*. T-shirts, posters, and programs touting the festival are sent to relatives in the States, and so are the fruits and vegetables that are the theme of the event. As videotapes made by visitors or local residents are sent to distant friends, these festivals are also finding their way into living rooms in New York, Delaware, and Connecticut as the latest samples of Puerto Rican culture. For example, I once saw a young man filming two small girls who were competing in a troubadour contest, a musical genre typically associated with older rural men. Charmed by the scene, he taped the competition for his parents, former residents of rural Puerto Rico now living in New York. Thus what people oftentimes see in these festivals are new elements being praised as "cultural" as people tap their communities for the symbolic raw material around which to organize their festivals and present them as community cultural events.

By now it should be evident that among representatives of the government's cultural and tourist institutions, such as the Institute of Puerto Rican Culture and Puerto Rico's Tourism Company, it is compliance with government-authenticated images of culture and its politico-partisan connections that most influence a festival's reputation as a cultural event. For their part, local politicians are generally more likely to dismiss government-authenticated definitions of culture, favoring instead the most popular activities or those celebrated by members of their political constituencies. This does not mean, however, that local politicians are unaffected by the dominant criteria about what represents Puerto Rican culture; they too discriminate against popular representations when assessing the value of competing events within their communities.

Consider the response given by a local politician in Caone (a member of the pro-statehood PNP) when I asked him to rank the activities that he would be most likely to support. In order of importance, he listed the Festival of Bomba and Plena (which was no longer being celebrated by the time I talked to him),[12] the Festival of Saint Cecilia (organized by Caone's cultural center), and last the Fisherman's Festival (celebrated by a fishermen's cooperative) and ARECMA's Breadfruit Festival.

He explained his ranking by saying that the Festival of Bomba and Plena honored nationally recognized musical genres deriving from the African heritage, or "the third root" of Puerto Rico's racial triad, and that the Saint Cecilia Festival was a Caone tradition that had been celebrated for over two decades. In contrast, the Fisherman's and Breadfruit Festivals, which had been celebrated for about seven years, were not only newer but also emphasized "regional" rather than "national" themes. By this reasoning, neither fishermen nor breadfruits, originally brought in to feed slaves on the island, fit the romanticized peasant view of national identity. The politician also noted that the Saint Cecilia Festival was organized by an ICP-affiliated cultural center whose mission is to represent national culture in the local community, whereas the independent groups' activities had no such mission and were mostly a source of entertainment.

These events, however, attract a variety of audiences with different notions of what is culturally meaningful. Some who expect more traditional elements in order to describe a festival as "cultural" formed part of what I call a "traveling audience" or a constituency that visits these festivals throughout the year. This audience is mostly composed of college students, university-educated professionals, middle-class families, and middle-aged women accompanied by friends. These visitors tend to concentrate on the daytime program (folk-art fairs, children's activities, vendors) rather than on the evening events that local residents attend in greater numbers. This audience of visitors was also more likely to express nationalistic reasons for attending different festivals, mentioning their wish "to back Puerto Rican culture," "to see our Puerto Rican things," or "to follow our culture." Visitors tend to show their "patriotic" motivations by wearing what I call the "festival uniform," consisting of straw hats and T-shirts from other cultural festivals or shirts that display patriotic logos ("It's an honor to be Boricua," "The star of my flag does not fit in the American one") or Taino iconography.

However, while the outward display of cultural elements was a common expectation for these festivals, often used to determine how authentically "cultural" they really are, these were not limited to elements that officially represent the national culture. Instead, visitors came to the festivals expecting something different and unique to an area, such as a new fried food or new ways of decorating kiosks. A couple of times I even witnessed visitors chastising local organizers for "letting Puerto Rico down" by not fully showcasing the cultural theme advertised in the program. A young man with his wife, residents of San Juan and evidently festival followers judging by their distinctive T-shirts, reprimanded organizers of the Festival del Panapén (Festival of Breadfruit Seeds, another festival in Vega Alta)[13] as follows: "There is nothing here that is made from breadfruit or from its seeds. What would happen if the press came to cover this festival, or a TV channel came to make a story about the event? They too would be disappointed. This is not only my point of view; this is the feeling of a *pueblo* that is disappointed with this."

These comments attest to the popularity many of these festivals have achieved beyond their own localities and to visitors' expectation of finding something representative of "culture" in them, whatever that may be. In contrast with these visitors from other parts of Puerto Rico, the festivals' local public tends to be more heterogeneous and to express other reasons for attending the events beyond their "cultural" content. Many identified the festival as cultural, but most people mentioned the opportunity it provides for sharing with the community while enjoying free public entertainment, as well as the commerce and activity that it fosters in the area. Thus, the woman who was chastised by the San Juan couple insisted that they had been the only ones who had complained about the festival. According to her, people may not always find the typical food or other things they are looking for, but then they begin to listen to the music, and "they get into the mood and they no longer complain. They leave satisfied."

As I discussed above, local interest in the festival is also intensified by the lack of recreational facilities and public areas on the island. A resident of a small interior town succinctly addressed this issue in explaining to me that she did not differentiate between the festival organized by the ICP-affiliated cultural center and that celebrated by another group in her town: "I never miss anything that happens in this town. To me all the festivals are good; they have music, and everyone is there. A festival is the only thing that ever happens in this town. I go to all of them, and I could not care less if they are cultural or not."

Overall, economic, cultural, and recreational concerns were always conflated in these festivals, which remain the most important aspect of the work of most grassroots groups. While many intellectuals regret this conflation, its existence is a well-known fact among corporate sponsors, whose involvement is examined in the next chapter.

Display of posters of the Breadfruit Festival in the home of ARECMA's director. *Photo by Arlene Dávila.*

Preparing breadfruit fritters for the 1993 Breadfruit Festival. *Photo by Arlene Dávila.*

A flat-bottomed boat being carried to the 1994 Flat-Bottomed Boat Festival competition. *Photo by Arlene Dávila.*

Street signs announcing corporate-sponsored local events, Vega Alta, 1993. *Photo by Arlene Dávila.*

Her Majesty Yesenia Meléndez, queen of the 1994 Flat-Bottomed Boat Festival, saluting the public. Her dress represents the sunsets of La Playa community. *Photo by Elizabeth Rivera.*

Silk-screened T-shirts with patriotic messages designed and sold by Luis Vázquez. The T-shirts depict the nationalist leader Albizu, the revered salsa musician Héctor Lavoe, and an indigenous Taino, among other images. *Photo by Arlene Dávila.*

Wood machetes printed with historical facts and over 50 patriotic messages, designed and sold by Wilzen Pérez. The machetes evoke the cane-cutting tool and the symbol of the Puerto Rican nationalist armed group, the *macheteros*. Photo by Arlene Dávila.

Chapter V

Culture, Politics, and Corporate Sponsorship

These messages are just trying to exploit commercially what is in fact a reality: that the Puerto Rican people feel great pride toward their national symbols. Though it elects and re-elects an annexationist governor, Puerto Rico is profoundly nationalist.

—Manuel J. González, *El Nuevo Día*

We decided to seek Budweiser as a sponsor. After all, Budweiser is *cosa de aquí* [from here].

—Festival organizer, Festival del Burén, 1993

U p to this point I have hinted that the corporate sector has become an important sponsor of cultural activities throughout the island, and that corporate involvement is creating challenges and contradictions in Puerto Rico's cultural politics.[1] This chapter further explores these issues by analyzing the interaction of culture, politics, and corporate sponsorship in the context of public events and activities throughout the island. This task involves treating corporate interests not as forces that are contrary to the development of ideas of cultural distinctiveness, but rather as added players elaborating conceptions of Puerto Ricanness.

169

As a primary consumer of U.S. products, importing over $12.2 billion in goods annually from the United States,[2] Puerto Rico is continuously inundated with publicity and marketing campaigns for a variety of products. A common theme in these campaigns is the association of products with Puerto Rican culture. The corporate sector appeals to nationalist icons and symbols in its product advertising, and it has become the primary sponsor of many cultural festivals throughout the island. These campaigns have become part of everyday life for most Puerto Ricans, who are daily exposed to company logos in the media, in bars and cafeterias, and on the hats, T-shirts, and paraphernalia that are given away at corporate-sponsored activities.

With these promotions, commercial products are becoming identified with the average Puerto Rican consumer in ways that make us rethink the objects, materials, and ideas through which Puerto Ricans construct and represent their identity, as well as contemporary processes of identity formation on the island. Consider, for example, one of the most popular floats during the 1993 National Folk Arts Carnival in Ponce, where steel signs advertising Winston cigarettes, old and rusted with age, became the key decorating element to transform a peasant-theme float into a "traditional" rural canteen. The float included characters dressed like *jíbaros* and drinking illegally produced rum (*ron caña*) under the aged Winston ads, centrally placed as symbols to connect the audience with a continuous and unbroken past.

Foreign and local companies have shown an interest in using Puerto Rican culture in their advertising since the beginnings of Puerto Rican radio and television. In fact, this practice predates the rise of the modern media and of the advertising and publicity industry, as noted by Edgardo Díaz's (1987) discussion of the use of Puerto Rican *danza* and local genres in the advertising of nineteenth-century Puerto Rican merchants. Since the 1970s, however, culturally oriented advertising campaigns have become an added requirement for the successful introduction of products into the local market, provoking in turn debates over the effects and scope of these campaigns among the greater population. As Lauria noted (1980), folkloric and rural images, as well as values traditionally associated with Puerto Rican culture—strong kinship bonds, hospitality, and respect for elders and superiors—became popular advertising themes in the 1970s, contributing to the dominant culturalist definition of Puerto Rican national identity. Ads in the 1970s for the locally produced Corona beer[3] featured "Cantalicio," a cartoon figure depicting a Puerto Rican national who outwits his competitors, representing Spanish, American, and Nuyorican characters. ("Nuyorican" is a name commonly used to refer to all expatriate Puerto Ricans in the States.) Also at this time, Don Q rum associated its product with the traditional peasant wedding, Mazola linked its cooking oil with Puerto Rico's indigenous population, and Eastern Airlines drew upon Puerto Rico's migratory experience to show emotional images of friends and relatives awaiting loved ones at the airport.

Several factors contributed to the prevalence of cultural themes in marketing after the 1970s. First among them is the growth during that period of the island's publicity industry. Transnational public-relations conglomerates had been establishing themselves in Puerto Rico and forging mergers and partnerships with local offices since the 1940s, so that by the 1960s the most important transnational advertising agencies in the world—firms including Leo Burnett Worldwide, Saatchi and Saatchi, and the J. Walter Thompson Agency—had initiated operations on the island.

However, since the mid-1970s there has been steady growth in the industry. Among other reasons, this was spurred by the internationalization of the island's economy after Section 936 of the Internal Revenue Code enacted in 1976 and the Industrial Incentive Law 26 of 1978, which extended tax exemption to export-related enterprises such as consulting services and public relations agencies on the island (Pantojas-García 1990). These advantages led to the restructuring of certain industries (such as finance and advertising) along transnational lines, and to the opening of many transnational public-relations conglomerates on the island. Thus, more than sixty of the seventy-three firms appearing on a 1996 list of Puerto Rico's advertising agencies were founded since the mid-1970s (Caribbean Business 1996). While these new agencies rarely accrue more than $1 million in annual billings and many of them are local agencies, much smaller than their transnational counterparts, they have added vitality to an industry that—with over $770.8 million in revenues annually and representing 11,680 direct and indirect jobs (S. Rodríguez 1994c)—is now perceived as one of the fastest growing on the island.

The nationalization of the publicity industry through the recruitment of local artists and intellectuals was another important factor in the turn to culture by publicity strategists. Today most agencies, regardless of whether they are owned by local or transnational interests, are dominated by a Puerto Rican staff and creative team who bring local knowledge to the publicity process. As a result, the industry has developed a Puerto Rican flavor that makes it impossible to distinguish sharply between Puerto Rican and transnational companies. As an officer of the local Association of Publicity Agencies explained: "Most of these agencies have been around forever, and no one sees them as foreign anymore. There are no gringo faces anywhere."

Another important element in the nationalization of the industry has been the incorporation of *independentistas* into publicity work. Of course, many publicists, without reference to their own backgrounds and political affiliations, incorporate aspects of Puerto Rican culture in their campaigns. Consider that the publicists who developed the PNP's electoral campaign, Ramón Flores and Steve Wachtel, relied heavily on the Puerto Rican flag, and that the American publicist Gary Hoyt was behind the aforementioned campaign for Corona beer in the 1960s, while Guastella Films and Guede Films, both owned by Cubans, have been involved in some of the most "nationalistic" advertising on the island (González 1997). Nevertheless, since the 1970s many *independentistas* have become involved in some of the most "Puertoricanizing" ad and promotional campaigns in the media. This, in turn, has triggered accusations, such as those by pro-statehood critic Luis Dávila Colón appearing in a major local newspaper, concerning the use of commercial advertising by *independentistas* as part of a concerted effort to push the ideals of nationalism and separatism to the average consumer (Dávila Colón 1997). Contrary to this view, however, I found that the involvement of pro-independence advocates in the publicity industry stemmed not from any "concerted effort" to propagate their political ideology but rather from their ongoing persecution on the island.

Discriminated against and unable to find jobs throughout the 1970s, many of them found employment opportunities in a growing publicity industry in constant need of artists, writers, and intellectuals. Many *independentista* publicists have since become important figures in the island's advertising industry, such as the director of Comunicadora Nexus, one of the largest of the locally owned public-relations companies, which is directed by former leaders of the pro-independence student organization FUPI (Federación de Universitarios Pro Independencia). José Torres, a pro-independence industry leader, recalls, "We had great writing skills, which we had used to mobilize people, and a deep appreciation of Puerto Rican culture as well as an awareness of the importance of Puerto Rican culture for the Puerto Rican. Those were our skills when we entered the marketing industry." In turn, *independentista* advertisers have long negotiated their place in an industry that is increasingly recognized for its pro–Puerto Rican stance, as evident by the accusations of the aforementioned critic. Formerly criticized by fellow *independentistas,* who originally saw them as "selling out," they now openly highlight the role of the media as a venue to enhance Puerto Rican culture and values. Consider these further comments from José Torres:

> The power of advertising is great. How do you have more
> power over it, alienating yourself from it or working with it?
> My concern is to exalt Puerto Rican culture. One does not al-

ways get to do it in this business, but it is great when one has
the opportunity to do it. They may say that we are profiting
from Puerto Rican culture, and that may even be the
company's concern, but it's not mine. I do not care about the
corporations' objectives. I care about my own, which is to exalt
the view Puerto Ricans have of their culture whenever I can.

The turn to culture since the late 1970s has also been influenced, among other factors, by brand competition and the restrictions on advertising imposed on the liquor and cigarette
industries by the Federal Communications Commission, to which
the island is subject (Subervi Vélez and Hernández López 1990:
169). These restrictions encouraged more aggressive campaigns
and a move toward grassroots promotions among the companies
that had developed more culturally specific campaigns on the
island. This turn to culturally specific promotions is, of course,
not unique to Puerto Rico but is part of a global trend in
advertising toward incorporating the culture-specific characteristics of a given market, whether along gender, race, ethnic, or
national lines (Alden et al. 1993, Appadurai 1990, Sveberny-
Mohammadi 1991). Moreover, this trend is not a new development but has paralleled the growth of international brands aimed
at international markets as part of a larger attempt to promote
brand loyalty and supersede cultural differences and inconsisten-
cies in the reception of standardized marketing (Maxwell 1996,
O'Barr 1989). In this way, culturally specific marketing is directly
related to structural shifts in the communications industry toward
growing internationalization. It responds to pressures to be more
specific in targeting diverse audiences (Mattelart et al. 1993,
O'Barr 1989), a trend that challenges, in turn, notions of capitalist
development as cultural homogenization (Tomlinson 1991).

While this marketing trend has been analyzed by some as an
example of the dissipation of hegemonic centers and the opening
up of spaces for the representation of marginal cultures, the turn

to the local is most often seen as evidence of the ubiquity and all-encompassing nature of global capitalism. It is often considered one more form of containment, one that "disguises the political nature of everyday life and appropriates the vulnerable new terrain of insurgent differences in the interests of crass consumerism" (Giroux 1993: 6). Doubtless, the primary motive behind these advertising tactics is sales: the need to address newer audiences and broaden the consumer base. However, and as García-Canclini (1992a) reminds us, the turn to culture among private sponsors has not taken the same direction in all countries, just as the outcomes of these strategies are not always easily predicted. Thus the new cloaks of capitalism are just part of a story that also includes the ways in which people manipulate the meanings that are put to its service.

For instance, the appeal to Puerto Ricanness attains even greater relevance because of the colonial situation, in which most issues, including language, sports, and commercial products, have been politicized. Consider that after the aforementioned criticism of these campaigns by Luis Dávila Colón, numerous letters in major newspapers accused him of subverting and censoring Puerto Rican culture. Two argued that not appealing to Puerto Rican culture in commercial advertising would represent a rejection of national symbols and a denial of Puerto Ricanness in favor of the imported and foreign. "Should it be eskimos [*sic*] that sell us beer in this tropical weather?" argued one such letter (Mercado 1997, González 1997). Advertising's turn to culture has also been an important force in popularizing national icons in a context where open appeals to Puerto Rican culture have been historically perceived as subversive. One example occurred shortly after the 1993 plebiscite, when it was argued that personal decorations depicting the Puerto Rican flag should be banned from the polls because the flag is an *independentista* symbol. The publicity team for Clorox developed an entire advertising campaign that highlighted the Puerto Rican flag to present Clorox as the number-one cleaning product on the island. In the end, the local electoral commission allowed the use of personal decorations displaying the Puerto Rican flag at the polls, deeming the flag a symbol of "all Puerto Ricans" and beyond partisan considerations. Yet in general, the corporate sector has been less constrained by political considerations in using national symbols than have other sectors of Puerto Rican society, such as the government's cultural institutions. The latter have been subject to changes in government cultural policy since, as I have discussed, they are commonly called on to express and promote the dominant party's political ideals.

Finally, the case of Puerto Rico provides an important example for understanding the effects of culture-specific campaigns on local cultural politics. The showcase for an export-promotion model of industrialization in the 1950s, the island continues to serve as a model, this time for advertising products in culturally specific markets. As the local president of a U.S. company operating in Puerto Rico commented, "Puerto Rico is the first step to explore a new market in a stable territory. It is different from standard U.S. markets but not as exotic or different from them as a Latin American country" (Ryan 1994). Agreeing with these comments, the CEO for a franchise restaurant in Puerto Rico stated, "Puerto Rico's Latin American heritage enables American franchisers, for almost any type of product or service, to test new and different ideas here to measure market acceptance before a stateside launching. In other words, Puerto Rico serves as a testing ground for products that will be launched in areas with a sizeable Hispanic population" (Ryan 1994).

Puerto Rico's telecommunications structure, its dollar-based economy, and its highly skilled labor force add to its appeal as a test site for companies preparing to launch marketing and public relations campaigns in Latin America and in the U.S. Hispanic market. One example of this is a Miller's beer ad campaign for the Latino market in the United States that was managed by the Puerto Rican agency Martí, Flores, Prieto and Wachtel, affiliated with J. Walter Thompson. The promotion revolves around the "Tongoneo," a dance competition inspired by the success of another ad campaign, this one featuring a custom-made dance called the *virazón* to promote Budweiser beer, a campaign that will be discussed later. In fact, Puerto Rico's role as a showcase for marketing strategies is one that local entrepreneurs are promoting to transnational corporations. A good example is provided by NAZCA S & S, a new Latin American advertising network founded by a Puerto Rican businessman and headquartered in Puerto Rico. It is the first transnational advertising network geared to the Latin market that is not stationed in either New York or Miami. This network aims to replicate the successes of other regional advertising networks such as Euro RSCG and Dentsu, which were successful in the European and Asian markets respectively (S. Rodríguez 1994b).

Considering that the corporate appeal to local and nationalist symbols, folklore, and popular culture is an ongoing enterprise, what is the effect of these marketing tactics on the "nationals" whose culture is being used to lure them into using new commercial products? In other words, as transnational companies and local marketing strategists increasingly capitalize on the booming cultural nationalism of Puerto Rican society, what views of Puerto Rican culture are these private companies advocating and for what purposes? What are some of the implications of the involvement of transnational interests, as mediated by local marketing strategists, in local-level cultural politics?

Recent analysis of the increasing integration of the world economy, which sees nationalism in the context of globalization not as a contradiction but as a complementary process, helps us grapple with this issue. This research has led to much theorizing about the relationship between local nationalism, identity politics, and global political economic processes (Foster 1991, Glick Schiller 1994, Hall 1991). A recurrent theme of this literature is the dual nature of global processes, a duality that calls for an analysis of commercial interests not solely in terms of their homogenizing tendencies but also in terms of how they may impact national identification. Specifically, global processes, far from homogenizing, work through the creation and recreation of differences, thus leading to new forms of inclusions and exclusions. Most of these may be preordained according to the greater demands of the global economy, but they nevertheless serve as bases for the creation and expression of difference (Appadurai 1990, Wilk 1995) .

Stuart Hall, for instance, has noted how the new situation is characterized by the decentering of old hierarchies, where capital "has had to renegotiate and incorporate and partly reflect the differences it was trying to overcome" (Hall 1991: 32). In this process, the marginal group's "difference" is often co-opted or folklorized at the same time that new opportunities for representation are created that can also serve as the first step into politics. Thus local identities remain a contradictory terrain, at once venues of politics and subject to appropriation (Hall 1991). It is in this context that the corporate turn to Puerto Rican culture can be understood.

Our entry point for examining these issues will be strategies used by the R. J. Reynolds company to advertise Winston cigarettes and by Anheuser-Busch to promote Budweiser beer. I chose to focus on these companies because they have developed some of the most successful culturally directed advertising campaigns on the island, thereby providing clear evidence that "culture sells." They also represent the kinds of products (beer, refreshments, cigarettes) that advertisers wish to associate with the enjoyment and sociability of cultural events and public festivals. In the case of R. J. Reynolds, one of the first companies to advertise its products by sponsoring public festivals, its identification with Puerto Rico was accompanied by systematic investment on the island since the 1950s. The example of Anheuser-Busch is more similar to that of other companies that represent products ranging from cars, Clorox, Pepsi, and Coca Cola and that have all developed culturally specific advertising in more recent years. In the next section I analyze these companies' early and most recent advertising strategies to discuss the use of Puerto Rican culture in advertising and corporate promotions.[4]

Advertising the Nation

Say "Winston y Puerto Rico" (Winston and Puerto Rico) on the island, and someone is likely to respond, "no hay nada mejor" (there is nothing better) to complete the company's familiar advertising slogan. This slogan—sung, printed, and superimposed over filmed scenes of rural landscapes, tourist spots, concerts, and other well-known Puerto Rican imagery—has identified R. J. Reynolds in Puerto Rico since the 1960s. The company, which has sold its brands on the island since the 1950s, has a manufacturing plant that currently rates as the third largest of its twenty-seven plants worldwide (Ruaño 1997). In 1993 the plant processed over 8 billion cigarettes a year. Between 65 and 70 percent of its products are exported; the remainder are sold on the island, where the brand controls over 60 percent of the market (Mier 1993). R. J. Reynolds has been so successful in Puerto Rico that the company is planning to expand its operations there, even though production is being discontinued in the United States. On the island R. J. Reynolds benefits from a variety of tax breaks offered for manufacturing and export-services activities under Section 936 of the Internal Revenue Code.

R. J. Reynolds developed its advertising and distribution strategy while its presence on the island was still small. The association of the product with Puerto Rico was strengthened in the 1970s when, as part of an international reorganization, the company opened a plant there. Then, the company placed a local team of publicists in charge of the Puerto Rican market. The Puerto Rican publicists brought local knowledge to the decision-making processes, and through this knowledge the "Yo y mis Winstons" campaign, originally derived from a campaign devised for the U.S. market, was indigenized and transformed from one evoking "the American way" into one almost tantamount to Puerto Rican culture.

Winston's first ads, filmed against a Puerto Rican landscape, featured jingles that incorporated local instruments and were sung by well-known Puerto Rican singers. Moreover, the models were all Puerto Ricans; local beauty queens were used in place of the American models who were and are still commonly used in other campaigns in Puerto Rico. Most important, the ads were produced with the understanding that Puerto Rican consumers are different. A Winston ad representative recalled: "Our campaign has always been different because the Puerto Rican is different. It is a country with many American things but many Puerto Rican things. What is done for the Puerto Rican market is done here and is unique." The same representative contrasted the culturally specific campaign developed for the Puerto Rican market with that for nearby countries: "In the Dominican Republic you cannot do 'Dominica y Winston' because it would not work. In the Dominican Republic, as well as in other countries, one appeals to the United States, to that which one does not have, to that which is imported, . . . whereas the vision here is different." Implied in his statement was a view shared by many involved in the island's publicity industry. This is the view that these types of advertisements fill a void—that while Puerto Ricans, like most consumers, crave the newest and most glamorous consumer product, they also crave for their culture to be publicly showcased.

The product's appeal to Puerto Ricanness is evident in the following slogan, which was used (with some alterations) from 1968 to the 1980s: "Me and my Winstons, and my Puerto Rico, there is nothing better. What great flavor. Winston and Puerto Rico have in common a great flavor, a unique flavor that never changes and that is why Puerto Rico is our pride, Borinquen is our *tierra* [country, homeland][5] and Winston is our cigarette.

Winston offers an exclusive blend specially chosen and manufactured for the best flavor . . . surrounded by history in Old San Juan [or whatever location was being filmed] there is Winston."

Especially at first, the product was associated with the same images of Puerto Rico that are used by the government's Tourism Office and the Institute of Puerto Rican Culture, images that gave it a direct identification with the local market. Easily recognized tourist spots, like Old San Juan and the Ponce Fine Arts Museum, or romantic beach scenes were most often featured in the advertisements. Similarly, in a series showing a young heterosexual couple visiting local artisans (used between 1984 and 1987) the artisans shown are the *maestros* (master artisans), all male and elderly, who create the folk arts that conform to the government's standards of Puerto Rican culture.

After two decades of such advertising, however, Winston's reliance on government-authenticated views of Puerto Rican identity backfired; the product came to be associated with old age and maturity. Bacardi's early campaign "Manos puertorriqueñas" (Puerto Rican Hands), which associated the making of Bacardi rum with the craftsmanship of a Puerto Rican artisan, met the same fate. Thus, since the late 1980s, Winston has attempted to rejuvenate its advertising without losing its identification with Puerto Rico. In this task it has drawn on aspects of contemporary popular culture while still maintaining the conservative image that the company aims to project for its product.

For instance, instead of the familiar landscapes and folklore identifying the product with Puerto Rico, Winston's 1994 campaign featured written captions referring to popular cultural icons, language, and associations that are only known by Puerto Ricans. In one ad the headline "Festival de las Flores" (Festival of the Flowers, alluding to one of the most popular festivals on the island) is superimposed over a photograph of four smiling young women wearing pastel dresses. In another *frituras* (fried-food snacks) are represented as young sunbathers, and in a third the headline "Pelea de Gallos" (cockfight) is superimposed over a photograph of two men arm-wrestling in a play of words and images easily discernible to the average Puerto Rican. The ads still drew on stereotypes about what a tourist spot is, who Puerto Rican artisans are, and which gender is like a flower and which like a "cock" (rooster), although this time they drew from popular icons, such as fritters, rather than from the authenticated images that had previously been associated with the product. A more recent campaign entitled "100% Puerto Rican" draws on street slang and colloquialisms. An ad showing young women rating the physique of two males on the beach reads: "94% *satería* [roughly translated to lowlife mannerisms], 96% *tasadera* [scoping], 100% *puertorriqueño*," words that convey an ambiance of banter associated with being 100 percent Puerto Rican.

Through this advertising focus, Winston has become the best-selling cigarette on the island, providing a good example that "la puertorriqueñidad vende" (Puerto Ricanness sells). This was corroborated by market research on the public reception of cigarette ads. It showed Winston to be the brand most easily remembered by the public. Winston and Salem ads, both of which feature Puerto Rican settings and icons, were also preferred by the public over ads for Camel and Marlboro, which use American motifs (Guevara Monge 1992). At present, Winston remains one of the top advertising brands in magazines and the print media (Public Records, Inc. 1994). Meanwhile, tobacco's health hazards and the industry's manipulations, so debated in the United States, are largely overlooked on the island, where Winston continues to strengthen its reputation as a culturally concerned company. The company maintains this image not only through advertising but, as we will see, through its sponsorship of events and cultural festivals and other culturally specific promotions. One example is the "Winston Medal for Culture" (recently renamed the R. J. Reynolds Medal), an annual prize instituted in 1983 that is advertised as the only national prize for cultural activity on the island.

Like Winston, Budweiser developed one of its most successful campaigns in Puerto Rico, increasing its market share from 2 percent in 1980 to over 48 percent in 1990. Behind this rapid growth was a local advertising firm, Lopito, Ileana and Howie, known for its emphasis on culture in the Popular Democratic Party's gubernatorial campaigns, which it had handled since 1972, and in the PPD's campaign in the 1993 status plebiscite, which strongly appealed to Puerto Rico's national culture and Olympic sports identity. Lopito, Ileana and Howie is currently the third-largest advertising agency in Puerto Rico, accruing some $35.5 million in annual billings, of which $4 million come from Anheuser-Busch (Zehr 1994b).

Also like Winston, Budweiser's early advertising campaign (from the early to mid-1980s) drew on images and symbols that had already been institutionalized as representations of Puerto Rican cultural identity. Aiming to "recognize, identify and embrace Puerto Rican values and lifestyles,"[6] the ads portrayed situations and settings that were clearly associated with the island, or, as an advertising representative put it, "puertorriqueños en sitios puertorriqueños" (Puerto Ricans in Puerto Rican settings). The jingles or text emphasized that Budweiser was a product that honors, exalts, and embraces Puerto Rican ways. For instance, one ad honoring the Puerto Rican woman depicts a country wedding and voices the message: "You have all the beautiful things that God made beautiful in a woman. Puerto Rican woman, because you are the purest expression of genuine quality, Budweiser honors your beauty." Another ad compares the quality of the Puerto Rican thoroughbred horse or "Paso Fino" to the excellence of the Budweiser Clydesdales: "Our 'Paso Fino' unique in the world, and the famous Clydesdales, two different races, reflecting the same pride, the search for excellence, nothing is compromised. Budweiser honors the excellence of Puerto Rico."

Besides identifying the product with valued aspects of Puerto Rico's national culture, Budweiser's campaign appealed to its popular culture by presenting "average" Puerto Ricans engaging in popular activities. One ad depicts the popular Feast of Saint James the Apostle in Loíza, which has historically been seen as an example of the Afro-Caribbean legacy on the island. The ad, with a jingle using *bomba* music, films people chanting and dancing and using colloquial language while they eat the cod fritters that are popular in the area.

In another set of ads, Budweiser appeals to the stereotypical heavy beer drinker (male, blue collar, and middle aged) in order to show "real people in bar settings and situations" in one of the first times in Puerto Rican advertising.[7] The ads use colloquial language and are written in story form to convey male camaraderie embedded in a joking environment. The ads show public situations such as country bars, people joking with one another, friendly customers, and rural family gatherings because the Puerto Rican is considered to be a social drinker and not a solitary home consumer.

The campaign worked. Sales of the brand soared, reaching 25.6 percent of all beer sales in 1982, 37.7 percent in 1987, and 48.1 percent in 1990. Anheuser-Busch claimed that the Puerto Rican market had the "largest single brand share for Budweiser anywhere in the world." More recent ads have turned to a younger audience, but they continue to rely on the same marketing strategy of "showing Puerto Ricans in Puerto Rican settings." However, the new ads use real people in real locations instead of actors or sets. A series beginning in 1995 features the *virazón*, a custom-made dance inspired by the comment of a participant in a marketing-research group, whom Budweiser's new upside-down label reminded of the swirl produced by Puerto Rican hurricanes. The campaign is based on traveling dance contests, held in over sixty locations throughout the island, in which people are encouraged to join in dancing the *virazón*. According to an account executive for the brand, the idea underpinning this participatory campaign is "barrio obrero meets Hollywood," or giving the "working-class barrio" and the average consumer a chance to show off and validate him- or herself in a public activity. "Budweiser's essence will always be to validate what being Puerto Rican is all about," stressed the same executive.

It is important to note, however, that the new diversity of representations is still managed and engineered by "merchants of style" according to notions of aesthetics, appearance, and politics that govern marketing practices worldwide (Ewen 1988). All of these ads depict dominant views of gender relations and aesthetics as they showcase youth, lighter Puerto Ricans, and women as symbols of sexuality. Even those ads aiming to represent people from working-class neighborhoods, which make a point of showing people from diverse racial backgrounds, show well-built youth, as in Budweiser's *virazón* campaign.

We cannot ignore either that these campaigns are geared to youth, who in Puerto Rico are legally allowed to drink at eighteen years of age, and that these products' health hazards are being overlooked in their identification with island culture. Yet, paradoxical as it may seem, until recently there has been little public objection to these campaigns on the island. As stated earlier, criticisms over the use of nationalist symbols and rhetoric in advertising have been countered by swift defenses; not appealing to these symbols is understood as a denial and censorship of Puerto Rican culture. Moreover, while local groups like Morality Media focus their criticism on sexually explicit materials appearing in the media, they have been less vociferous about the presence of cigarette and alcohol promotions at grassroots activities or about the overall commercial saturation of everyday life. Similarly, while cigarette and alcohol advertising has been increasingly subject to government restrictions, following the general trend in the United States toward regulation of the two industries, these initiatives have neither aroused nor been accompanied by grassroots appeals and manifestations.[8]

Again, we need to understand this situation in terms of the

island's colonial context and in relation to the reputation that these companies have built for their products on the island. As we have seen, public assertions of the distinct qualities of Puerto Rican culture attain great relevance in contemporary society, even if it is as consumers that Puerto Ricans are being addressed. Moreover, many of these culturally specific campaigns have achieved such high identification with the public that products long promoted with this type of advertising, such as Budweiser, are popularly perceived as *cosa de aquí* or *del pueblo* (something from here and from the people).

This trend was vividly apparent in the comment of one ICP promoter, who, while lamenting the involvement of beer advertising in cultural events, justified that of companies such as Winston because "Winston cares about Puerto Rican culture." The promoter was smoking a Winston cigarette as he spoke with me, a brand he claimed to prefer because of the company's involvement with "our culture." This comment, which could well have come out of a Winston ad, attests to the high identification with the Puerto Rican consumer that many products have achieved. Indeed, companies seem well aware of this in their continued identification of their products with the local culture.

Thus, while advertising trends are ever changing, they have continued to maintain their focus on connecting with the average consumer in culturally specific ways. In the process, the new campaigns are turning away from representing Puerto Rico through the dominant images fostered by the government's cultural policy and toward contemporary popular culture. Specifically, contemporary campaigns have moved away from traditional markers of identity such as folklore, images of the peasant household, or the peasant past (used by Budweiser in its initial campaign), and toward images of everyday life. This trend, however, is not about moving away from Puerto Ricanness, as I was assured by numerous advertising agents, but about refurbishing corporate advertising while maintaining a product's association with the island. Tapping into everyday experience and showing situations where "people see themselves" were also commonly used to associate Puerto Rico with a wide range of products. A local representative for Badillo Saatchi Advertising explained this as follows: "We give our campaigns a touch of Puerto Rico, which is not about the *güiro,* the maracas, the plantain, or the Spanish garrison, but about a local flavor, with local music, local talent, and Puerto Rican vignettes." He added, "Our last campaign for Schaefer [beer] was a hit, with a Caribbean beat, and beach vignettes with a lot of Puerto Rican elements: guys in the bar, an old woman dancing with a guy, a sign that read 'No Talking about Politics Allowed,' a cockfight, all of which associated my product with Puerto Rico without including a flag, or a *güiro,* or a maraca because that was the stereotype of fifteen or twenty years ago."

In informal interviews about Budweiser's 1993 "reality campaign" (which filmed "real people in real settings"), some respondents named the music, the feeling, the overall mood, the sharing with friends, and the idea that "we Puerto Ricans like to *parisear* [party]" as the aspects most closely identified with Puerto Rican culture. Others thought, however, that this shift to reality advertising marked a departure from Puerto Rican images, and claimed that only campaigns that had relied on overt nationalistic icons and images were *puertorriqueñistas.* One informant asked me, "What is Puerto Rican about this campaign? This is not about conserving or raising consciousness about something. This is about showing people and their ways of life. This is about the everyday." Indeed, the emphasis in contemporary advertising is not on conserving culture, as the government's cultural policy stresses. The appeal is rather to the everyday and even the commonplace. Nevertheless, people felt a subjective identification with Puerto Rico in the ad even though they could not point to specific icons or concrete images of Puerto Ricanness.

In fact, a common strategy employed by the publicists I talked to was the identification of Puerto Rican culture with "values," which involves associating products with well-known Puerto Ricans, or with ways of being or acting. As another publicist explained: "What we do is not about nostalgia. It is more modern. It is about values that recognize the youth, the country in general. It is about the things we do, not about overt patriotism or *cursilerías* [clichés]. The audiences would not buy into that. That has been done already."

This strategy was evident in ads prepared by this local agency for the pro-independence party (PIP). Most of them featured young people, both male and female, representing different class and racial backgrounds, in ordinary settings (the beach, pool bars, someone's kitchen). Yet their most popular ad depicted a young *independentista* singing rock in English, denoting that he is not only pro-Puerto Rico but also a bilingual rock fan. These identities are perceived as irreconcilable in Puerto Rican society, where political affiliation is often associated with attitudes about Puerto Rican culture. The youth is shown defending himself against his parents (shown wearing blue and red shirts to identify them with the PNP and PPD parties respectively), who accuse him of betraying his independence ideals. The youth replies, "Independence is not opposed to any language, but our language has to be Spanish, now and always, officially." The ad received a lot of attention, and, although it did not lead to the PIP's victory, it successfully conveyed an updated vision of what independence would mean for the island, one that accounts for the many *independentistas* who are also English-speaking Puerto Ricans.

Raymond Williams suggests that subjective experiences are among the first indicators of change: "[A]ll that seems to escape from the fixed and the explicit and the known is grasped and defined as the personal: this, here, now, alive, active, 'subjective'" (1977: 128). This encourages us to ask if contemporary advertising is tapping into emerging ways of experiencing and expressing nationality in contemporary culture. Given that cultural activities more and more tend to depart from concrete nationalist icons and symbols, and are conceived as cultural more because of the food, the music, or the familiar community environment, the success of these advertising campaigns can be attributed to their skillful manipulation of popular expressions and representations of Puerto Ricanness. These rely on aspects of popular culture and everyday life, and on subjective identifications with values or images that have not yet become objectified as representations of culture, more than on the traditional components of culture as defined in government policy. A discussion of the way in which different cultural groups throughout the island tap into the corporations' promotional turn to culture may help clarify these issues.

Marketing the Nation

Increasingly, cultural activities organized by independent groups throughout the island are funded by corporate sponsors. Featuring commercial rhythms and departing from the official cultural policy, these events are often shunned by government funding sources, making them candidates for less discriminating commercial sponsors.

Again, a variety of factors contributed to the corporate interest in funding cultural events in the 1980s. Among these were brand competition among alcohol and tobacco companies and the need to circumvent advertising controls. An example of the effects of brand competition on this type of sponsorship is what came to be known as the *guerra de las cervezas* or the "beer wars," prompted by the government's 1992 termination of a regulation against long-neck bottles. Upwards of seven new brands arrived on the beer market soon afterwards, provoking fierce competition. In 1993 Budweiser alone sponsored some 206 grassroots activities, ranging from sports competitions to cultural festivals, in an attempt to maintain its position as the leading beer in the market. (This does not include the "happy hours," during which beer distributors offer discount prices, that are the most commonly sponsored promotional activity.)

Competition among companies sponsoring public events has also led them to seek out small-scale cultural festivals. As it became impossible for companies to attain exclusive exposure for their products in a stiff and aggressive market, most liquor and cigarette companies diminished or eliminated their sponsorship of the *fiestas patronales* (patron-saint festivities) and began to favor the cultural festivals instead. These were considered easier to tap because they were organized by local groups with little or no experience in negotiating contracts, rather than by the municipal governments that sponsor patron-saint festivals and have often established commitments to specific brands. As a commercial promoter for Bacardi explained:

> Before [in the 1970s], there used to be respect between the companies, and if I sponsored the patron-saint festivities the competition would stay away. We vendors knew and helped one another out. But then, this company bought our main competitors and became really aggressive. It was a matter of "You get out because here I come." If they had to break your van, they would break it. People spent millions on promotions, and the market was spoiled. Before, you could sponsor the patron-saint festivities of a town just by offering the mayor a cocktail for the *ausentes* [former residents of the town], and the mayor would give you exclusive exposure. Now those people [publicists representing new products] come and they offer a salsa show that is worth twenty-five thousand dollars, and they keep exclusive control of the patron-saint festivities.

Despite its close involvement with the cultural festivals, corporate sponsorship in Puerto Rico remained diverse, ranging from classical-music concerts to beach-volleyball tournaments to tours by amateur comedians. Sponsors drew from similar promotions used throughout the world whereby products are associated with modernity, enjoyment, entertainment, and Western lifestyles (Nath 1986). However, the pro–Puerto Rico advertising histories of Budweiser and Winston have earned them reputations as "culturally sensitive" companies that are concerned with Puerto Rico's culture and its *gente de pueblo* (common people). This is one of the goals of advertising, which, if successful, transforms the meaning attached to the goods so that "the viewer/reader attributes certain properties he or she knows to exist in the culturally constituted world to the consumer good" (McCracken 1990: 77).

It is their reputation for being "culturally concerned" that, in turn, motivates local events organizers to seek out these firms to fund their cultural activities. This was confirmed for me not only by the many people who identified the same companies as prospective funders but also by my observation of the distribution center of one such company in San Juan, where people from all over the island traveled to request funds for their activities. One way for groups to establish contact with this company is through a member who might sell its product in a local shop and have contact with the distributors in San Juan. Or the member might work directly for the company or have previously visited the San Juan office to present a funding petition. The involvement of private companies with grassroots events and festivals has also been facilitated through regional promotion and distribution offices, which allow them to monitor and gain access to the most popular activities in different areas.

The new cultural activities provided corporate sponsors with new venues through which they could associate their products with pleasure and entertainment while reaching their target consumers, the "common people." In return for a contribution of between two and five thousand dollars, companies obtain the exclusive right to sell their class of product (cigarettes, beer, soft drinks, and liquor) as well as to display and distribute items bearing the company's logo—tents, T-shirts, hats, sunglasses, banners, and

inflated balloons shaped like beer cans or cigarette boxes. Bene-
fiting the most from this arrangement is undoubtedly the product
representative, who, at the nominal cost of a small monetary
contribution and free marketing paraphernalia, can make thousands of dollars from selling his or her product free from competition and enjoy maximum exposure for the duration of the
festival. I was told by one product representative that festivals are
"the best advertisement. People come and they know your product and they associate it with the community. It makes my product
a household and community item, and they are thankful to you
for making that possible." In this way, the promotion of cultural
festivals becomes an extension of the companies' identification
with Puerto Rican culture, one that allows them to maintain their
cultural image while diversifying their advertising strategies.

For their part, the new grassroots celebrations can increasingly
tap into indiscriminate sponsors who will fund "pure national
culture" (folklore and peasant music) and popular culture equally,
so long as a mass public is involved. But while the appeal to folklore
is always a good advertising tactic, what is popular and attractive
to the largest public is what rules corporate promoters as they
seek maximum exposure, product exclusivity, and the association
of their product with pleasure and entertainment. In this quest,
private companies are leaving behind the romanticized images of
folklore and turning to popular culture and the realm of everyday
life, thereby favoring the same activities that are shunned by the
official organs of culture on the island.

Popular and Commercial Culture

The term "popular culture" has become a contentious one in
contemporary studies. It has variously been defined as folklore, as
the alternative expression of subordinate classes, and as the "de-
generate" product of mass culture, among many other definitions
(Mukerji and Schudson 1991, Storey 1993). In this work I define

popular culture as the realm of social practice and everyday life and, following Hall (1981), as the ground on which transformations between imposed orders and resistances are played out. This focus analyzes popular culture not as something that has an intrinsic nature in and of itself but that is defined in relation to existing cultural hierarchies, against which it is placed in a subordinate position.

This view of popular culture does not differentiate or dichotomize "pure" popular culture from mass culture, but rather emphasizes the "mediations" between the two or the insertion of the popular classes in a mass society where popular forms of expression are immersed and intersected within new technologies or commercial expressions (Barbero 1993). In this way, contemporary popular culture in Puerto Rico is but a product of the mixture of forms that may be otherwise regarded as folkloric, oppositional, or commercial.[9] Accordingly, popular interests and alternative ways of representing Puerto Rican culture are integrated with and not necessarily opposed to commercial cultural expressions. Yet dominant ideas about what are the appropriate elements to represent Puerto Rican culture continually disregard the possibility that commercial music and forms of entertainment could be channels for constructing or communicating local identities.

Popular culture thus remains the realm that needs to be subverted, contained, or appropriated by nationalist programs. It is in relation to these ideas that we can consider the impact of corporate interests in events and activities associated with the "cultural" realm. Specifically, corporate support of commercial music for cultural activities both defies government disapproval of these genres and contributes to ongoing discussions about which musical styles can appropriately represent Puerto Rican culture. Consider the case of the popular rhythms of salsa, merengue, rap, and reggae. These rhythms are seen as foreign to Puerto Rican culture and are therefore not promoted or funded as cultural activities by government institutions. Salsa, the popular rhythm that has gained the most acceptance as a representation of Puerto Rican culture, is still not perceived to be "original" to Puerto Rico but is mostly associated with "Nuyoricans," who are in fact subjected to racism and classism by islanders. In Puerto Rico, being *nacido y criado* (born and raised during one's formative years) on the island are the primary criteria for defining Puerto Ricanness, rather than self-identification with Puerto Rico and its culture. While most Puerto Ricans have relatives in the States and maintain active links with their U.S. counterparts, as evidenced in the many *ausentes* celebrations on the island, expatriate Puerto Ricans also constitute the other against which racist, sexist, and classist conceptions of Puerto Ricanness are constructed. These views are based on the belief that island Puerto Ricans speak a "purer" Spanish, or are less crime-ridden, more knowledgeable about their culture, and more conscious of "proper gender roles" than their New York, Philadelphia, or Chicago counterparts. Thus the ICP budget allocates no funding for salsa groups to participate in ICP-sponsored cultural activities, just as it neglects other expressions associated with the Puerto Rican U.S. diaspora, such as Nuyorican writing.

However, salsa is used strategically by political parties to appeal to the greater Puerto Rican population. The PNP used salsa in its campaign jingles and in official celebrations of the Central American and Caribbean Olympic games held in Puerto Rico in 1993. Salsa has also been used selectively to represent Puerto Rico abroad, as when the PPD administration of Rafael Hernández Colón, guided by the popularity of salsa music among Europeans, included salsa rather than the traditionally favored peasant music during "Puerto Rico Day" activities at the 1992 International Expo in Seville, Spain. In addition, salsa has become more widely accepted as authentic to Puerto Rican culture as people are revaluing the rhythms against the increased local popularity of Dominican merengue. Nevertheless, while salsa and other popular rhythms are often used to appeal to the greater Puerto Rican population, they remain excluded from officially sanctioned representations of Puerto Rican culture, which always highlight Puerto Rico's peasant past. These decisions are often motivated by racist considerations. Consider the explanation I was given by the organizer of an ICP-backed festival, who justified not inviting salsa groups to the activity by arguing that they might attract *cocolos* (blacks), youth, and disorderly elements. According to him the inclusion of salsa would create "disarray in a family-type setting, because it attracts *cocolos* that have no respect for anything" and would only lead to disarray, disorder, and lack of control.

Salsa, however, is far better received than merengue, another Afro-Caribbean rhythm, which is criticized for being an "inferior rhythm" and an example of *chabacanería* (what is cheap and inferior). This rejection is closely tied to the racism to which Dominicans, who are associated with this rhythm, have been exposed since their immigration to the island. On many occasions I heard people request unsuccessfully that merengue not be played at certain events because it would "turn the festival into a Dominican rather than a Puerto Rican cultural festival."[10] Similarly, rap and reggae, which are popular rhythms among Puerto Rican youth and are closely identified with Puerto Rico's migratory experience and Afro-Caribbean roots, are considered foreign and Americanized rhythms.[11]

Yet, while many popular rhythms are considered by the ICP inferior to the pure national culture, people constantly validate them by including them in their own activities. In this way, salsa, reggae, and rap, which are not intrinsically oppositional in their lyrics and content, attain added value and are politicized through what Stallybrass and White (1986) have called the "dialectic of antagonism," in which popular forms attain oppositional implications when subjected to constraint or governmental intervention.[12] That is, the inclusion of these musical genres in festivals that are overtly identified as "cultural" helps to revindicate aspects of the popular within the national and to politicize these genres through their inclusion in cultural activities despite their exclusion from many "official" settings. An example of the discourse by which salsa and other popular rhythms are revindicated at the local level was provided by a civil worker and organizer of the Festival of Breadfruit Seeds in Vega Alta:

> We believe it is a mistake to think that the only typical music is string music and the *seis chorreao* [a peasant rhythm] because our music comes from Afro-Antillean rhythms and there is a continuity with salsa and merengue. We always include as many typical elements in our cultural festival as we can, but in terms of music, it is with salsa and merengue that we identify, and we try to bring in the local artists because we are a community and we want our people and Puerto Rico to develop, and we achieve this by giving opportunities to our local artists.

Similar processes are at play with other aspects of commercial culture in Puerto Rico. The island's most popular TV shows are also heavily sponsored by the same corporate interests that promote its cultural festivals. I do not analyze these shows in any depth here, except to note that they are an important topic in contemporary discussions about Puerto Ricanness. It is in contrast to these shows, which are regarded as cheap, full of sexual innuendo, and overly commercialized, that conservative sectors of Puerto Rican society define the "true character" of Puerto Rican culture. Less often discussed, however, are the factors that mediate the involvement of commercial sponsors in local television. One is the history of corporate TV sponsorship, which dates back to the origins of Puerto Rican television. Comedy shows like the *India Tavern, Libby's Show,* the *Coca Cola Show,* and, most recently, the *Kiosko Budweiser,* have somewhat naturalized the company/comedy junction, especially in a bar or canteen setting. Another factor is that the same shows that are marketing tools for consumer products also constitute important sources of identification for Puerto Ricans.

Locally produced and drawing on Puerto Rican popular culture, language, satire, and humor, most of these corporate-sponsored comedies revolve around everyday situations, to which elements of the Bakhtinian carnivalesque are added: hierarchies are overturned, politicians are debased, clientelism is exposed, and sexual double meanings inundate the dialogue.[13] Some of these shows include *¡Qué bacilón!* (loosely, What a Raillery!) recently rated as the most popular show on Puerto Rican television, which proudly presents itself as "Puro de aquí" and "Hecho en Puerto Rico" (authentically Puerto Rican); *El kiosko Budweiser,* whose setting is the popular *kiosko* or standing eatery that is the center of activity in most festivals; and the new *El gran bejuco* (The Greater Trickster), whose main character's uniform is a T-shirt displaying the Puerto Rican flag.

The popularity of these shows benefits from and feeds cultural nationalistic ideas, as played out in the ongoing preoccupation with hiring Puerto Rican artists ("artistas de patio") over foreign artists and with countering the U.S.-dominated local entertainment industry, which limits space for displaying Puerto Rican mannerisms and colloquialisms. These debates pervade the letters to the editor in the major newspapers. One such letter chastised the Puerto Rican merengue singer Jailene Cintrón for hiring Miami artists rather than Puerto Rican dancers and choreographers for a new video. In her letter the female fan scolds Cintrón's "unpatriotic move" and advises her that, if "you say you are from the people and for the people, then use your people. . . . You know how much cause of pride it is for a Puerto Rican dancer to be seen in his/her land and to work for his/her people" (Ríos 1996).

Last, many of the new cultural festivals celebrated by independent groups are also corporate sponsored, are dominated by popular rhythms and forms of entertainment, and are therefore perceived to be less patriotic and more commercially motivated and *chabacano* (cheap). One informant, a local legislator, showed his contempt for these festivals and criticized their tendency to display "vulgar" forms of expression: "We have to be more selective about these festivals, which confuse culture and education with other things. We have to be watchful not to fall into things that could clash with the beautiful things that the ICP should project."

This informant did not specify what the "other things" are that these festivals display that clash with Puerto Rican culture, yet his immediate association of "beauty" and culture with the Institute of Puerto Rican Culture was evident. Independent celebrations were categorized and devalued not only by my informants working in the ICP but also by officers of the Tourism Company and government representatives working in the Culture Commission in the Senate, and, of course, by many political activists favoring "pure" cultural activities.

Some of the activities I heard people dismiss were the "staple-vegetable festivals," which include the Festivals of the Plantain, the Breadfruit, and the Yam, which are often mocked because these products are seen as "mundane" staples that are not as evocative of a romanticized peasant culture as is, for instance, coffee. These products, mostly minor fruits rather than important export crops (as coffee once was), are so commonplace that they are not recognized as part of a legacy and are seen instead as fads or excuses for celebrating yet another festival. Moreover, as I have noted, festival themes that tend to emphasize aspects of regional and popular culture are often in direct opposition to the official view of national culture. A worker at a municipal office in charge of providing technical support (lights, trash collection) for local public celebrations expressed his frustration with these festivals: "Who has heard anything about a Festival of Yuca or Breadfruit or anything else? People are just inventing reasons to celebrate festivals. If it were a festival of typical music or folk arts or *bomba y plena* music, which are nationally recognized cultural values, then we would not have a problem with these festivals." The problem, according to this informant, is that people are not emphasizing the nationally recognized cultural icons but are arbitrarily "inventing" things. Such views ignore the importance of these activities for distinguishing communities and miss the meaning organizers attach to them, however varied their content. In turn, these are the events that corporate sponsors are tapping into as they seek to identify their products with local constituencies.

Sorting through Culture and Dollars: The Making of a "Cultural Festival"

There is great debate over the influence of commercial interests on Puerto Rico's cultural politics. Among government cultural workers one matter of concern is how the same companies that sponsor officially sanctioned events featuring folk art and traditional music also support *fiestas patronales,* beach festivals, and the most popular TV shows—or the infamous three B's of *baile, botella, y baraja* (drinks, dancing, and gambling)—which are considered to be examples of consumerism, social decay, and disintegration by conservative sectors of Puerto Rican society. The companies' flexibility also surfaces in their different strategies for advertising and promotions. In their advertising, companies often reinforce images and ideas that have been institutionalized as representative of Puerto Rico, whereas in their promotional strategies they often harbor a different conception of what is a "culturally relevant" program, one that greatly relies on popular culture. This flexibility is at odds with the ICP and with many island intellectuals, who, irrespective of their political beliefs, seek a rigidly delimited and secured view of what rightfully represents Puerto Rican culture.

Nevertheless, the government has praised and recognized the cultural work of companies such as Winston and Bacardi, which hold large-scale annual activities on the island, while both welcoming and encouraging the financial assistance of other major corporations. Examples of this governmmental encouragement are the letters of praise and recognition sent to R. J. Reynolds by the then governor, Hernández Colón, and the president of the Senate, Miguel Hernández Agosto, and published in January 1992 in "Las Artes," an annual bulletin published by this company to announce its cultural work throughout the year. Governor Pedro Roselló (1992-), whose focus has been on the "reinvention of government" through increased privatization, has also encouraged the role of private corporations in funding cultural festivals and cultural work within the communities.

Moreover, private corporations assure the government's positive evaluation of their work by maintaining close personal ties and good relations with government cultural officials. For instance, three of the five medals awarded by R. J. Reynolds to cultural groups always go to government-affiliated cultural centers, and the awarding committee often includes a government cultural representative (often the director or an officer of the ICP office in San Juan). Furthermore, as one organizer explained, the winners always represent a balance between fine-arts organizations, such as ballet companies or symphonies, and folk-art institutions, thus bridging the gap between the universal and folk art that have been associated with the pro-statehood PNP and pro-commonwealth PPD, respectively. Winston's criteria for its awards also adhere to the highest standards, as stipulated by the different political officials. As a result, this prize is highly respected among local groups, as I was able to confirm by the many times I was proudly shown the medal during my visits to centers that had won the prize.

Similarly, Bacardi's annual Folk Arts Fair invites only artisans affiliated with and recommended by the Institute for Puerto Rican Culture. In turn, awarding the 1993 Budweiser Prize to a master artisan entailed gathering representatives of the government's folk art institutions and including as a main speaker a renowned ex-director of the Institute for Puerto Rican Culture. These activities fail to include the salsa and merengue groups that these same companies support heavily at the local level.

Yet while all administrations welcome corporate funding of activities that are regarded as "culturally meaningful" according to dominant standards, commercial sponsorship has ultimately created controversy over what, after all, is an authentic cultural activity. As many more unaffiliated cultural centers are growing outside the guidelines of the ICP, government cultural officials are questioning the commercial tendencies of these new groups and their legitimacy as representatives of Puerto Rican culture. In this way, old discourses about legitimacy and authenticity in Puerto Rican culture are being recycled in response to the growth of these groups and their activities.

As we have seen, representatives of the government cultural entities have repeatedly tried to defend their position vis-à-vis the independent groups by maintaining distinctions between ICP festivals and commercial activities. One ICP official stated, "In our festival everything is cultural and it is not commercialized. What you see is typical music, not shows to draw the masses. The activity is for a small group, and it is educational. It is about cultural resistance." Another official went further: "You have to make a distinction when you talk about cultural festivals. Ours are cultural, but not the others. Those are sponsored by people who are culturally underdeveloped. They cannot tell a cultural activity from a commercial activity."

In this way, the involvement of corporate sponsors, who are seen as attracting commercial forms of entertainment, was generally seen by ICP staff as a threat to the cultural objectives of the activity. Organizers of independent events, however, did not always perceive the same threat. Nor was drawing on municipal and governmental funding always perceived as compromising the groups' autonomy and independence. Rather, autonomy was based on the ability of the organizing group to obtain the greatest credit for its work and effort, as well as control over the content of the programming. This view was evident in the explanation given by the organizer of the Festival of the Pineapple Cutter, who echoed what I was repeatedly told: "All festivals have regional characteristics; the substance of the activity is cultural. What happens is that it is impossible for local commerce to sustain the festival. But the activity itself, what is presented—besides the commercial promotion of products that are not from here—is Puerto Rican; and what people come to see is the folk arts, and the groups that come to play. Even if it is a merengue group, it has to come from here; it has to be Puerto Rican."

It is important to note, however, that not everybody drew a sharp distinction between foreign products and the Puerto Rican content of a show, as this informant did. For many organizers, products like Budweiser and Winston have attained such a strong pro-Puerto Rican identity through their advertising histories that they are perceived to be *cosa de aquí* (from here) rather than as foreign imports. Thus, many take for granted their involvement in these events and dismiss suggestions that they disrupt their programs. Some organizers were even puzzled at my questions regarding the involvement of products like Budweiser in their festivals.

This does not mean that corporate sponsorship provokes no conflict. A common preoccupation among organizers is that "the corporations are remembered but individuals are anonymous." Corporate sponsorship of local festivals carries prestige for some people; it is often interpreted as a sign that the organizing group has connections or that its members "know what they are doing." At the same time, however, public acknowledgment for the effort and time that local organizers put into a given festival is publicly diminished in relation to the contribution of these sponsors. Thus the question of credit, rather than the involvement of corporate sponsors per se, is debated among groups. This was also the case with municipal and governmental funding, which in itself was not perceived as compromising the groups' autonomy and independence. This contrasts with the ICP stance that sees the involvement of the corporate sponsors as a threat to the cultural objectives of its activities but never regards the influence of partisan politics in the festivals as an issue.

Overall, however, I found local groups to be quite publicity literate and able to negotiate corporate demands for maximum public exposure without sacrificing the cultural nature of their festivals, however defined. Organizers employed a variety of strategies to limit the credit that corporations obtain for their involvement and to accommodate the advertising in ways that harmonize with their activity. Mainly, this involved manipulating their funding conditions at the local level. Common strategies involved covering the most prominent areas of the event, such as the center stage and the most visible kiosks, with the activity's distinctive banners before the corporate staff were allowed to put up their logos and announcements. The latter are always posted by the corporate staff themselves, never by the festivals' organizers, which limits their ability to control their festival's look once the corporate staff begins their decorating. Another strategy involves concentrating all advertising around the drinking areas, leaving the typical food and artisanal kiosks—deemed most representative of the cultural aspect of the activity—free from advertisements. One group I met even cut off the sponsoring company's logo from a poster announcing the festival before posting it around the community.

Other groups bought products directly from their local grocery stores to avoid making deals with a corporation that would then press for advertising exposure in the event. This was a measure taken by ARECMA, as one member explained: "We always discussed this issue of corporate funding because we wanted our festival to be a cultural event because we were a cultural organization. We did not want a commercial festival. So we never allowed just one company to sponsor the whole event. Instead we would make a deal with the local merchant and we bought the product from him. That is how we kept the purity of the event as a cultural event of the community, not a marketing tool for corporations."

Many groups prioritized local firms by seeking the sponsorship of the locally produced Don Q rum, Suiza fruit juices, or their local shopowners prior to approaching other corporate sponsors. However, the efficacy of this measure is questionable considering that the island's manufacturing and export-led economy constantly blurs distinctions between local and foreign products. For instance, Medalla beer, made in a local brewery and regarded as a Puerto Rican product, is distributed exclusively by Bacardi and Martini Caribbean, the local distributing subsidiary of Bacardi Corporation, which is a Delaware-based transnational corporation. Groups hoping for Medalla's sponsorship have to go through Bacardi and Martini.

A most threatening development for the autonomy of local groups are the new "corporate promoters" that have rapidly emerged in recent years and act as intermediaries between the organizing groups and the corporations. Using these promoters is becoming highly popular due to the importance that corporate support has attained in a more competitive environment. Promising groups more funding than they had previously obtained from their own efforts, these promoters are being hired at a rapid pace, often with devastating consequences.

Both the Lancha Festival and ARECMA had problems with promoters during my fieldwork. Each had decided to hire a corporate promoter for the first time as a way to increase corporate funding. In the case of ARECMA, the corporate promoters greatly compromised the organizing group's decision-making power vis-à-vis the corporation. They increased the amount of advertising placed in the festival's surroundings, thus diminishing the group's control over the appearance of the festival, which is one of the most important aspects of the event. In the case of La Lancha, the promoter failed to bring one of the trendy bands that it had originally promised the group as well as other spectacles for which the group had already paid. The Lancha Committee, however, was oblivious to the added advertising placed by the promoter, just as many other groups do not mind the companies' inundating their festivals and activities with advertisements because these are also thought to give a more festive and contemporary feel to the activities.

This attitude is also tied to the importance that these cultural activities attain for people in the informal economy, for whom printed ads, posters, and publicity paraphernalia are an important way of attracting consumers. I even saw people request that the corporate staff add more posters or decorations here or there, and at other times, people added more such decorations themselves to make their kiosks stand out. Corporate sponsorship is also sought to increase the effectiveness of these festivals as fund-raising tools for larger projects. This is how the Claridad Festival, organized to generate operating funds for the *Claridad* newspaper, which is the widest-read print medium among pro-independence sectors and the Puerto Rican left, became sponsored by Budweiser and other corporations in recent years.

Meanwhile, cultural centers that depend most heavily on the ICP for their funding are continually seeking compromises between the requirements of the government's cultural policy and the funding conditions of commercial companies. For example, the government's educational priority is constantly obstructed by the corporate funders' display of advertising banners, which according to a local leader "tend to turn the cultural festivals into a Schaefer or Budweiser beer activity." Another critical issue is how to reconcile the government's preference for a no-alcohol policy at cultural events and the corporate sponsors' expectations, especially in the case of beer and soft drink companies. These sponsors typically arrange a huge display of freebies promoting their products and always expect heavy sales as a condition for future financial support.

Some groups have chosen to remain at the margin, and they reject external funding in order to avoid both governmental and corporate regulation; but most groups are forced to rely on nongovernmental funders to support the popular-entertainment aspect of their activities. While the government endorses folk music and troubadours, it is salsa and more often merengue music that attracts audiences to the "cultural" programming. Thus folk music and *trovadores* are often featured during the day, but the night belongs to rum drinks, salsa, and merengue. As a leader of one local cultural center stated, "Through salsa you bring people in so that they participate in the cultural activities," openly voicing the official discourse that distinguishes salsa from legitimate "cultural" activities.

Considering that rejection of corporate financial support is almost inconceivable for most groups interested in organizing cultural activities, corporate sponsorship will continue and is likely to increase. Corporations continue to benefit from this publicity strategy, and even the government encourages their involvement as public funding for cultural work shrinks. In 1993, the Institute of Puerto Rican Culture experienced a cut of over $2 million by the commonwealth government, and most legislative assignments to cultural groups for local festivals and cultural activities are being discontinued.

Yet, far from eroding national culture, these companies are another source that local groups tap in the ongoing struggle over defining and representing Puerto Rican culture. In this process, people draw on corporate funding to highlight aspects that are excluded due to their more popular and less "cultural" outlook, and that can become a venue for the validation and recognition of different elements of Puerto Rican culture. Corporate sponsorship is also sought after for a variety of purposes that are not always at odds with the meaning of these events for their organizers or participants.

As we have seen, private corporations are after faithful consumers, just as the ICP favors those groups who accept its precepts on culture. Ironically, however, it is through the intervention of capital in these cultural activities that popular expressions of nationality are obtaining a voice and a space. The authenticated but static and folklorized conception of Puerto Rican culture is not able to resonate and attract popular support from classes that continually challenge the purist conceptions of Puerto Ricanness that nationalist ideologies depend on. Increasingly consumer oriented and leaning toward the *chabacano*, a large segment of contemporary Puerto Rican society is less interested in strict definitions of pure culture and more eager to embrace everyday representations of Puerto Rican identity. In turn, lacking the nationalist preoccupation with "pure" culture, the corporate sector can be "polluted" by the popular classes from which it accrues support in the form of consumers.

Accounting for these new developments pushes us to rethink the processes of constructing national identities in contemporary society, where the publicity industry constitutes an added channel elaborating definitions of Puerto Ricanness and where multinational products can appear more or less "Puerto Rican" to the average consumer. Yet far from being contradictions, these new processes are intrinsic components of contemporary cultural politics on the island where corporate sponsors continue to sell products through culture and culture through products.

View of the Fiesta Criolla del Panapén in Vega Alta, with giant balloons depicting consumer products. *Photo by Arlene Dávila.*

Troubadour contest flanked by corporate advertising, Fiesta Criolla del Panapén, Vega Alta. *Photo by Arlene Dávila.*

Silk-screened poster for the Budweiser event by local artist Samuel Lind. The poster was commissioned by Anheuser-Busch for its corporate Prize to the Master Artisans. *Photo by Arlene Dávila.*

Winston advertisement showing couple visiting Jayuyano artisan Ariel Soto. The advertisement was produced in the 1980s as part of a campaign developed by Ammirati Puris Lintas, San Juan, Puerto Rico. *Photo by Arlene Dávila.*

Winston advertisement drawing on the Festival of the Flowers. The advertisement was produced in 1995 as part of a campaign developed by Ammirati Puris Lintas, San Juan, Puerto Rico. *Photo by Arlene Dávila.*

View of the Bacardi Folk Arts Museum inside the company's headquarters in Cataño. *Photo by Arlene Dávila.*

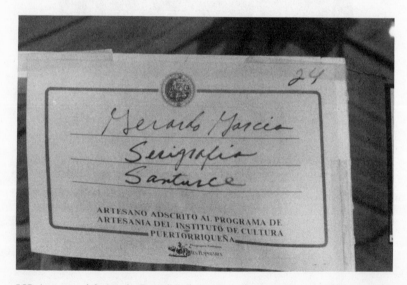

ICP signs posted during the Bacardi Folk Arts Fair. The signs distinguish those artisans who are officially registered with the Institute of Puerto Rican Culture's Folk Arts Program. *Photo by Arlene Dávila.*

Street markings painted by participants to claim space in the "outside fair" during the Bacardi Folk Arts Fair. *Photo by Arlene Dávila.*

Mariana Ortiz Montero, queen of the National Indigenous Festival in 1995. Her dress of corn, clay, pumpkin seeds, yucca, and starch achiote was made by Jorge Figueroa and represents the *guatú* or indigenous fire symbolizing the "life light of our people." *Photo by Orializ Rodríguez.*

View of the audience, Barranquitas Folk Arts Fair. Notice the flag and corporate logo T-shirts, which are commonly seen side by side in cultural festivals. *Photo by Arlene Dávila.*

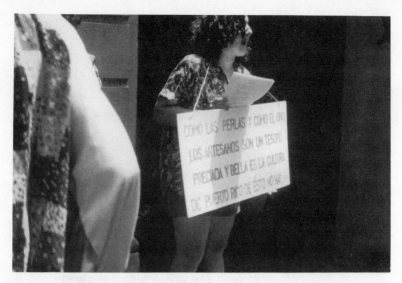

Folk artist and activist Eislee Molina. Her sign reads, "Like pearls, like gold, artisans are a treasure. Valued and beautiful is Puerto Rican culture. Of this there is no doubt." *Photo by Arlene Dávila.*

"Puerto Rico Is My Nation." The sign was painted on a car during one of three July 1996 marches over the issue of Puerto Rican nationhood. *Photo by Arlene Dávila.*

Chapter VI

Contesting the Nation, Contesting Identities

> Pero es el circuito de las escaramuzas, las estratagemas y
> argucias de que ha estado siempre hecho el camino de los
> dominados hacia el reconocimiento social. [It is out of
> artifices, schemes and skirmishes that the route of the domi-
> nated toward social recognition has always been shaped.]

—Jesús Martín Barbero, *De los medios a las mediaciones*

The delegitimation of many new cultural expressions as commercial clearly serves to limit their influence on dominant conceptions of identity. Fear of commercialism is therefore not only an outcome of the continued involvement of commercial interests in Puerto Rico's cultural politics but also part of larger attempts to establish and maintain hierarchies among forms and genres that claim to represent Puerto Rican culture. These expressions are either legitimized as cultural or rejected as commercial.

The division between cultural and commercial forms is embedded in a larger field in which standards are set for the production, circulation, and consumption of goods that aim to represent Puerto Rican culture.[1] As we have seen, what is considered cultural, according to official standards, is associated with a "traditional" past in which utopian precapitalist and noncapitalist forms have the strongest claim to authenticity.

Precapitalist forms are a common foundational element for defining cultural authenticity (Alonso 1994, Ferguson 1992, García-Canclini 1993), as is the opposition between the modern and the traditional (Olwig 1993). As we have seen, this opposition has been heightened in Puerto Rico as a result of the island's colonial relationship with the United States (so that modern culture and consumption are associated with the dominant American "other," which provides the reference against which authentic culture is forged) and also because of the high involvement of corporate sponsors in the island's cultural politics. Recall that a primary motivation for the creation of the Institute of Puerto Rican Culture was to protect the Puerto Rican soul from the ills of consumerism, which were seen to lead to Americanization and culture loss. Thus, consumerism and materialism have become constructed as major threats to Puerto Rican culture, which itself is constructed as the local "domain of sovereignty."

The cultural policy's standards also state that patriotism should be the motivation for producing cultural forms that aim to represent Puerto Rican culture and that the production of "authentic" cultural forms should be divorced from economic and commercial motives. What is defined as authentically cultural thus becomes what Bourdieu has termed the "economic world reversed," or the "disavowal" of economic value—that is, the separation of economic interest from the creation and production of cultural goods and practices (Bourdieu 1993). Bourdieu's discussion refers mostly to high culture rather than to folklore or objects and expressions that aim to represent a national identity. Nevertheless, just as disassociating culture from commercial values in order to safeguard taste and distinguish the "authentic" from mass commercial products has been documented since the origins of mass-consumer culture (Handler 1992, R. Williams 1982),[2] the "disavowal" of economic interest in the production of symbols of national identity also helps to sanction and "consecrate" dominant interests under the unquestionable standards of authenticity.

In terms of circulation and consumption, similar standards help to legitimize dominant views of authenticity. These standards demand that "cultural" activities should promote education and be consumed as educational products rather than as mere entertainment. Accordingly, what is legitimized as cultural according to institutional standards ends up reproducing social hierarchies and excluding popular ways of expressing and consuming "Puerto Rican culture." This results in intersecting dichotomies that equate authenticity with the individual and inauthenticity with mass production, folk art with high culture and popular culture with the everyday.

This chapter analyzes the contemporary distinctions created by official cultural policy between "authentic" and "commercial" expressions as part of a greater process of struggle over the content of legitimacy in the nationalist ideology. In this context, the distinctions between legitimate and heretical, and between high and low culture, serve as axes to legitimate dominant culture and exclude subordinate culture, just as other classist and racist distinctions serve to delimit and exclude people from a national community, however defined. I argue that these contemporary distinctions between "cultural" and "commercial" forms provide a new terrain for recycling discourses about legitimacy and inauthenticity in Puerto Rican culture, and that they serve as a veil for the subversion of alternative views of nationality originating from subordinate groups.

I address these issues through two case studies: of the National Indigenous Festival, an ICP-sponsored activity, and the corporate-sponsored Bacardi Folk Arts Fair. These represent two of the most important activities supported by the ICP and a commercial sponsor respectively. I argue that a commercial component is an inescapable aspect of all cultural expressions on the island, rather than a qualitatively different domain; and that the assessment of cultural products as legitimate and authentic or commercial and inauthentic is most important for legitimizing or disqualifying different claims. As such, these categories are arbitrary and can be shown to be situationally deployed and constituted.

The National Indigenous Festival: In Search of the "Purest" Indigenous Queen

The National Indigenous Festival was founded in 1969, four years after the inauguration of the ICP-affiliated cultural center of Jayuya. Since its inception, the festival has been the activity that most directly celebrates the legacy of Taino culture through a massive display of its dress, music, foods, dance, and games. The activity is nationally famous, and is considered one of the most authentic festivals among government cultural officials and the one event that highlights an important component of Puerto Rican nationality.

As such, the festival has been a priority of the ICP, which regards it as a model for other cultural centers to follow. In turn, the cultural center of Jayuya has become the home of one of the regional offices of the ICP and has produced some of its most influential regional promoters. The National Indigenous Festival also enjoys more government funding than other local ICP celebrations, which has allowed the cultural center to reject or exert greater control over corporate sponsors and ensure the festival's image as a purely cultural event. Besides the ICP and the municipal administration, it is mostly the locally owned businesses and the two manufacturers in Jayuya (Boots Pharmaceuticals and Baxter Laboratories) that support the festival. Big commercial sponsors, like Winston, have supported the festival in the past, but their advertising is controlled by the cultural center. The festival I witnessed had no visible advertising from local or external sources. The few commercial sponsors involved in the festival are not allowed to advertise and obstruct the decoration of the festival.

Yet even within this culturally sanctioned domain there is evidence of struggle over the definition of authenticity. It is manifested in the different popular perceptions of the activity (as a tourist attraction, a cultural event, or a political act) and in the participants' rejection of imposed and unattainable standards of authenticity.

I first became aware of these issues when I heard people commenting on the festival during my fieldwork in remarks that ranged from open admiration to indifference. The feelings of people involved in organizing the festival clashed with those of people I met later in Jayuya, who were generally less enthusiastic about the event. Most people pointed to the event's entertainment value and said the festival was important because it was one of the few shows offering a diversion for Jayuyanos. These perceptions of the festival as a "show" or a leisure activity, rather than a culturally significant event, suggested early on that, for many, it was not the purely cultural occasion envisaged by the organizers.

I later learned that there had been some skepticism about the legitimacy of the festival ever since its inception. Some saw it as ridiculous and contrived, given that the Taino had been officially extinct since the 1600s; they perceived it as a heresy, as "digging up the dead." As Chapter II discusses, this belief is directly tied to the official nationalist ideology, which holds that the Taino have been extinct since the Spanish colonization of the island, and that only "traces" of them and their "contributions" remain in Puerto Rican culture. This common perception has maimed the authenticity of the festival because in the name of authenticity the best that can be achieved is a performance of cultural forms attributed to the Taino.

The second point of contention was the festival's identification with the PPD and PIP parties. This further undermined the legitimacy of the festival for some people, especially PNP advocates, who saw it as a politically motivated event rather than a culturally worthwhile activity. Although partisan elements are commonly associated with ICP-funded events, Jayuya's history as one of the bases of the harshly suppressed nationalist uprising of 1950, and the place where Puerto Rico was declared an "independent republic," has given the festival a nationalistic image that attracts thousands of visitors from all over the island.[3] The area's cultural promoter said that the festival especially attracts "those who want to express their *nacionalismo solapao* (hidden nationalism), without having to be open *independentistas,* which they would be afraid of." And indeed, the festival I witnessed was extremely crowded, even though it was competing with two other blockbuster events with nationalistic overtones: the 1993 Central American Olympic games and the government-funded quincentennial celebration of the island's "discovery." The festival's politically charged environment has often turned it into a public competition between the PNP and the PPD municipal administration. At the festival I attended, this tension was evident when a palm tree, the political emblem of the PNP, was burned. The incident was interpreted by some as the act of crazy kids and by others as the work of nationalists. It led to rumors and references to the 1950s uprising, indicating the fear that is still associated with open expressions of nationalism in Jayuya.

The political identification of the festival is also strengthened by the close ties between the local cultural center and two government offices: the local branch of the Education Department and the ICP's central office in San Juan. Because of its controversial nature and local political connotations, these agencies have been involved with the festival since its origin. The ICP in San Juan has been particularly important in sustaining it. Anthropologists and archaeologists employed by the ICP were an important factor in the cultural center's decision to highlight the city's Taino heritage. It was ICP staff members who originally told the cultural center about the cacique who ruled the area prior to Spanish colonization. Since then, archaeologists have unearthed materials documenting Jayuya's indigenous history. The town displays some well-known Taino artifacts, including an Indian tomb where a Taino skeleton is on display; and the Museo del Cemí (Cemí Museum) is shaped after the sculptured stone deities of the Taino.

Its reputation as a pure cultural event has turned the National Indigenous Festival into a nationalist and tourist activity and Jayuya into the "Taino capital" of Puerto Rico. The festival is very important for tourism and brings life to the small town of Jayuya, where economic growth has been hampered by lack of accessible roads and industry. Unemployment is close to 35 percent, and the population has remained constant at around fifteen thousand inhabitants since the 1940s, because youth leave the economically depressed area in search for work. Seventy-six percent of the population live below the poverty line (Negociado del Censo 1990). But during the festival local people and visitors crowd the town square, hostels fill up, and commerce booms.

The festival's key role in the local economy has molded the event to appeal to the outside public rather than to local residents because, as I was told by the director of the cultural center, "People come to Jayuya to see the festival and they expect to see certain things." This emphasis on outside visitors was evident in the cultural center's programming, which was not discussed at the meetings of the cultural center's leadership, but was decided by the director of the festival and the ICP regional promoter. As a result, the musical and artistic elements are predictable, and locals complain that the same artists appear year after year, a fact that the cultural center staff defends on the basis of the performers' authenticity.

Yet one aspect of the festival has continued to attract local residents and provides a good example of the way in which authenticity is contested and reformulated: the celebration of a *Reinado indígena* (Indigenous Pageant) to select the Indigenous Queen for the festival. Since its introduction in 1973, the pageant has been the most popular addition to the festival and has attracted the greatest community participation. For our purposes, this event provides a rich context to analyze some of the hierarchies at play in contemporary society. As Ballerino Cohen et al. have argued (1996), pageants vary widely, but they always provide a forum for displaying values, concepts, and issues involved in the constitution of the identity of their organizers.

The pageant was added to the festival on the initiative of the first woman director of the cultural center, a renowned school superintendent who, despite her influence, faced opposition from the other members of the cultural center, who saw the pageant as a modern event opposed to the traditional image of the Taino. As the founder of the pageant remembers:

> People associated the pageant with Miss Universe and Miss
> Puerto Rico, something modern. People in the center thought
> it was out of place to do this. Yet I explained to them that
> Taino society was organized around kings and queens and that
> their daughters must have been princesses of the tribe. Then
> people realized that they had nobility and that it was probably
> in these types of societies that pageants initially originate, in so-
> cieties with queens and princesses, and I finally convinced them.

The decision was also influenced by the popularity that pageants were attaining among the public, which peaked after Puerto Rico won the Miss Universe beauty pageant for the first time in 1970.

The initial idea was to select an indigenous queen (a *cacica*) on the basis of the themes represented in the candidate's costume—very much like carnival contests celebrated in other cities, although in the Indigenous Pageant the costume design had to be related to indigenous culture. The first pageant dresses combined cloth, sequins, glitter, and other synthetic decorations into confections that aimed at representing Puerto Rico's flora, fauna, and ways of life. By 1976, however, the center turned toward native materials, and the authenticity of the dress was judged according to its use of materials found in the local environment, like feathers, seeds, shells, earth, roots, shells, and pebbles. Dresses were made of *majagua* (bark) with flower or seed trimmings and complemented by tiaras made of seeds, corn, and other natural materials. The use of synthetic or manufactured materials like glue, sequins, cloth, or plastic was banned and made grounds for disqualification.

The strengthening of the Taino identification in the pageant, through the use of the purest local materials in the design of the dress, occurred as the Taino were becoming an important symbol of cultural identity in Puerto Rican society in the mid-1970s. This shift was evident in the resurgence of archaeological and historical studies of the Taino, the popularization of Taino themes in artistic work, and the representation of the Taino in commercial advertising.[4]

The popularization of the Taino as a symbol of national identity contributed to the festival's reputation as the guardian of indigenous culture on the island, a reputation that required a continuous searching of the past for further bases of authenticity. Indicative of the festival's emphasis on strengthening links to the past was the founding, by the members of the cultural center, of the Indigenous Band and the Indigenous Dancers in the mid-1970s. Clothed in Taino dress—loincloths, body paint, and shell decorations—these groups are in charge of replicating *areytos* (Taino ceremonial dances) and exhibiting the *batey* (communal ball) during the festival's celebration. The added importance of the event nationwide was explained by a high school teacher who has been involved in the organization of the pageant for over ten years: "The festival was so pure, so pure that everything had to be natural. If we were going to select an indigenous queen, naturally we had to choose something that was congruent with the festival, with the culture, with the customs, something virgin. It was no longer possible to select an indigenous queen with a sequined dress."

Additionally, the center decided that in an indigenous pageant, physical resemblance to the Taino should be the main criterion for the selection of the queen. Until then the participants were mostly young white women, and I was told that the favorites were blondes wearing dark wigs and skin paint to represent Taino characteristics. After the change in policy, candidates were chosen according to their "indigenous" characteristics, among which long straight hair, a narrow forehead, elongated eyes, a short nose, pronounced cheekbones, and copper coloring were identified as criteria for authenticity. These features were based upon historical descriptions and the bust of a local high school boy selected for his indigenous appearance in the 1970s.

Thus, the selection of an "authentic" Taino queen emerged as another way of showcasing authenticity in the festival. However, the criteria for selecting the queen have been contested because the performance aspects of the activity rather than the queen's physical appearance attract the most popular interest. The dress and its presentation have become the most important aspect of the pageant, not the physical appearance of the *cacica* that the ICP-affiliated cultural center stresses.

After the adoption of the new policies, the cultural center gave primary emphasis to physical characteristics in the selection of the *cacica*. Young women representing competing schools in the final pageant are first selected solely on the basis of their facial features and hair and skin color. Their dress only became important during the competition itself, which took place before the public in the middle of the plaza. But in response to criticism from people involved in making the costumes, the cultural center later gave equal weight in the selection process to physical traits and to the dresses. Nonetheless, the center retained its preference for physical traits as the true mark of authenticity. As one organizer explained, "The dress also represents the culture, but we have to make people understand that we are after those physical characteristics, because that is the true root. Sometimes the schools say that they cannot find candidates, but after a while they always find one. As long as we find the characteristics, we will continue to emphasize them as the defining aspect of the festival."

The center's concern about physical characteristics does not mean that it espouses the view that there are living descendants of the Taino in modern Puerto Rico, but only that physical traits will be the basis for selecting those who look more "authentically" Indian. This was evident in the reaction of one of the organizers of the activity, who declined to present on stage a group of Puerto Ricans from New York who asserted a link to the Taino through spiritual descent. This group claimed to have developed a religious connection with the Taino that went beyond physical features. Rejecting the group's request to make a public announcement inviting local people to a ceremony they had planned by the Taino burial monument, the organizer explained, "Our goal is to make people feel Puerto Rican, not to turn people into indigenous people. This festival is scientific and cultural. Only scientifically and officially validated indigenous people get to be announced in the festival."

In fact, indigenous people from South America and the Caribbean have participated in the festival; but the "spiritual" Tainos, or any group claiming genetic relatedness to the Taino, are dismissed as inauthentic. In this way, the cultural center is following the ICP's official policy of emphasizing the contribution of the Taino legacy to contemporary Puerto Rican culture, rather than the mobilization of Taino identity for political purposes. This view also serves to invalidate the attempts of local and expatriate Puerto Ricans to look to the Taino for symbolic material with which to construct a contemporary Puerto Rican cultural identity. In fact, a variety of groups now claim Taino descent through a range of means, including blood ties, "spiritual descent," or commitment to furthering Taino interests. Most of these groups are located in the United States — one example is the Taino Inter-Tribal Council in New Jersey — although there are some on the island as well, such as the Consejo General of Borinquen Tainos (General Council of Puerto Rican Tainos). Some of the U.S.-based groups have appealed to Jayuya's cultural center as a means of enhancing the legitimacy of their claims vis-à-vis other groups claiming Taino descent. These appeals are perceived as aberrations, however, and are not given voice in the festival. Thus the festival affirms persons who look "authentic" without ever believing themselves to be real Tainos, as their "fake" counterparts do, although the latter cannot possibly be authentic given Puerto Rico's official position on the Tainos' extinction. Because the physical characteristics required of the pageant candidates are not represented as a genetic link to the Taino, they are not perceived as threatening the official view of the Tainos' extinction nor dominant racial ideals of whiteness; *looking* Taino is never equated with *being* Taino.

In selecting the *cacica*, members of the cultural center visit the different schools to make sure that candidates are chosen according to the specified physical standards. The women in charge of the contest pride themselves on having educated the town to recognize "Taino traits," and claim that there is little controversy about their selections. I was told: "They themselves know which are good candidates; we no longer have to tell them what to look for. Some of the darker girls are disappointed, but things are explained to them, and usually they have selected some good candidates before I go to advise them on what to look for." What is striking is that it is still easier for lighter-skinned girls to represent accepted Indian traits and be selected as candidates than it is for darker ones. This is mostly because skin color and hair texture (the two phenotypical characteristics most commonly used to distinguish race on the island) are the predominant criteria for selecting the queen; other characteristics are more easily ignored. A candidate with "bad" (curly) hair was unlikely to be selected, even if she had such Taino traits as high cheekbones, a narrow forehead, and elongated eyes. The requirements of straight hair and copper coloring discriminate most against black Puerto Ricans (who are identified principally by their hair type and skin color).

The same selection process is discernible in the composition of the Indigenous Band and Dancers, which also chooses participants according to supposed Taino traits. Composed of about thirty adolescent boys and girls (many of whom were former *cacicas* or candidates in the pageant), the band is also sponsored by the cultural center. Yet whiter-skinned girls, either wearing makeup or long dark wigs, were included in the group while black and darker-skinned girls were absent. There were also male dancers whose dark features would otherwise disqualify them, who wore wigs to the performances. It was easier for darker males to be accepted as performers than for women because most males felt too embarrassed to participate in dances that clashed with traditional gender roles. This led to the relaxation of entry requirements for men in the dance troupe although not to the elimination of racial markers as a major determinant for participation. Thus, the wig of one of the oldest members of the group, who has been part of the band and dance group since its inception, always occasions laughter and explanations about the "real" texture of his hair.

In this way, the overt inconsistency of accepting that white and Taino can merge but black and Taino cannot belies the cultural center's claim that the emphasis on the candidate's physiognomy is innocuous. Meanwhile, the importance of imitating Indian characteristics, which was never challenged by the organizers of the festival, was continually debated in practice because people placed less value on these criteria as a legitimating factor. In reality, despite the cultural center's emphasis on the candidates' physical traits, it is the dresses that steal the show. These are still created with natural products, but they have become more elaborate in their production and in their themes. There are far more arguments about which is the best, most original, and creative dress than about who is the most "Indian looking" candidate. Arguments about the dresses have sometimes escalated, and jurors have been physically threatened by people unhappy with their voting.

Such controversies actually led to my involvement in the pageant. I was asked to serve as a juror because it was believed that, as an outsider, I would be an impartial judge. My background as an anthropologist also gave me some weight as someone who "knows about culture" in Jayuya, where archeologists have been pivotal in constructing its Indian past. I can therefore confirm from experience that it is the performance aspects of the contest that draw the most popular attention, and not the candidates' physical features. I had to review and talk to all the candidates in my role as a juror, and it became clear that they and the people who made their dresses were following different standards from those of the pageant organizers. For instance, "Indian" features were generally disregarded as they focused on how the dress was made, the different materials used, how they were found, whether they were novel or had been used before, and, most important, who was involved in the creation of the dress.

The amount of time people put into making the dresses (which were created by students from the participating schools or by someone hired for the job,) as well as the inspiration for the various dress themes, were also important issues that came up spontaneously during my meetings with the contestants.

In contrast, none of the candidates or the people around them (mostly those involved in making the dresses) drew attention to the candidates' physical features. These became a secondary aspect of the contest and were referred to only in order to legitimize the jurors' decisions. However, people seemed generally aware that the candidates tended to be light skinned, as evidenced in the generalized explanation I commonly heard to explain a juror's disregard of a favorite candidate, which was by calling attention to her whiteness. I often heard "she was too white; that's why the other candidate won," comments further suggesting the predominance of whiter "Indians" in the pageant, who at the end had to be screened out to safeguard the Taino authenticity, which certainly is not black but neither is too white. In this way, the fact that racial features were popularly invalidated and overlooked as a determining category in the pageant may be evidence of a tacit recognition of the "whiteness" of the queens. This left the dress and its manufacture as the real contested element during the pageant, even though the organizers maintain that it is the physical features that carry most weight during the pageant.

The priority that the dress has attained over physical features in selecting the pageant's winner was a cause of tension for people who preferred a more "purist" festival. "This is not a festival, this is a carnival," said an outraged proponent of this view, who was once very active in the organization of the festival. He complained that people no longer cared about the educational purposes of the festival, or the authentic indigenous features that it aims to highlight, but were only concerned about "giving a show" and performing rather than enhancing the legacy of Taino culture. These claims reproduced the same dichotomies by which what is thought to be educational and authentic is deemed cultural and what is for show or entertainment is perceived to be "tainted" and purely for "wasteful" consumption.

The concern to control the carnivalesque aspects of the activity in order to preserve its purity was also evident in the reaction of cultural center members to the costumes that I reviewed in my role as a juror. One of my first choices was a "bat dress" made of black feathers, earthy crushed stone, carbon, and hair. It was inspired by a Taino legend about a young woman who takes the form of a bat to be able to fly to her lover. However, I was initially discouraged from this choice by one of the organizers of the event, who thought it was "ugly" and too much like "Batman." My attention was directed to contestants who were thought to look more "Indian" in their dress (such as a contestant dressed with in earth-colored materials, such as seeds and bark, assembled to represent a more standard theme, the sun) and away from the bat, which was based on a mythical story and was thought to be too unconventional.

To conclude, although the National Indigenous Festival is commonly represented as a pure and educational activity, it is not entirely without entertainment aspects, commercial content, or conflict. The entertainment component is assured by the nationalist ideology, which limits the Taino identity to a performance of Taino lifestyles. Meanwhile, the festival's commercial component is assured by its role as one of the most important economic activities in Jayuya, which helps strengthen the area's tourist appeal as the "Taino capital of Puerto Rico." Yet while the cultural, educational, entertainment, and economic aspects of the activity are all intertwined, boundaries are still maintained between those aspects of the activity that are more or less cultural. Thus, during the pageant, physical traits are deemed the determinant of authenticity by the cultural center's staff rather than the dress that is constructed by participants as the most important aspect of the event. The relevance of this distinction in maintaining hierarchical notions of authenticity is obvious when one considers that it helps disqualify the dress, the one aspect of the pageant that subverts the emphasis on physical traits and the racist implications of favoring "whiter make-believe" Tainos.

The Bacardi Folk Arts Fair

> Artisan
> Man, Essence of Borinquen
> Flower of the "ilan," "ilan"
> you emerge from the earth
> Artisan
> Naboria [Taino worker], Patriotic jíbaro.
> (Pierluissi de Rodríguez 1989)

In Puerto Rico almost everyone knows that the Bacardi Folk Arts Fair involves two different events: the "inside fair," organized by the company on its own premises in the town of Cataño, and the "outside fair," which has developed outside the company gates as a spontaneous creation of the informal economy.

The inside fair was founded in 1976 as part of a broader promotion strategy aimed at identifying Bacardi rum with Puerto Rico. It was the outcome of company research in the mid-1970s, which revealed that the product's image as a Cuban product was hampering sales on the island. Even though the company had been operating in Puerto Rico since the mid-1930s, where it had come in search of better tax conditions, it had not been able to shed its Cuban identity and compete with other Puerto Rican–produced rums on the local market. This image problem became particularly problematic with the increase of Cuban immigrants to the island, which began after the 1959 Cuban revolution and peaked in the 1970s. As Duany (1995) has noted, the earliest Cuban immigrants to the island came mostly from the upper classes of Cuban society; in consequence anything Cuban came to be associated with a stereotype of arrogance and exclusivity.

The fair was part of a broad public-relations effort intended to solve Bacardi's image problem and identify its product with Puerto Rico. The advertising component of the campaign, entitled "Manos puertorriqueñas" (Puerto Rican Hands), equated the process of making Bacardi rum with the craftsmanship of nationally recognized Puerto Rican artisans, painters, and other artists. Launched in the mid-1970s, this campaign continued until the mid-1980s, when the advertising strategy for Bacardi rum shifted to more modern themes, abandoning overt folkloric and nationalistic imagery. Once again this move was informed by research, which revealed that the product's identification with folklore had led it to become associated with maturity and old age. However, the company continued to link its product to Puerto Rico through the sponsorship of cultural events, folk art exhibits, and most importantly through the annual fair, which has since evolved into a national event attracting thousands of visitors.

The identification of the product with Puerto Rican culture helped increase Bacardi's market share on the island from 3 percent in the 1970s to 45 percent in the 1990s.[5] The campaign has nationalized the product to such a degree that the rum is popularly perceived as a Puerto Rican product both locally and in the U.S. market, even though Bacardi is in fact a multinational company incorporated in Delaware and benefits from tax breaks under Section 936 of the Internal Revenue Code, just as other multinationals on the island do. Bacardi is produced not only in Puerto Rico but also in Mexico, Trinidad, and Nassau, and is bottled and distributed in over a dozen other countries, a network that has contributed to making Bacardi one of the best-selling rums in the world.[6] Thus, Bacardi's identification as a Puerto Rican product is as spurious as the perception that Winston cigarettes are a local product solely because they are manufactured on the island.

The continued identity of the rum as a national product is nevertheless a pivotal aspect of Bacardi's operations on the island. Besides changing the product's image, this identification ultimately enables the company to profit from the excise tax on rum imported to the United States, which is returned to the Puerto Rican government. In 1992, according to a spokesperson from Fomento (Puerto Rico's Economic Development Administration), a total of $195 million in taxes were returned to the Puerto Rican government, of which $17 million was awarded to various enterprises for promotion purposes. As the number-one rum importer, Bacardi is a primary beneficiary of this tax benefit, which translates into millions of free promotional dollars for the company.

In order to identify its product with the most authentic representations of Puerto Rican folk arts, the company sought from early on the collaboration of the Institute of Puerto Rican Culture in the organization of its fair. This collaboration is highly publicized in the fair through signs announcing ICP's co-sponsorship of the event and by small signs displaying the logo of the ICP in front of each artisan's space. These connections with the ICP allow the company to legitimize the event as cultural while relinquishing the most controversial aspect of its organization—the actual selection of the artisans who will participate. In fact, the ICP has been the subject of numerous criticisms about the reappearance of the same artisans in the fair, to the exclusion of many others who have never been invited. This exclusivity is the result of the event's emphasis on authenticity and the stipulation that participants must be the best representatives of Puerto Rican master artisans, despite the increasing number of artisans whose work diverges from official definitions of authenticity.

Official definitions of Puerto Rican "master artisans," which are recycled in the government's cultural institutions, promote the image of a male, elderly, rural white peasant who inherited the craft from his immediate family and is a true lover and defender of Puerto Rican culture. As a radio interviewer punned during the 1993 National Folk Arts Fair, artisans are creators of *arte sano* (healthy art). The folk arts are perceived as good and wholesome, as are their creators, by extension. Not surprisingly, the crafts that are identified as "representations of culture" are mostly limited to rural-identified, handmade, preindustrial products — crafts associated with the rural peasant rather than the urban and coastal workers. These traits, of course, are directly related to Puerto Rico's peasant-based national myth. Accordingly, Puerto Rico's master artisan carves *santos* (wooden images of Christian iconography), or does other forms of woodworking, or makes hammocks, but he does not rely solely on his craft for sustenance. The economic role that crafts have historically played on the island is ignored by this construct, which emphasizes only the patriotic role of folk artists as the bearers of Puerto Rican cultural traditions.

Needless to say, many contemporary Puerto Rican artisans differ from the government's conception of a master artisan, and most of these are therefore perceived as commercially motivated and not as true defenders of Puerto Rican cultural values. According to a study conducted by a previous director of the ICP's Folk Arts Division (Vargas 1991), 52.9 percent of contemporary Puerto Rican artisans are women, most are between thirty-one and forty years of age, and 56 percent live in urban areas. The study referred to these artisans as "neo-artisans" because 51 percent were found to have been working at their craft for less than ten years. Most of these neo-artisans learned their craft from friends, at technical schools, or even at the university. Most took up their craft as a means of solving unemployment problems; but whatever their motivations, most respond to economic pressures. As a result, it is what sells best that influences the items they produce: typically souvenirs in clay and leather or silk-screened T-shirts expressing Puerto Rican themes, Taino iconography, and nationalist phrases or poetry. Jewelry and other easily manufactured goods are much more common than the "traditional" folk arts (wood carving, embroidery, mask making), which require more time and training to produce and are therefore less profitable for the artisans. Moreover, the primary materials of contemporary folk arts, such as leather and clay, are mostly cheaper imported goods rather than the more expensive locally produced materials, which challenges governmental dictates that authentic crafts be made from indigenous materials.

Attempting to maintain high standards for its event, Bacardi follows the official distinction between "cultural" and "commercial" folk arts, inviting only those artists who have met ICP standards. These are based on Law 99 of 1986, which lists general criteria for the evaluation of artisans. Among other things, these stipulate that Puerto Rican artisans should be residents of Puerto Rico, a clause that excludes U.S.-based artisans who travel back and forth. The law also states that products must be "made in Puerto Rico, that one should use primarily Puerto Rican material, and that the themes should be related and should reflect Puerto Rican culture, such as its history, its fauna, flora, and the symbols of the traditional life of our people." The law also stipulated that ID cards should be issued to artisans who passed the evaluation process to identify them as authentic representatives of Puerto Rican culture. This evaluation process is supposed to be coordinated by four governmental agencies (the University of Puerto Rico, the Folk Arts Division of Puerto Rico's Development Corporation, the Tourism Office, and the Institute of Puerto Rican Culture); but it is usually referred to as the "ICP evaluation" because that agency presides over the process. This law has since been changed in response to controversies aroused by the evaluation process, although I was told by members of the artisanal community that the changes were basically a "technicality" and that evaluations still followed the overall guidelines listed in Law 99.[7] Specifically, cards attesting to an individual's authenticity as a folk artist are still required for participation in most ICP-organized events, and the standards for defining authentic Puerto Rican artisans and their work remain unchanged.

By showcasing only "quality" folk art, the Bacardi Folk Arts Fair has obtained a reputation as one of the most "cultural" events nationwide, one whose standards of excellence and authenticity are measured by cultural workers even though it is openly corporate sponsored. The event is highly praised in the media as an "autochthonous homage to the island," "an activity filled with cultural value," and "an indigenous manifestation of our culture." Besides the backing of the Institute of Puerto Rican Culture, the activity has the support of other government institutions such as the Tourism Office.

Its reputation is strengthened even further by the showcasing of *artistas nacionales*—that is, popular artists who have a national reputation, either because they have brought fame and recognition to the island by becoming internationally known and representing Puerto Rico in international settings, or because their music and songs develop nationalistic themes. (Examples of the latter are Danny Rivera, Lucecita Benítez, and Andrés Jiménez.) Although the program generally excludes popular music like salsa, it has showcased internationally recognized salsa groups like El Gran Combo, or performers of what has been called "elegant salsa" for its romantic lyrics and the more elegant dress of the performers. Since 1984 Bacardi has also reinforced the fair's cultural image by holding a troubadour contest and involving the most renowned *trovadores* in the event.

In contrast to the official "inside" fair, which is held on the company's spacious premises, the outside fair is made up of hundreds of artisans and vendors clustered along the two main roads leading to the company's facilities. The outside fair began after word spread that the invited artisans had found the inside fair particularly profitable and could sell all their products in two days. Uninvited artisans (both uncertified and ICP-certified) then began to claim a share of the market. One of the first to "take over" the fair recalled, "We had just arrived from New York with no way of making a living. I realized that they sold a lot in the Bacardi Fair. I used to make a living knitting bedcovers, so I put up a table at the entrance. I sold everything that day. Back then it was only me and someone else selling *pinchos* [shish kebab]."

As artisans became increasingly attracted to the area, informal organizers began to take on the task of structuring the event and charging fees to different vendors. Among these organizers are people native to the area, as well as the vendors and artisans themselves. Almost anyone who pays a fee—the amount ranges from a voluntary contribution to over $300 for food and drink vendors—is assured a space in the activity. I myself was offered a space of about three square feet by one of the participants for a fee of $250—no questions asked.

One of the first informal organizers was a former fisherman and native of the area who took on the role of finding spaces for exhibitors, building wooden stands for them, and picking up the trash, functions he assumed to ensure his wife a place to sell her things. He remains involved in the fair and in charge of organizing the artisans, albeit according to an entirely different logic from the one governing the inside fair. The outside fair's standards for authenticity were explained by the same informal organizer, who claimed not to "see the material, or the person, or whether he is black or white or yellow or ugly or pretty, or if he has an ICP card or not, or if they sell kitsch or not, because this is *pa'l pueblo, pa' todos* [for everybody]." This greater inclusiveness is one of the main aspects that has made the outside fair so popular with the public. For one thing, while fewer than two hundred artisans can participate in the inside fair, there are more than four hundred artisans and countless food vendors outside. Artisans are greatly attracted by the sale conditions, which many consider better than at the inside fair. Inside, the artisans are concentrated in a section of one tent, relatively close to one another, in an area that becomes extremely crowded with onlookers. The artisans are located away from the stage and the food and drink kiosks, serving almost as a show in their own right, with little connection to the other activities associated with the event. This organization contrasts with the outside fair, where artisans are located closer to food and drink vendors on a street where traffic flows in both directions and there is plenty of space for social interaction. Other attractions that have made the outside fair the public's favorite are cheaper prices and the greater diversity of folk-arts merchandise for sale there.

Although the outside exhibitors may enjoy better selling conditions, these advantages have no bearing on standards of authenticity, which relegate them to the status of mere "vendors" rather than "true artisans." To understand the implications of these categories, it is important to note that while the folk arts have undergone great transformations, the dominant ideology still holds that artisans should be motivated by cultural and not commercial concerns.

Specifically, the growth in the number of people claiming spaces to sell in these events is leading many vendors to uphold these same standards to claim their own authenticity vis-à-vis other similar vendors. Thus many artisans are embracing the same distinction between culturally and economically oriented artisans, reinforcing in turn government-sanctioned standards that they simultaneously challenge in practice. Abi, a college graduate working as a bead jeweler, explained: "You have to take into account that there are two types of artisans: *el de ocasión y el de vocación*. Those who do this *de vocación* do it for life whereas the others only seek the extra income. The true artisan wants to improve his or her art, represent our culture. Folk arts should not be the refuge of the unemployed." According to these views, true artisans are patriotic, an emphasis that downplays their economic concerns. These are the standards that many "outside" artisans, not only at the Bacardi Fair but throughout the island, are concerned to challenge in order to assert their right to participate in such events. At stake is the ability of artisans either to challenge the dichotomy between the cultural and the commercial, or to assert their identity as authentic Puerto Rican artisans on the basis of different standards and criteria.

To shatter the distinction between the commercial and cultural, it was common for "outside" vendors to define their productions as authentic and cultural according to more flexible standards than those propounded by the ICP. Being made by a Puerto Rican and having some relationship to Puerto Rican themes — whether peasant, Afro-Caribbean, or reminiscent of Taino imagery — helped to define products as Puerto Rican. These more flexible criteria often represent an accommodation between the cultural content required of folk art and its economic function as a source of income in a context of increasing unemployment. An informant who had been working on jewelry since she was fifteen years old, and who relies on the income from her craft to supplement her part-time job, stated, "My work is folklore because it is made here and by myself, a Puerto Rican. I obtained my ICP card doing something else, but I continued adding beads because it is what I like and it sells much better. I am indeed a representative of Puerto Rican culture, but one who represents a contemporary aspect and a historical moment in Puerto Rican culture and history, unemployment and the socioeconomic situation."

Another woman who had passed the ICP evaluation by presenting a traditional cloth doll now makes clown dolls because they sell better. She described her clowns as cultural because they are part of a tradition that can be traced back to the African, Spanish, and Indian components that make up the blending myth of identity in Puerto Rico. As she put it, "My clowns are a Puerto Rican folk art because I make them with my hands, and our ancestors, the Spanish, African, and Indian mothers, also made them with their hands for their daughters. They made a variety of designs, just like the clowns I make today." Practices like this woman's reveal how aware my informants were of the importance of presenting their work as "cultural" and authentically Puerto Rican. Their manipulations of ICP policies also represented a questioning of the cultural policies themselves, which were seen as impractical and not always possible to adhere to or as enforced in arbitrary and biased ways.

For instance, the cultural policy's stipulation that artisans should use indigenous materials was openly dismissed by some artisans as an impossible condition. This requirement is thwarted by the island's colonial situation, which limits local decisions about production and trade and imposes federal regulations on the removal of natural materials. As a result, the leather used by most Puerto Rican artisans is imported from Latin America, even though Puerto Rico produces unprocessed leather for export. In addition, artisans cannot freely collect natural materials from certain government-controlled and private areas, as another informant discovered when she attempted to gather seashells for her work from a tourist beach. Ultimately she abandoned her quest for indigenous materials and asked a daughter living in Florida to send her Florida seashells. The ICP's selection of participating artisans is presented in terms of mastery and authenticity, which are also regarded by some as a cloak for favoritism along politico-partisan lines: "We know that only their friends [referring to the ICP] get invited to the inside fair. I have never been invited, not because my work is not good enough—I have an ICP card that says I am a proper artisan, and

I make the best seed rosaries there are—but because I am a PNP activist, and they already have their lists of who they like to invite."

Finally, the rapid changes undergone by the folk arts have also challenged the cultural policy pertaining to them, and served to delegitimize the distinction between cultural and commercial forms. For instance, the ICP's authentication of forms once perceived as purely commercial has set an important precedent that highlights the arbitrariness of the distinction between authentic and commercial folk-art forms. This is the case with silk-screened T-shirts, which were excluded when they were first popularized in the 1970s but have now become a new category of folk art.[8] These shirts have been responsible for introducing many innovations to the themes associated with Puerto Rico, and have been a particularly important medium for the introduction of Afrocentric themes.

While most artisans tried to present themselves as "cultural" in order to assert the legitimacy on which the profitability of their work is based, the commercial value of folk art was no secret among artisans in the "outside" fair. It is generally understood that people are there to make a living, and most participants felt artisans should be given a "break" instead of being expelled if their work is deemed "unfit," as commonly happens at ICP-organized events. This economic concern overrides government concerns about authenticity, particularly because, as we have seen, almost anything can be presented as "authentic" and its economic value raised by cultural claims.

At first, the Bacardi Corporation ignored the outside fair because, as I was told by a company representative, they "never thought it would become so popular and so strong." However, the outside fair soon became a threat to the inside one. It is incredibly popular with the public, many of whom regard the outside event as the real fair and do not even bother going onto the company's premises to visit the corporate-sponsored fair. The ICP representatives I talked to found this highly problematic because, as one said, "people leave with the impression that Puerto Rican folk arts are just plastic." The Bacardi representatives worry in turn that people may confuse the outside fair for the "real" fair, and then get the "wrong impression" of the activities the company sponsors.

The outside fair also challenges the company's attempt to obtain exclusivity for its products. Only the company's products are sold inside (Bacardi rum drinks, and products for which the company serves as exclusive distributor, such as Medalla beer), but the outside fair is filled with all the brand competitors, who have been known to give the outside vendors special deals to induce them to feature competing products on Bacardi's terrain.

Most of all, the outside fair presents a threat to the company because it signals the incursion of the nearby community, one of the poorest on the island, onto the company's premises. While Cataño is one of the areas with the highest concentrations of industry in Puerto Rico (over twenty-five manufacturing plants are clustered in a mere five square miles), 58 percent of its population lives under the poverty line, and there is little public space for leisure and entertainment. Yet, similar to Jayuya, during the fair the company's outside premises are turned into a communal vending and recreational area by community residents as well as by people from all points on the island. These vendors stake their claim in the area through a complex system of colored paint marks on the roads leading to the company's main entrances. The marks identify vendors' spaces and help maintain the continuity of the fair year after year. The spaces are secured by some organizers and residents of Cataño, who often remain outside the company's premises to guard the marks or paint over those that have been tampered with or erased. As a result, the two main entrances to the company are covered with a growing profusion of white, yellow, red, and blue paint marks that further establish the outside fair's stake in the event. This visual incursion, combined with fears that the outside fair would get out of control and damage Bacardi's reputation, and suppositions about the informal organizers' connections with crime, were major preoccupations of the Bacardi representatives I talked to, who showed great frustration at not being able to tame what has emerged as a self-sustaining annual event.

The corporation has tried to evict the fair from the company's entrance, using various means that include summoning the police, destroying the *kioskos*, painting over the place marks, and pressuring the municipal government. They have also invoked laws banning the sale of drinks on local and state roads. However, by the time these measures were taken, the fair was sufficiently popular for the informal organizers to appeal to politicians, neighborhood connections, and the strength of the informal economy the fair helps to sustain. Indeed, the very fact that the outside fair lacked institutional and municipal approval had won it a base of support among the people who benefited from it and among the public, who regarded it as a self-generated cultural expression. Even one consultant for the Bacardi Corporation said, "I have a lot of sympathy for the outside fair. I believe it is an authentic and autonomous expression of the people. How could you prohibit that expression, and a call to culture that goes overboard because it does not fit in the inside fair? I don't know why they do not like it. Maybe it is to protect the artisans who are selling inside."

This consultant had advised Bacardi to "win over their competitor" by making the outside fair part of the overall activity. He suggested helping the vendors with trash collection and placing speakers in the outside area as a way to entice the public to go inside to hear the music. Most important, he suggested giving outside vendors discounts on Bacardi products to reduce their competitors' sales. The company did reach out to the outside fair, but only after their attempts to suppress it had failed. By then the offer was rejected outright by the informal organizers, who could now get back at the company not only through their presence but also through their open rejection of the company's discounts on Bacardi products.

At present, the outside fair has acquired a local reputation as a "cultural event" in its own right. This in turn assures its continued presence because it deters Bacardi from taking a public position against the fair. To do this would jeopardize its image as a "culturally concerned" company, which Bacardi tries hard to project. However, among the informal organizers the community value of the activity was never in dispute. A sense of entitlement was evident among those I talked to; they asserted their rightful place as long-term residents of Cataño with a legitimate duty to organize a "community" event. As one organizer argued, "They do not know what they are up to. Bacardi's new president has only been here for three months, but I have been here for eighteen years, and this has been our fair all this time. The fair stays and will live on."

Contesting the Nation, Contesting Identities

The case studies above describe two very different events. One is an activity whose authenticity is controlled by the ICP; the other is a corporate-sponsored event that ironically enforces even stricter standards of authenticity than other local groups I came in contact with. However, both cases illustrate the contradictions of contemporary cultural politics on the island. First, it is clear that "authenticity" in the context of the Indigenous Pageant is just as contested as the boundary between cultural and commercial folk arts is in the Bacardi Folk Arts Fair. In both events, legitimacy was officially defined as adherence to cultural policy as defined by the ICP-affiliated local cultural center or the ICP in San Juan. These standards favor forms that evoke a "traditional" past and whose cultural and educational content is not tainted by economic interests or leisure purposes. However, these standards generate their own contradictions because they also require local participation and a public. These local participants increasingly challenge the standards and introduce disagreements about the bases for determining legitimacy. Thus, disregarding physical features as a criterion for selecting the *cacica* during the National Indigenous Festival represents an unspoken rebuttal of the racist biases embedded in the pageant, just as the development of the outside fair during the Bacardi Folk Arts Fair transgressed strict divisions between "cultural" and "commercial" artisans. Thus it is apparent that ample subsidiary production has arisen from the consumption and adoption of imposed orders, spaces, and regulations (de Certeau 1984). These processes involved validating new practices for defining what constitutes a legitimate celebration or folk art as "cultural," while formal standards for "authenticity" are rendered less important.

The standards upon which authenticity is based were also popularly discredited simply on account of their unattainability in contemporary society; it is impossible to find a "pure" indigenous queen or produce authentic folk arts that conform perfectly to the romanticized official version of folk art. As a result, despite the official standards, it is the entertainment aspect of the National Indigenous Festival that attracts most attention, and it is the "outside fair" at the Bacardi Folk Arts Fair that is gaining in popularity. Meanwhile, most folk art fairs are saturated with jewelry, T-shirts depicting reggae and salsa musicians, souvenirs, and other forms of folk art that the ICP dismisses as commercial and of little cultural value. Even the National Folk Arts Fair in Barranquitas, widely known for displaying only traditional forms of Puerto Rican art, included the same genres that were described to me as commercial or economically motivated by ICP officials.

The distinction between more and less authentic forms is thrown into further doubt by the ironies of contemporary cultural politics. Here we find corporations like Bacardi upholding the ICP's standards of authenticity to assure the fair's reputation as a cultural event and the success of its own marketing strategy. The praise given to the fair by the press proves that the company has successfully veiled its own economic motive behind the event and succeeded in presenting the activity as purely cultural. Meanwhile, the increment of corporate funding in most cultural activities assures that a commercial component is an inescapable aspect of most cultural expressions rather than a qualitatively different domain. Thus the discursive categories that distinguish what is "cultural" or "commercial," or more or less "authentic," which are made irrelevant in practice, still need to be understood as part of a greater struggle over the content of legitimacy. In this process, these distinctions serve to invalidate cultural expressions that involve entertainment or do not conform to dominant standards of "authentic" cultural content, irrespective of whether they provide a basis for legitimating different ideas about culture. Thus, in the end, what is legitimized as cultural according to institutional standards ends up reproducing social hierarchies and excluding popular ways of expressing and consuming "Puerto Rican culture."

Cassettes, Posters, and Bumper Stickers

The setting is the National Folk Arts Fair of Barranquitas, sponsored by the ICP-affiliated cultural center of Barranquitas, the hometown of Luis Muñoz Marín, one of the ideological forefathers of the Popular Democratic Party. This is the most important fair organized by the ICP, and only the most "authentic" representatives of Puerto Rican music and folklore are invited to participate.

It is the middle of the afternoon, and Guabey, one of the invited folk-music groups, has finished performing and stops to converse with the audience gathered in the middle of the plaza. The musicians ask for volunteers to come up to the stage and sing along with the group, for which they will be awarded prizes. A female performer calls to the audience while the rest of the group follows a musical beat:

FEMALE PERFORMER: We need three volunteers to come up on stage. Come up and we will give you a "cassette," a "poster," and a "bumper sticker" of the group.

Although she speaks to the audience in Spanish, she uses English words for the three items. The male performer and leader of the group immediately corrects the woman, mocking her use of English and remarking sarcastically,

MALE PERFORMER: *¡Ay bendito!* We are a cultural group and this is a cultural activity and she just said three English words in a row!

FEMALE PERFORMER: Well, speaking half English and half Spanish is also part of Puerto Rican culture.

The audience laughs and cheers, totally absorbed in the interaction between the performers.

MALE PERFORMER (didactically to the audience): How do you say "poster" in Spanish?

AUDIENCE: "Afiche."

MALE PERFORMER: How do you say "cassette" in Spanish?

AUDIENCE (Silence. No one knows the word. Someone finally responds): "Casetera" [the Spanglish word for tape player].

The answer provokes giggles from the audience.

MALE PERFORMER (correcting the person): No, that is the name of the "cassette player."

Finally, someone in the audience remembers.

MEMBER OF AUDIENCE: "Grabación."

MALE PERFORMER: Yes, that is how it is said. We are making culture, we are learning how to say things in Spanish, as it should be done.

Although I have not focused on language in this work, I begin my conclusion with this vignette of wordplay because it captures some issues that have been central to my research. Here is an instance in which a popular convention, the spontaneous mixing of English and Spanish, is validated in practice yet decried on moral grounds as unpatriotic. On being critized for speaking "half English and half Spanish," the woman's response — to justify her actions by presenting them as "part of Puerto Rican culture" — displays a popular tendency in Puerto Rican society to associate culture with ideas that go beyond the official national ideology. In turn, the male performer found himself validating yet another Spanglish word, *casetera,* when he spontaneously corrected a member of the audience by saying that *casetera* is "the word for a tape player"; in fact, "tape player" is *tocacintas* in Spanish.

I also want to draw attention to the promotional culture that has developed around the contemporary folk arts. Posters, recordings, and publicity paraphernalia have become an important part of the promotion of cultural groups. Considering that those who seek the status of "authentic" representatives of Puerto Rican culture must demonstrate patriotic rather than commercial motivations, these developments are sure to complicate claims of authenticity even further.

Yet the ambiguities at play today are not altogether new. Since the 1950s, industrialization, growing consumerism, and materialism have been important factors influencing Puerto Rico's cultural policies. Seen by many Puerto Rican intellectuals as threats to Puerto Rico's spirit, culture, and values, they were a driving force behind the foundation of the Institute of Puerto Rican Culture. In turn, the ICP was part of a broader governmental program aimed at limiting the cultural impact of export-led industrialization. However, the utility of these conceptualizations is questionable when transnational interests are as likely to use cultural forms to assert and legitimize their claims as are local interests; and when, within the "commercialized" context of contemporary Puerto Rican society, people continue to assert Puerto Rican culture more openly than ever.

Thus, with respect to the question of national identity construction in an increasingly global context, the Puerto Rican case illustrates that what is of interest is not the prospect for the development of new identities (in Puerto Rico processes of identity formation have been active and ongoing) but rather the potential for these constructs to transform restrictive definitions of identity. I have shown that expressions of Puerto Rican identity are numerous and diverse, although many do not meet the specifications of the government's cultural policy. Instead, new expressions of Puerto Ricanness emerge around regional identities, as shown by ARECMA and the Lancha Committee, and in the "commercialized" terrain of the many cultural festivals. The search for a collective identity becomes a search for "secure moorings in a shifting world," as David Harvey would describe it (1989: 302), but with commercial culture and mass-mediated cultural expressions serving as motivational forces alongside "traditional" cultural expressions.

Exposing the Colonial Veil

This work has shown how a range of agents are actively engaged in elaborating cultural nationalist discourse, a process that feeds the growth of divergent views of Puerto Rican identity and struggles over legitimacy. Framing these struggles were assumptions about proper nationalist discourse that have developed within a colonial context. Among other things, these assumptions posit a pure nationalist discourse in opposition to the "disruptive" external forces of commercialism, perceived as the embodiment of Americanization and the most potent threat to the purity of Puerto Rican culture. Yet the "external" transnational forces of the media and corporate commercial advertising have not been the only entities involved in depoliticizing and neutralizing identities and sectors of Puerto Rican society. The government's cultural policy and institutions have also engaged in similar processes by defining authenticity according to racist and classist evaluations that exclude different aspects of Puerto Rican culture.

Thus, the same views of Puerto Rican culture that are seen as threatened and in need of protection by official cultural policy are intrinsic components of Puerto Rico's colonial project. Locally led government attempts at defining and asserting Puerto Rican identity were never independent from U.S. prerogatives. Specifically, U.S. colonialism shaped both the content of Puerto Rico's nationalist ideology and the scope and manner in which nationalism could be expressed on the island. Thus, Puerto Rico's nationalist ideology drew on the ideas developed by its Hispanophile elites, who, in an anticolonial response to U.S. imperialism, ended up embracing their previous colonizer, the Spanish.

Embedded in these sanctioned definitions of culture are cultural hierarchies in which the blending myth, the male peasant, and folklore have served as important metaphors to reproduce ideas of common identity while simultaneously limiting the representations that can be associated with Puerto Rican culture. These standards have been inscribed and reproduced in government cultural policies and institutions. There we saw hierarchies around the claims that there are authentic and spurious defenders of Puerto Rican culture, as evident in the distinctions between promoters and local groups, between ICP-affiliated and independent groups, and between those who are or are not entitled to defend Puerto Rican culture because their political affiliation, discourses, and practices are perceived to be incompatible with it.

Within these hierarchies, the remnants of the 1950s nationalizing project lingered in the positioning of the PPD, the ICP promoters, and the ICP-affiliated groups as "true" guardians of Puerto Rican culture. These views are part and parcel of the pro-commonwealth PPD's appropriation of the nationalist discourse and imagery of the times, which led to the neutralization of independence as a political option and the exclusion of supporters of statehood from the nationalist discourse. Thus this position contributed to legitimizing the status quo of commonwealth and the ICP, and the ongoing containment and neutralization of overt separatist sectors into cultural work was largely obscured.

Even the terms in which debates about culture have been framed have contributed to the permanence of the present status. The discussion is framed in terms of the major conflicting political options for the island: statehood and commonwealth, a framework that discounts independence as a political possibility. In this model, the pro-commonwealth PPD is associated with a more folkloric view of Puerto Rican culture and presented as the true defender of Puerto Rican nationality, while the pro-statehood New Progressive Party (PNP), associated with a "universalist" view of culture, is seen as the major threat to Puerto Rico's cultural integrity.

This close identification of the two dominant parties with particular views of culture veils the way in which both have, at different times, deployed both similar and divergent views of culture to further their political interests. As we saw, the PPD originally held a more "universalizing" view of culture, and the PNP has appealed to different conceptions of "creole" statehood since the late 1960s. Cultural struggles divided along partisan lines have also veiled similarities between their economic and political policies. Ultimately, the furthering of local interests through compliance and conformity to U.S. policies has continued to be ingrained in the island's political culture.

The colonial imprint of contemporary cultural politics was also evident in the primacy of cultural policies and institutions as loci of local power. The promotion of cultural nationalism was linked to the creation of cultural policies and institutions as channels for political legitimization, which as such could never be fully popularized. Government policies and institutions were an important medium through which people asserted their views of Puerto Rican culture, attempted to direct the island's political future, and advanced particular agendas at all levels of Puerto Rican society. Those in control of Puerto Rico's cultural policies have therefore tended to defend their position by imposing standards of authenticity through cultural policies and legislation while limiting the numbers of people who can take part in the cultural domain via these special claims to knowledge and authenticity. Here lies the strict association of partisan political interests with the government cultural policies, which was shown to have undermined the dissemination of an uncontested view of Puerto Rican national identity. Instead, the government's assertion of standardized views of Puerto Rican culture was often perceived to cloak partisan interests rather than express the national identity. In this way, rather than generalize a "content" for Puerto Rican culture, what the government cultural policies accomplished was the consolidation of culture as the dominant medium for political discourse and the dissemination of some generalized hierarchies about who and what are its most appropriate representatives.

Last, initiated under American colonialism by modernizing elites, Puerto Rico's cultural policies of nation building were more accommodating toward than critical of the colonial situation. These policies were aimed at countering the Americanization of the island, exemplified as the processes of industrialization and mass migration that were initiated by Puerto Rican colonial elites in the name of progress and modernity. While "modernity" itself was encouraged, its by-products—the rise of mass culture, the transnational community of Puerto Ricans, and hybrid forms of language and culture—were considered direct challenges to the image of the nation constructed around a folklorized and utopian peasant past. Today, similar processes of inclusion and exclusion are in place. Groups seeking commercial sponsors are shunned by the same governmental elites who themselves associate with corporations that seek to legitimize the cultural content of their own promotions (as in the case of the Bacardi Folk Arts Fair and the Winston Medal of Culture, which are coordinated with the help of the ICP). As a result, contemporary distinctions between forms and genres that aim to represent Puerto Rican culture, whether they are legitimized as cultural or rejected as commercial, respond to the accommodating nature of the cultural policies of nation building. This is particularly so because the distinction between cultural and commercial serves more to authenticate the official view of Puerto Rican culture than to reject the involvement of corporate sponsorship, a process that, once again, reveals the relationship between the government's cultural projects and U.S. interests on the island.

Moreover, divisions between cultural and commercial forms do not necessarily correspond to any objective states, given that a commercial component is an intrinsic element of most cultural activities on the island. These arbitrary divisions are instead part of the process of cloaking and subverting difference. In particular, "commercial" serves as an all-purpose label for aspects of popular culture perceived as challenges to the purity of the nation. In this way, the case at hand supports the observations of Latin American scholars who have argued that, due to the historical appropriation of popular culture by nationalist and populist projects in the area, mass-mediated forms of expression have often been more useful sources of popular expression (Barbero 1987). Perceived as unattractive to these projects and to their search for pure and unadulterated representations of culture, mass-mediated culture remains a potential foundation for alternative representations. Thus we saw that it is through the mediation of forms defined as "cultural" and "commercial," or more or less authentic, that people give meaning to their cultural expressions and negotiate relationships with political and commercial interests in ways that are not perceived to hinder their identification with these activities. What we cannot stop documenting, however, is the continued devaluation and appropriation of such representations by nationalist and governmental projects. These processes, as the case at hand shows, are likely to become increasingly contested in the commercialized context of contemporary society.

Much More Puerto Ricanness

I have argued that, although they openly contest the official cultural policy, most agents involved in contemporary cultural politics still operate within the dominant parameters of discussion on the island, with culture as a subject and object of contention. It is through appeals to culture that a wide variety of interests are being advanced. These range from raising funds for the establishment of physical facilities, as many independent groups do; to supplementing one's personal income, in the case of Puerto Rican artisans; to seeking greater representation for one's community, which was the goal of ARECMA and the Lancha Committee; and even to selling beer, which was the aim of Budweiser sponsorship.

In a similar manner, the "building blocks of nationality" are still the surest markers of authenticity, while popular ways of representing Puerto Rican culture are still more likely to be rejected as low and "polluted."

However, while the parameters for practice and resistance have been defined, the nationalist discourse has not been left untouched by the advent of new actors in Puerto Rico's cultural politics. This development has contributed to a growth of the discourses of authenticity about Puerto Rican culture and identity. Perceived as a threat to the image of homogeneity that the government cultural policy strives to project, the growth of new groups has led many to uphold government-sanctioned definitions of Puerto Rican culture as a way to distinguish among the many players who now claim to be *puertorriqueñistas*. These processes have also led to a reformulation of the nationalist discourse. This was evident in the involvement of corporate sponsors in local cultural politics, which has led not only to the enhancement of the criteria for establishing legitimacy but to an emphasis on commercialism as a salient element against which authenticity is defined. This view reproduces old themes of pollution and adulteration prevalent in nationalist ideologies, now directly voiced concerning the involvement of corporate sponsors.

However, the involvement of more actors in Puerto Rico's cultural politics has also helped challenge and expand definitions of cultural identity. In particular we saw that through their use and appropriation of culture to further particular interests, independent groups generate new ways of identifying Puerto Rican culture, some of which cut across major distinctions promoted by the government cultural policy. By drawing from popular culture and everyday life, rather than on predetermined representations of nationality, the new actors in Puerto Rico's cultural politics are also more likely to blur or bypass distinctions between popular and high culture and folk and commercial forms. Local groups such as ARECMA and the Lancha Committee also provide arenas for the validation of different communities and the dissemination of aspects that are neglected in official accounts of history and nationhood. Specifically, they confront dominant views about the subordinate position of their communities with respect to Caone's urban-biased history, by incorporating the idioms of community and marginality—in economic terms, or in relation to their respective municipal centers—as added bases for the representation of their communities. Moreover, they are also part of a process of contention over the legitimate basis upon which to define Puerto Rican culture and the ways in which that definition might be expanded.

Ultimately, it is the very flexibility of these grassroots groups, in their organization and in their representations of Puerto Ricanness, that enables them to curb the power of government cultural policy to define nationality through fixed notions of Puerto Ricanness. If we analyze resistance in terms of its capacity to limit the extent of power to define action (Abu-Lughod 1990, Foucault 1983), these new groups can be seen as agents of resistance to a "technique of power" represented by the nationalizing tendencies of the ICP conveyed through its cultural directives. Specifically, the very emergence of newer groups, committees, and organizers of cultural activity simultaneously pushes the limits of the cultural policy by associating new ideas and objects with Puerto Rican culture while it limits the attempts of the ICP, the political parties, and other agents to shape cultural directives or secure strict definitions of national identity. Moreover, popular use and manipulation of the government's cultural policies give rise to representations of culture that rely less on dominant selective traditions. For example, folk music is increasingly composed of "hybrid" musical forms; and while government policy still limits the musical forms that may officially represent Puerto Rican culture, in practice folk music is greatly influenced by the same rhythms and instruments that are shunned by cultural policy standards. Similarly, in the folk arts, objects described to me as commercial have been finding their way into the most official domains, such as the National Folks Arts Fair in Barranquitas, known for displaying only traditional art forms and for serving as the standard for authenticity among folk artists.

Of course, while these heterogeneous practices contradict the homogeneity promulgated by the government cultural policy, they are far from replacing dominant views of cultural authenticity. This transformation would require changes in the fundamental premises of identity construction, presently founded upon the idea of culture, as well as in the island's colonial and subordinate position in relation to the greater world community. As we saw, the present ambiguous political status preserves the relevance of culture as an idiom to define sovereignty and perpetuates the need for an "official" view of Puerto Rican identity. These popular practices, however, remind us of the vulnerability of official conceptions of identity. This is most evident in the way in which grassroots cultural groups are feared and condemned by those trying to enforce the government's cultural policies. Recall that among the practices most feared by representatives of the cultural policy is the presentation as "cultural" of popular practices, events, and products that disregard standards of authenticity. These fears evidence the limits and lack of cohesiveness of institutional attempts at securing official definitions of national identity.

In short, transformations in the conceptions of Puerto Rican culture are taking place in popular contexts, while official constructs of national identity need to be safeguarded as pure, traditional, and therefore unchanging even as they are updated through the incorporation of elements from popular culture that serve to preserve their dominant position. These are the processes through which symbols associated with the Nationalist Party, such as the flag, were incorporated as symbols of the commonwealth, and the peasant culture was romanticized in Puerto Rico's blending myth, and Nueva Trova was ultimately "peasantized." Efforts at incorporating the new groups and practices representing Puerto Rican culture were also evident in the ICP's attempt to affiliate or work with some of its independent counterparts. Most of these strategies, however, were directed at reinvigorating their program by drawing in new actors—although not necessarily with the new material delivered by many of these groups.

Thus, as popular culture becomes more and more "what we make out of the products and practices of mass-produced culture" (Storey 1993: 201), and it thereby becomes increasingly "contaminated" with commercial culture, we are led to ponder the prospects for the incorporation of these new elements into the "content" of Puerto Rican culture. Does the Puerto Rican case imply limited prospects for nationalist ideologies that rely on ethnic components and traditional pasts to establish legitimacy when culture becomes "commercialized," globalized, or "adulterated"? Are there limits to the incorporation of forms that are perceived to be commercial when the nationalist constructs depend on establishing continuity with a utopian precapitalist past? From our discussion the answer seems to be that only attempts at securing an official nationalist discourse around traditional principles of purity and authenticity are threatened by these developments. As we saw, the always-fragile process of bounding a national identity is becoming increasingly difficult for Puerto Rico's cultural workers and institutions. The latter fail to present themselves as both inclusive and anticolonial, as they shun elements of popular culture and remain unable to renew themselves by incorporating more inclusive definitions of identity. At the level of popular culture, however, global processes have continually served as a reference to local strategies of self-assertion and have been negotiated in daily life, thereby illustrating that the increasingly global, commercialized, or mass-mediated context of contemporary society does not suggest the end of collective constructs of national identity.

Of course, the fact that many popular representations of Puerto Rican identity are currently being dismissed or rejected does not preclude them from future appropriation. Commercial interests, who are generally less concerned with cultural authenticity, already make use of popular expressions, from popular festivals to colloquial language. The case at hand thus reminds us that constructs of identity are never free from contention nor from future appropriation—if not by a nationalist program, then by global capital. However, the permanence and the increase of cultural struggles attest to the significance of the idiom of culture for debating and communicating claims, even if these are subsumed within a larger process, be it a nationalizing process led by governmental elites or the marketing of culture spurred by corporate interests. Specifically, the idiom of culture is likely to continue to be used to voice claims for greater representation within particular communities; to sustain or supersede partisan political divisions; to assert the right to participate in the informal economy; or to challenge the frameworks of authenticity through which popular representations of culture are delegitimized. Analyzing these issues, however, requires considering the battle for culture not solely in relation to traditional paradigms of nation building, where cultural struggles are analyzed in relation to the processes of securing a nation-state or a generalized political program, but also in relation to other claims and processes. This involves going beyond analyzing "nationalisms" and cultural movements as unitary movements to account for the different interests that compete through culture within a particular context.

In the case of Puerto Rico, the same political ambiguity that perpetuates the growth of cultural nationalism and the need for an "official" view of Puerto Rican identity continues to open up strategic spaces for the development and mobilization of more inclusive definitions of identity. These are the processes that explain the success of the turn to popular representations of Puerto Ricaness among marketing strategists and the ability of different groups to articulate a variety of local interests through cultural claims.

Moreover, the case at hand also directs us to overcome the dichotomized thinking that has pervaded analysis of cultural identity and globalization, in which nations are perceived by cultural critics to be superseded and identities tamed and depoliticized or more optimistically reconstituted under new guises. It points to the exclusionary nature of nationalist projects, which limits their efficacy and their value as alternatives to the advancement of contemporary capital, which in turn operates more and more through culture and difference. Through this focus we are in a better position to assess the reconfiguration of hegemonies and the opening of alternative spaces. Thus, in Puerto Rico, at the heart of local preoccupations about the permanence of the island's national identity are not solely anticolonial preoccupations but also racist concerns that our language could become "rotten" or, as one ICP official told me, that we might become a "cultural phenomenon" like the Nuyoricans. These fears signal a general awareness of the societal "contradictions"—such as the transnational community of Puerto Ricans or the mass-mediated popular culture—that will continue to challenge traditional constructs of identity and may potentially affect reconfigurations of power.

Thus, at stake in the present context is the possibility that the new forms through which people are asserting national identities could translate into more inclusive and expanded definitions of identity and national communities. In assessing these issues, studies of divergent expressions of national identity that do not conform to traditional definitions remain important for assessing expressions that may be involved in a larger cultural nationalist process, either in a subverted or in an emergent form, and that may lead to alternative definitions of national communities. This is particularly the case in the current global context, in which culture remains a popular discourse for social movements, identity politics, and marketing campaigns alike, and tropes of culture and nationhood are likely to remain relevant for many kinds of politics. In Puerto Rico, where nationalism is often dismissed as "neonationalism" because separatism is not favored by most Puerto Ricans, cultural nationalism has played an important role in shaping and maintaining a colonial project and serves as the terrain for contemporary struggles. Meanwhile, as long as culture remains the dominant medium for divergent political or economic interests, other ways of defining identity are likely to present challenges to traditional formulations of national identity. For as local intellectuals attempt to control the new agents elaborating views of Puerto Rican identity, the content and nature of official definitions of nationality are likely to be affected by these new developments, which slowly intrude into the totalizing view of national identity, even if not yet into the colonial or subordinate position that envelops them.

NOTES

Introduction: Making and Marketing National Identities

1. Cultural politics will be defined here as the social and political struggles waged through culture (Yúdice, Franco, and Flores 1992: xiii), where culture is conceived as consisting of elements of symbolic identification. These struggles have also been referred to as the "politics of culture" or "cultural struggles," terms that highlight the political aspects involved in the definition and authentication of culturally relevant images and representations. See the work of García-Canclini (1992a, 1992b), Verdery (1991), Domínguez (1990), and B. Williams (1991), among others who have studied culture as a site of ideological and political struggle.

2. The terms "neonationalism" and "*nacionalismo* light" are used for a variety of purposes, but they always denote a pejorative attitude toward the popularization of nationalist discourse. This popularization is perceived either as a product of politico-partisan manipulations (see newspaper editorials such as that of Luis Dávila Colón in *El Nuevo Día*, December 8, 1993), or as leading to a rise of essentializing constructs of nationhood (Pabón 1995). These critiques are similar to those voiced by a variety of scholars of contemporary nationalism, who emphasize its intersection with exclusions related to race, class, and gender, which function to limit their democratic possibilities. For a recent debate on these issues see Stolcke's (1995) discussion of European "new nationalism" and the responses to her argument in the same issue. See O'Barr (1989) for an analysis of how the idiom of culture has emerged as a global marketing medium (and Chapter V in this book).

3. Throughout this work I use "American" to refer to the United States rather than to the entire hemisphere because my informants generally used "American" rather than "North American" to refer to U.S. companies and products. This reflects the Puerto Rican/"American" dichotomy that lies at the heart of Puerto Rico's nationalist ideology.

4. Consider the different typologies advanced according to the historical stages in the manifestation of nationalism (Heyes 1968), the motivation and political goals of its proponents (as in the oppressive, liberatory, minority, or

263

majority nationalisms analyzed by Symmons-Symonolewicz [1965]), or to how the relationship between state and ethnic group gets resolved as noted by Worsley (1984). Similarly, scholars analyzing the potential of nationalism as a tool of colonial liberation have been adamant in distinguishing nationalism for purposes of liberation from the imperial kind of nationalism (Cabral 1973, Fanon 1963), while other scholars have drawn distinctions according to whether they take their base from a territorially marked state or from an ethnic community (Smith 1986).

5. Philip's (1980) study of European nationalist movements, for instance, highlights the cultural standardization involved in them—starting from the development of an interest in history and folklore by a literate elite and leading to the spread of this interest among political leaders and its communication to a greater population as a basis for political change.

6. One example is provided by Dominguez's (1990) study of the central place of Zionism in Israel's nationalist ideology. As she argues, even while the history of Zionism as the dominant version of Israel's history was under scrutiny, with Sephardic elements of Israeli society attaining voice and political power, the debate never challenged its position as the central discursive construct. Instead, all contestations responded to and departed from Zionism, strengthening its central place in Israel's national imagery.

7. I am drawing here on Brackette Williams's (1991) reelaboration of Gramsci's term "transformist hegemony" and its application to her study of nationalism in Guyana. See also Mouffe (1979) and A. Alonso (1994) for discussions of this term.

8. While all hegemonies are products of compromises and class alliances, I want to emphasize here the limits upon these processes imposed by a colonial relationship. Chatterjee has documented similar circumstances in pre-independence India. As he noted, where an emergent dominant class "lacks the social conditions for establishing complete hegemony over the new nation, it resorts to a 'passive revolution,'" or forming alliances to enhance its local power through the creation of a state that controls the capitalist forms of production (Chatterjee 1993: 30).

9. For a discussion on the creation of boundaries between high and popular culture through institutions, such as museums and theaters, that serve as means of class legitimation, see Levine (1984) and DiMaggio (1991).

10. This view counters some postmodernist approaches to identity, which see a shift to identity politics and more fluid forms of identification as marking a demise of nationalism and nationalist forms of identification characteristic of modernity. See Billig (1995: 128-53) for a review of these issues, and Lash and Friedman (1992) for criticisms of paradigms that see identities in modernity as fixed and bounded, and postmodernity as characterized by movement and fluidity.

11. A review of the literature on Puerto Rico's national identity is beyond the scope of this work. Readers may consult Díaz-Quiñones 1993, Flores 1979, Gelpí 1993, and Ramírez 1977.

Chapter I: Securing the Nation through Politics

1. The Puerto Rican Independence Party won 126,228 votes in the 1952 general elections, placing it second to the Popular Democratic Party (PPD), the landslide winner with 431,409 votes. The New Progressive Party (PNP) won only 85,591 votes and the Socialist Party 21,719 (Bayrón-Toro 1989).

2. For instance, the immigration policies of 1815 allowed Catholics from any nation friendly with Spain to settle free of taxes in Puerto Rico, which had the effect of increasing conservative forces on the island. Political repression by the Spanish colonial government was also evident in the banning of literary works with nationalistic overtones, such as the works of Daniel Rivera and Eugenio María de Hostos.

3. As mentioned earlier, it is not my intention here to review the cultural nationalist writings of the times. See the works of Pedreira (1985) and the discussions of the 1930s literary work of Ferrao (1990), Flores (1979), and Gelpí (1993) for essays on this literature. See also Chapter III for analysis of how the cultural nationalist climate of the time affected cultural productions at the local level.

4. This discourse is evocative of patterns found in other colonial contexts where the equation of the local with the moral or spiritual and the foreign with the modern and material provides room for colonial resistance and national assertion vis-à-vis the invader (Chatterjee 1993).

5. Other political parties at the time favored independence but failed to make it a priority and ended up favoring U.S. assimilation formulas instead. Thus, the Union Party, which dominated local politics from 1904 to 1928 and represented the interests of coffee growers and landowners, advocated a U.S. assimilation political formula by the late 1920s, whereas the Liberal Party (a reorganization of the Union Party in 1932) initially favored independence but later settled for increased local autonomy.

6. While the involvement of the Nationalist Party was limited to the recruitment of Albizu Campos for the negotiation process with the sugar corporations, this act did have political consequences for the possible junction of labor and nationalist forces.

7. See Acosta (1987, 1992) for a discussion of the use of this law for political persecution in Puerto Rico. For a report of such persecution, see Commonwealth of Puerto Rico, Comisión de Derechos Humanos (Civil Rights Commission) 1991.

8. Muñoz was the son of a former leader of the landowner-dominated Liberal Party, which had also attracted advocates of independence. Muñoz had split from

the Liberal Party, drawing a base of supporters from the Liberal Party to the PPD because of disagreements over the Tydings Independence Bill in 1936, by which Puerto Ricans would have had to vote to gain immediate independence while forgoing any economic restitution from the U.S. government.

9. *Melonismo,* a phenomenon of the "watermelon intelligentsia," is the tendency of the (green-bannered) Independence Party to align itself with the (red-bannered) PPD while adopting *independentista* stances (Torrecillas 1994).

10. These processes are characteristic of the development of nationalism in the service of a modernizing project. For the case of India, Chatterjee (1993) discusses them as the moment of "maneuver," which he regards as key for the consolidation and subsequent development of nationalism and its linkage to the demands of a given state.

11. As Bonilla and Campos (1985) found, during the first fifteen postwar years, Puerto Rican migration to the United States averaged over forty thousand people annually as Puerto Rico's agricultural sector lost thousands of jobs to the industrialization created by Operation Bootstrap.

12. The Departamento de Recreación (Recreation Department) organized the first folkloric dance groups, which paralleled the development of Puerto Rico's Olympic sports program. These groups accompanied teams as tourist icons for the island.

13. See Aguiló (1987) for a discussion of the cultural policies of the 1940s and 1950s and a more detailed discussion of the agents and interests embodied in them.

14. I owe this image to Antonio Lauria, with whom I discussed the early perceptions of the ICP held by Puerto Rican intellectuals.

15. It is common for local organizations, not only cultural centers, to change personnel whenever there is a change of government. Local mayors support these manipulations because they are ways through which new administrations establish control and client relationships within their constituencies. What was unique about this episode is that local centers had traditionally been excluded from these manipulations because they were publicly perceived as PIP strongholds.

16. This law was reversed by the following PNP administration, which reinstalled English as the second official language.

17. The results of the 1976 election gave the PNP 703,968 votes, the PPD 660,301 votes, the PIP 83,037, and the PSP (Socialist Party) 10,728 votes.

18. See Ramos (1987) and Meléndez (1993) for reviews of the changing social and cultural claims in the PNP's political program.

19. As documented by Pantojas-García (1990), PPD and PNP economic policies have historically been aligned with the interests of U.S. capital. Their political policies, he argues, have become increasingly similar since the 1980s, when the island's economy was consolidated around what he calls the "high finance strategy."

This strategy relied on structuring the island's economy around federal tax policies and tax breaks extended to investments and profits on the island.

20. See Commonwealth of Puerto Rico, General Legislative Budgets from 1978 to 1990.

21. This is particularly the case when considering illicit and criminal activities as part of the informal economy, as Ortiz (1992) does for Puerto Rico.

22. Salary averages obtained from the Departamento del Trabajo y Recursos Humanos, División de Estudios y Estadísticas, July 1993. I was told by kiosk vendors that they could make over five hundred dollars a day in a profitable activity. Of course, vending is also a risky endeavor and incomes vary according to what is being sold and the nature of people's involvement. Those working as contractors or subcontractors (which involves organizing vendors and selling permits) make more than independent vendors. Similarly, kiosks specializing in piña coladas, soft drinks, and beer earned far more than food kiosks, which required more work and investment.

23. In fact, although most vendors need to obtain permits and pay governmental fees to sell at public events, I was told that lack of coordination among the three or more agencies involved in disbursing permits—including Hacienda (the Department of the Treasury), ARPE (Administración de Reglamentos y Permisos, or the Regulations and Permits Administration), and the Negociado de Bebidas Alcohólicas or Bureau of Alcoholic Beverages—largely precludes governmental verification of payment and filing of individual permits.

24. It was the director's intention to create community councils composed of representatives of different cultural groups in a given community. Because, in her plan, local mayors and municipal cultural workers would be part of these councils, they were soon criticized as easily swayed by local partisan politics.

25. This is partly because criticisms were being levied instead at the local cultural centers rather than directly at the more visible Institute of Puerto Rican Culture, as they were in 1980. In addition, it was rumored that the director's political identity as a known *independentista* helped curb criticisms of her reforms by *independentista* sectors.

Chapter II: The Institute of Puerto Rican Culture and the Building Blocks of Nationality

1. In the nineteenth-century novels *Agüeybana el bravo* (Agüeybana the Brave) by Daniel Rivera and *El pilgrimaje de Bayoán* (The Pilgrimage of Bayoán) by Eugenio María de Hostos, Taino Indians were principal characters through which each author conveyed a message of opposition to the Spanish authorities. The cacique, Agüeybana, is the main character of the former novel, in which the author urges those not born on the island to leave Puerto Rico.

2. See Instituto de Cultura (1960) for a list of the institute's programming during its first five years.

3. For a discussion of countersong as a medium of social protest and liberation in Latin America, see Reyes Matta (1988).

4. See Santiago (1994) for a discussion of 1970s cultural production. In particular, he discusses the "indigenization" and local appropriation of the same commercial rhythms perceived as foreign threats by my ICP informants.

5. For a discussion of the dissemination of popular rhythms on Puerto Rican radio and TV, ranging from boleros to *la nueva ola* (the 1970s Spanish rock boom), see among others Torregrosa (1991), Malavet Vega (1987), and Santiago (1994).

6. The informant refers to the research on folk music done by Rosa Nieves (1967) and López Cruz (1967).

7. My intent here is not to ascertain the actual historical contributions to Puerto Rican culture of these "building blocks." (As we shall see, these issues are highly contentious on the island, although the dominant view that these racial and cultural elements have long merged into a single culture since the Spanish colonization hinders assessments about what is original to each group, beyond those traits that have become stereotypically associated with each one in the ICP program.) Instead, my purpose is to point to the fallacy of the myth of harmonious cultural integration by bringing attention to how these building blocks are unevenly valued within official definitions of the national identity.

8. The peasant and the countryside are common elements used to evoke continuity with an agrarian past (Ferguson 1992, Raymond Williams 1973). The association of peasant life with the essence of the nation has been traced by Quintero Rivera (1988b) to the island's Spanish colonial era, when the countryside provided space for development separate from the island's colonial bureaucracy. I believe, however, that this romanticizing of rural life should also be seen in relation to geographical notions of race that associate the interior mountainous areas with "whiteness," as I discuss in this chapter.

9. A musical group that has incorporated recent innovations is Jíbaro Jazz, which mixes peasant and jazz rhythms in its compositions.

10. Promoters are also expected to attend activities within their assigned area, many of which take place at night. This has also contributed to the underrepresentation of women promoters, who are more likely than men to be apprehensive about night travel.

11. Because of the suppression of race in the national ideology, few studies analyzed race and racism on the island until recent times, when the subject has begun to receive more attention. Noted exceptions are the work of Blanco (1942), who was one of the first to examine the existence and scope of racism on the

island, and Zenón Cruz (1975), who analyzed racial attitudes in Puerto Rican literature. For discussions of race in relation to Puerto Rico's national ideology see Flores (1979) and J. L. González (1987). See also ethnographic works by Arlene Torres (1995) and Isar Godreau (1995).

12. It should be noted that changes of administration between the main political parties have not affected the total amount given to the ICP itself. In fact, the ICP's operational budget has increased slowly but steadily since the 1960s. Instead, the fiscal priorities of the different parties have been most reflected in the amounts they either disburse or withhold for special projects and cultural initiatives, which when allocated also fall under the custody of the ICP.

13. *Fiestas de pueblo* is the name popularly given to grassroots public festivals and festivities that are open to the public.

14. These regulations, although approved by a general assembly of cultural centers in 1986 and ratified by the ICP staff a year later, were originally conceived by the ICP staff in accordance with the PPD's cultural nationalistic policies of the mid-1980s. The regulations were aimed at reinforcing the ICP's ties with the centers and limiting their vulnerability to partisan politics at the local level, after local centers became battlegrounds in the national cultural wars of the 1980s. Thus, one of the most important regulations prevents new members from joining less than three months prior to elections; its purpose is to limit the recruitment of partisan supporters right before the voting.

15. Scarano suggests that the contacts established by eastern residents with their insular neighbors were quite generalized among the population and differed from the exchanges with foreigners in the southern and western parts of the island, which occurred mostly at the elite level. These more generalized contacts with the Anglophone neighbors to the east may also have contributed to the perception of the east as somehow "foreign" (personal communication). See Scarano (1989) and Quintero-Rivera (1988a) for a discussion of the influence of immigrants on the economic life of the southern city of Ponce.

Chapter III: From the Center to the *Centros:*
Cultural Politics from Below

1. Later, the University of Puerto Rico served as a breeding ground for new cultural centers. In the early years, the director of the ICP traveled throughout the island with his officers to found local cultural centers himself.

2. The identification of Latin American culture with Ariel has since been challenged by many writers, such as the Cuban Roberto Fernández Retamar (1973). While agreeing with Rodó's focus on the United States as the dominant other, Fernández Retamar argues that Rodó erred in selecting Ariel to symbolize Latin culture. It is Caliban, he argues, who turned against the master who taught

him to speak and thus most appropriately represents the area's history of colonization and revolt.

3. Behind this concentration of land were two sugar mills: Pasto Viejo, owned by the American Eastern Sugar Associates, and El Ejemplo, owned by a Caone family of seignorial origins who managed to establish links with American interests.

4. See Scarano (1993) for a discussion of the "sugar age" and its effects on the island's overall economy.

5. Caone's population decreased from 34,853 to 33,381 inhabitants between 1950 and 1960. This is the only period that the population has shown a general decrease since the 1940s. Since then, the population has steadily grown to 55,203 inhabitants in 1990 (see Negociado del Censo, municipio de Caone 1940-1990).

6. Organizations of *ausentes* (former residents) are very common in Puerto Rico, where one or more such groups can be found in every town. They vary in degree of organization and the class composition of their membership. In Caone the organization is dominated by educated urban professionals, most of whom now live in San Juan. *Ausentes* meet during the town's annual patron-saint festivities and increasingly during the celebration of local festivals, which also dedicate activities to the former residents.

7. During my fieldwork, the Disney Store had just opened in the largest shopping center in San Juan. As a result, the fashionable Mickey Mouse became a common reference through which people expressed their fears of Americanization on the island.

Chapter IV: Just One More Festival: New Actors in Caone's Cultural Politics

1. Before ARECMA there had been other informal organizations in the area, such as a cultural group called the Taino Circle and an ecumenical movement of religious renewal (active in the 1970s). These groups were organized by some former and present members of ARECMA, also to solve problems neglected by the municipal government, including the community's lack of recreational facilities and a municipal water supply. However, ARECMA was the first formal organization in the community, in the sense that it has a constitution and is registered as a not-for-profit organization with the Puerto Rican State Department, which makes it eligible for governmental grants.

2. The evolution of pro-statehood elements within the Socialist Party in Mariana was traced by different informants to the 1930s Coalition Party formed between Republicans and Socialists, who then represented the major opposition to the landowner-dominated Liberal Party in Caone.

3. This is a group of Puerto Rican teenage male singers that gained interna-

tional popularity in the late 1980s and has given rise to a variety of similar groups throughout the island.

4. Indeed, most coastal residents of Caone migrated to the United States in the 1950s, with the decline of sugar and the closing of the port in Caone. This pattern of migration contrasts with that of rural communities in Caone, who fled to the United States in the 1940s with the island-wide decline of sugar and agriculture.

5. This was the case for the towns of Arroyo and Barcelona, which separated from Guayama and Manatí respectively.

6. District senators represent the area muncipalities contained within the district. There are two senators for each of the eight senatorial districts.

7. It is becoming common among politicians to give money to local groups as a means of simultaneously shifting responsibility to them for delivering and maintaining public projects and services. As a local senator in Caone told me, "I know I can give money to ARECMA because they have proven themselves to be people who work. Today they are working within their community, but tomorrow, who knows! They may even begin to help with the community next to them, or the rest of Caone or the whole eastern area, and I say, better for me and for all."

8. For a discussion of the negotiations and engagements of festival participants and of how their experiences diverge from those intended by festival organizers, see Bauman and Sawin (1991).

9. In 1993 Puerto Rico ranked third among U.S. cities and territories in the numbers of murders and Type I crimes committed (violent crimes, armed robberies, carjackings, and the like) with 73.7 murders per 100,000 inhabitants or 946 killings that year (Pointi 1994).

10. See the works of Milagros López (1994) and Ivelisse Rivera (1996) for analysis of crime and fear in relation to issues of social class and local politics.

11. See Manning (1990) for a discussion of the transnational component of public celebrations in the Caribbean linked to the migratory history in the area.

12. The Festival of Bomba y Plena was one of the most important festivals celebrated in Caone until the early 1990s. It was originally organized by a group of musicians and artisans. Its discontinuation was linked to hearsay about mismanagement of government grants and problems among its leadership.

13. The Vega Alta group and ARECMA developed festivals evoking the breadfruit independently from one another. They have since learned about each other's festivals but have not cooperated as their work is geared to their respective communities.

Chapter V: Culture, Politics, and Corporate Sponsorship

1. A preliminary version of this chapter appears in *The Puerto Rican Jam:*

Rethinking Colonialism and Nationalism, ed. Frances Negrón Muntaner and Ramón Grosfoguel (Minneapolis: University of Minnesota Press, 1997) and forms the basis for "Negotiating Culture and Dollars: The Politics of Corporate Sponsorship in Puerto Rico," *Identities: Global Studies of Culture and Power* 4, no. 1 (1997).

2. Commonwealth of Puerto Rico, Junta de Planificación 1995. The United States is the number-one source of consumer goods for Puerto Ricans, whose consumption of U.S. products, some argue, is greater than that for the entire Hispanic market in the United States (Hernández 1991).

3. Corona is a now discontinued, locally produced beer. The campaign was developed by Young and Rubicam Associates in Puerto Rico in the 1970s.

4. Unless otherwise noted, all information about the advertising campaigns for Winston and Budweiser is based on my analysis of their campaigns and first-hand interviews in 1993 and 1994 with advertisers and publicity agents involved in these campaigns. The development of these campaigns is considered confidential information by the advertisers, who declined to provide me access to internal marketing studies about the material presented here.

5. Borinquen is a popular name for the island derived from Puerto Rico's indigenous name prior to Spanish colonization.

6. See video documentary (*Case History: A Story of Success,* 1990s) produced by the Lopito, Ileana and Howie Advertising in San Juan to describe the "successful" promotion of Budweiser through the right combination of advertising, marketing, and other forms of publicity.

7. Lopito, Ileana and Howie Advertising, *Case History: A Story of Success.*

8. Law 62, which bans cigarette advertising in all movie theaters, public parks, billboards, and within five hundred meters of public and private schools, was approved in 1994 by the commonwealth government and went into effect in August 1995. Its impact is still to be ascertained (S. Rodríguez 1994a).

9. See the work of García-Canclini (1993) and Barbero (1993) for a discussion of mass-mediated popular culture in Latin America. With these terms they challenge the idea that popular culture can be identified or contained, highlighting instead the hybrid transformations of cultural forms with commercial culture, mass media, and new technologies.

10. For a discussion of the government's love/hate relationship with salsa, see Flores (1992).

11. See Rivera (1993) and Flores (1991) for a discussion of rap music in Puerto Rico and among Puerto Ricans in the United States.

12. The misogynist character of popular music has been noted, along with the processes by which people receive and transform its messages to make them suitable to their specific contexts (Aparicio 1997, Lipsitz 1993). What is interesting here

is how these genres take added significance around their inclusion or exclusion of "cultural" activities.

13. The oppositional character of Puerto Rican TV comedy has been discussed by Eliseo Colón Zayas (1990) in a Bakhtinian analysis of "Sunshine's Cafe," a discontinued program that was at the top of local ratings in the early 1990s.

Chapter VI: Contesting the Nation, Contesting Identities

1. I follow Bourdieu's (1993) discussion of the legitimacy of cultural goods and practices considered in relation to the position they occupy within the field of cultural production. This field is defined as "the site of the struggles for the monopoly of the power to consecrate" (78). It encompasses the agents and the conditions involved in the production, circulation, and consumption of cultural goods. Because in Bourdieu's model the field of cultural production is subordinate to the field of power, it serves to establish definitions of legitimacy by veiling the underlying power relations that sustain it and by reproducing oppositional relations between dominant and dominated factions.

2. These processes are manifested in different guises. See for instance Rosalind Williams's (1982) discussion of the ethos of consumption developed in eighteenth-century France to distinguish "healthy" luxury (characterized by diversity, elegance, and intellectual pleasure in consumption) from the more vulgar forms of consumption developed by the working classes as a result of the "democratization of wealth" (and characterized by sheer numbers and superfluous consumption). The authentic is here constructed through "disinterestedness," thus basing claims to legitimacy on freedom from material constraints (Bourdieu 1993).

3. In November 1950 a nationalist uprising occurred in Jayuya and in other municipalities on the island, along with attacks on the Blair House in Washington, D.C. Municipal offices and police headquarters were occupied by the nationalists, who in Jayuya declared Puerto Rico to be an independent republic.

4. Recall for instance the mid-1970s ad for Mazola corn oil, which depicted members of Taino society harvesting and worshiping corn, represented as *oro de dios* or God's gold.

5. Sales figures provided by a public relations officer for the Bacardi Corporation.

6. For information on Bacardi's economic position as one of the world's most valuable producers of spirits in terms of sales, profitability, and growth potential, see J. C. Maxwell (1993) and Underwood (1993).

7. Law 99 was replaced by Law 166, which was passed on August 11, 1995. Law 166 differed most from Law 99 in the formal evaluation process, which was eliminated. Now before cards are issued artisans are evaluated more informally (on a per-request basis) by the Folk Arts Division of Fomento; evaluations are no

longer done by a full committee representing various government organizations (Commonwealth of Puerto Rico 1995).

8. In Puerto Rico, the graphic arts have been an important means of communication since the days of DIVEDCO, which introduced graphic-arts workshops as educational tools. The ICP has contributed to this development by commissioning a commemorative print for each of its sponsored activities since the 1950s. Today most festivals create event-related T-shirts rather than printed posters, which are more costly to produce, although the ICP still subsidizes the posters for the programs of its affiliated centers.

BIBLIOGRAPHY

Abreu-Vega, Salvador. 1984. *Apuntes para la historia.* Santo Domingo: Corripio.

Abu-Lughod, Lila. 1990. The Romance of Resistance: Tracing Transformations of Power through Bedouin Women. *American Ethnologist* 17: 41–55.

Acosta, Yvonne. 1992. Hacia una historia de la persecución política en Puerto Rico. *Homines* 15(2): 142–51.

———. 1987. *La Mordaza.* Río Piedras: Edil.

Aguiló, Sylvia. 1987. *Idea y concepto de la cultura puertorriqueña en la década del 50.* San Juan: Centro de Estudios Avanzados.

Alden, Dana, Wayne Hoyer, and Chal Lee. 1993. Identifying Global and Culture-Specific Dimensions of Humor in Advertising: A Multinational Analysis. *Journal of Marketing* (April): 64–75.

Alegría, Ricardo. 1973. *El Instituto de Cultura Puertorriqueña 1955–1973: 18 años contribuyendo a fortalecer nuestra conciencia nacional.* San Juan: Instituto de Cultura Puertorriqueña.

Alonso, Ana Maria. 1994. The Politics of Space, Time and Substance: State Formation, Nationalism, and Ethnicity. *Annual Review of Anthropology* 23: 379–405.

Alonso, Manuel. [1849] 1968. *El gíbaro.* Río Piedras: Editorial Cultural.

Althusser, Louis. 1971. *Lenin and Philosophy and Other Essays.* New York and London: Monthly Review Press.

Alvarez, Luis M. 1992. La presencia negra en la música puertorriqueña. In *La tercera raíz: Presencia africana en Puerto Rico,* 30–41. San Juan: Centro de Estudios de la Realidad Puertorriqueña and Institute of Puerto Rican Culture.

Alvarez-Curbelo, Silvia, and María Elena Rodríguez-Castro, eds. 1993.

Del nacionalismo al populismo: Cultura y política en Puerto Rico.
Río Piedras: Huracán.

Anderson, Benedict. 1983. *Imagined Communities: Reflections on the Origin and Spread of Nationalism.* London: Verso.

Aparicio, Frances. 1997. *Listening to Salsa: Gender, Latin Popular Music, and Puerto Rican Culture.* Middletown, Conn: Wesleyan University Press.

Appadurai, Arjun. 1990. Disjuncture and Difference in the Global Cultural Economy. *Public Culture* 2(2): 1-24.

———. 1986. *The Social Life of Things: Commodities in Cultural Perspectives.* Cambridge: Cambridge University Press.

Appadurai, Arjun, and Carol Breckenridge. 1988. Why Public Culture? *Public Culture* 1(1): 5-11.

Auger Marchand, José M. 1987. Apuntes metodológicos sobre la medición de actividades que eluden la detención para propósitos fiscales y estadísticos. Paper presented at Seminario 2001 conference, San Juan, sponsored by the Departamento de Recursos Humanos, Trabajo y Economía.

Babín, María Teresa. 1973. *La cultura de Puerto Rico.* San Juan: Instituto de Cultura Puertorriqueña.

Badone, Ellen. 1992. The Construction of National Identity in Brittany and Quebec. *American Ethnologist* 19(4): 806-17.

Bakhtin, Mikhail. 1984. *Rabelais and His World.* Indiana: Midland.

Balibar, Etienne. 1991. Is There a New Racism? In *Race, Nation, Class: Ambiguous Identities,* ed. Etienne Balibar and Immanuel Wallerstein, 17-28. London: Verso.

Ballerino Cohen, Colleen, Richard Wilk, and Beverly Stoeltje, eds. 1996. *Beauty Queens on the Global Stage: Gender, Contests, and Power.* New York: Routledge.

Barbero, Jesús Martín. 1993. Latin America: Cultures in the Communication Media. *Journal of Communication* 43(2): 18-30.

———. 1987. *De los medios a las mediaciones.* Barcelona: Gustavo Gil.

Barnett, Marguerite. 1974. Creating Political Identity. *Ethnicity* 1: 237-65.

Basch, Linda, Nina Glick-Schiller, and Cristina Blanc-Szanton. 1994. *Nations Unbound: Transnational Projects, Postcolonial Predicaments, and Deterritorialized Nation States.* Basel: Gordon and Breach International.

Bauman, Richard, and Patricia Sawin. 1991. The Politics of Participation in Folk Art Festival. In *Exhibiting Culture: The Poetics and Politics of Museum Display,* ed. Ivan Karp and Steven Levine, 288–314. Washington, D.C.: Smithsonian Institution Press.

Baver, Sherrie. 1993. *The Political Economy of Colonialism: The State and Industrialization in Puerto Rico.* London: Praeger.

Bayrón-Toro, Fernando. 1989. *Elecciones y partidos políticos de Puerto Rico.* Mayagüez: Ediciones Isla.

Beeman, William O. 1993. The Anthropology of Theater and Spectacle. *Annual Review of Anthropology* 22: 369–93.

Bhabha, Homi. 1990. *Nation and Narration.* London and New York: Routledge.

Billig, Michael. 1995. *Banal Nationalism.* London: Sage.

Blanco, Tomás. 1942. *El prejuicio racial en Puerto Rico.* San Juan: Editorial Biblioteca de Autores Puertorriqueños.

Bonilla, Frank, and Ricardo Campos. 1985. Evolving Patterns of Puerto Rican Migration. In *The Americas in the New Division of Labor,* ed. Steven Sanderson, 177–205. New York: Holmes and Meier.

Bourdieu, Pierre. 1993. *The Field of Cultural Production.* New York: Columbia University Press.

———. 1977. *Outline of a Theory of Practice.* Cambridge: Cambridge University Press.

Brau, Salvador. 1978. *La colonización de Puerto Rico.* San Juan: Instituto de Cultura Puertorriqueña.

Breuilly, John. 1982. *Nationalism and the State.* New York: St. Martin's Press.

Buci-Glucksman, Christine. 1982. Hegemony and Consent. In *Approaches to Gramsci,* ed. Ann Showstack-Sassoon. London: Writers and Readers.

Buitrago-Ortiz, Carlos. 1982. Anthropology in the Puerto Rican Colonial Context: Analysis and Projections. In *Indigenous Anthropology in Non-Western Countries,* ed. Hussein Fahim. Durham, N.C.: Carolina Academic Press.

Cabán, Luis. 1980. Alegría: Puerto Rico va camino a perder cultura nacional por la universal. *El Mundo* (San Juan), June 6, 10-B.

Cabral, Amilcar. *Return to the Source.* New York: Africa Information Service.

Calhoun, Craig. 1993. Civil Society and the Public Sphere. *Public Culture* 5: 267-80.

———. 1992. *Habermas and the Public Sphere.* Cambridge, Mass.: MIT Press.

———. 1991. Indirect Relationships and Imagined Communities: Large Scale Social Integration and the Transformation of Economic Life. In *Social Theory for a Changing Society,* ed. Pierre Bourdieu and James Coleman. Boulder, Colo.: Westview.

Caribbean Business. 1996. Puerto Rico's Advertising Agencies, 24-33. In *The Caribbean Business Book of Lists.* San Juan: Caribbean Business.

Carrión, Juan Manuel. 1993. Etnia, raza y la nacionalidad puertorriqueña. In *La nación puertorriqueña: Ensayos en torno a Pedro Albizu Campos,* ed. Juan Manuel Carrión, Teresa García-Ruiz, and Carlos Rodríguez Fraticelli. Río Piedras: Editorial de la Universidad.

———. 1980. The Petty Bourgeoisie and the Struggle for Independence in Puerto Rico. In *The Puerto Ricans: Their History Culture and Society,* ed. Adalberto López. Cambridge: Schenkman.

Castells, Manuel. 1983. *The City and the Grassroots: A Cross-Cultural Theory of Urban Social Movements.* Berkeley: University of California Press.

Castells, Manuel, and Alejandro Portes. 1989. *World Underneath: The Origins, Dynamics and Effects of the Informal Economy.* Baltimore: Johns Hopkins University Press.

Chatterjee, Partha. 1993. *The Nation and Its Fragments.* Princeton, N.J.: Princeton University Press.

———. 1986. *Nationalist Thought and the Colonial World: A Derivative Discourse?* London: Zed Books.

Cohen, Abner. 1993. *Masquerade Politics: Explorations in the Structure of Urban Cultural Movements.* Oxford: Berg.

Cohen, Jean, and Andrew Arato. 1992. *Civil Society and Political Theory.* Cambridge, Mass.: MIT Press.

Colón Zayas, Eliseo. 1990. Sunshine's Café y el poder del espectador. *El Mundo (Puerto Rico Ilustrado)* (San Juan), April 1, 6-8.

Comité Organizador del Festival de la Lancha Planúa. 1994. Programa del sexto festival. Punta Santiago, P.R.: By the committee.

Comité Organizador del Festival del Trabajador de la Piña. 1993. Programa del noveno festival. Vega Alta, P.R.: By the committee.

Commonwealth of Puerto Rico. 1995. Ley Número 166, House of Representatives. Proyecto de la Cámara 1799.

———. 1992. Composición industrial por municipio. Informe especial E-78. San Juan: Departamento del Trabajo y Recursos Humanos.

———. Comisión de Derechos Humanos. 1991. Informe sobre discrimen y persecución por razones políticas: Las prácticas gubernamentales de mantener listas, ficheros y expedientes de ciudadanos por razón de su ideología política. Revista del Colegio de Abogados 52 (January–March).

———. Office of Budget Administration. 1978–90. General Legislative Budgets (1978–1990). Library of the Puerto Rican Senate, San Juan.

———. 1955. Second Legislative Assembly 1953–1956 of the House of Representatives. Proyecto de la Cámara 1381.

Connor, Walker. 1978. A Nation is a Nation, is a State, is an Ethnic Group, is a . . . Ethnic and Racial Studies 1(4): 379–88.

———. 1973. The Politics of Ethnonationalism. Journal of International Affairs 27: 1–21.

Corrigan, Philip, and Derek Sayer. 1985. The Great Arch: English State Formation as Cultural Revolution. Oxford and New York: Basil Blackwell.

Dávila Colón, Luis. 1997. Publicidad comprometedora. El Nuevo Día (San Juan), January 18, 79.

———. 1996. Giro decisivo. El Nuevo Día (San Juan), July 17, 61.

———. 1993. El neonacionalismo. El Nuevo Día (San Juan), December 8, 73.

De Certeau, Michel. 1984. The Practice of Everyday Life. Los Angeles: University of California Press.

de González, Manuel. 1997. Nacionalismo que paga. El Nuevo Día (San Juan), January 25, 83.

de la Rosa, Luis. 1986. Los negros del Brick-Barca Magesty: Prohibición del tráfico de esclavos. Revista del Centro de Estudios Avanzados (San Juan) 3: 45–57.

Díaz, Edgardo. 1987. Música para anunciar en la sociedad sanjuanera del siglo XIX. Revista Musical Puertorriqueña 1(1): 6–13.

Díaz-Quiñones, Arcadio. 1993. *La memoria rota*. Río Piedras: Huracán.

Dietz, James. 1986. *Economic History of Puerto Rico: Institutional Change and Capitalist Development*. Princeton, N.J.: Princeton University Press.

DiMaggio, Paul. 1991. Cultural Entrepreneurship in Nineteenth-Century Boston. In *Rethinking Popular Culture,* ed. Chandra Mukerji and Michael Schudson, 374–98. Berkeley: University of California Press.

DIVEDCO (División de Educación de la Comunidad). 1968. Isla y pueblo. San Juan: DIVEDCO, Departamento de Instrucción Pública.

————. 1967. La familia. 2d ed. San Juan: DIVEDCO.

————. 1966a. Emigración. 2d ed. San Juan: DIVEDCO.

————. 1966b. El guardarrayas. San Juan: DIVEDCO.

————. 1961. La trampa. San Juan: DIVEDCO.

————. 1952. Alimentos. San Juan: DIVEDCO.

————. 1951. La ciencia contra la superstición. San Juan: DIVEDCO.

Domínguez, Virginia. 1990. The Politics of Heritage in Contemporary Israel. In *Nationalist Ideologies and the Production of National Cultures,* ed. Richard Fox, 130–47. Washington: American Anthropological Association.

Duany, Jorge. 1995. *Los cubanos en Puerto Rico: Economía, etnia e identidad cultural*. Río Piedras: Editorial de la Universidad de Puerto Rico.

Dufrasne-González, Emanuel. 1996. Afrofobia. *Claridad* (San Juan), Aug. 23–29, 25.

Englis, Basil. 1994. *Global and Multinational Advertising*. New Brunswick, N.J.: Rutgers University Press.

Escobar, Arturo, and Sonia Alvarez, eds. 1992. *The Making of Social Movements in Latin America: Identity, Strategy, and Democracy*. Boulder, Colo.: Westview Press.

Ewen, Stuart. 1988. *All-Consuming Images: The Politics of Style in Contemporary Culture*. New York: Basic Books.

Fanon, Frantz. 1963. *On National Culture: The Wretched of the Earth*. New York: Grove Press.

Featherstone, Mike. 1995. *Undoing Culture: Globalization, Postmodernism and Identity*. London: Sage Publications.

Ferguson, James. 1992. The Country and the City on the Copperbelt. *Cultural Anthropology* 7(1): 80–92.

Fernández Retamar, Roberto. 1973. *Calibán: Apuntes sobre la cultura de nuestra América*. Buenos Aires: La Pleyade.

Ferrao, Luis Angel. 1990. *Pedro Albizu Campos y el nacionalismo puertorriqueño*. Río Piedras: Editorial Cultural.

Flores, Juan. 1992. Cortijo's Revenge. In *On Edge: The Crisis of Contemporary Latin American Culture*, ed. George Yúdice, Jean Franco, and Juan Flores. Minneapolis: University of Minnesota Press.

———. 1991. Latin Empire: Puerto Rap. *CENTRO Bulletin* (Center for Puerto Rican Studies, Hunter College, New York), Spring.

———. 1979. *Insularismo e ideología burguesa*. Havana: Casa de las Américas.

Flores, Juan, and Milagros López. 1994. Dossier Puerto Rico. *Social Text* 38: 93–95.

Foster, Robert. 1991. Making Cultures in the Global Ecumene. *Annual Review of Anthropology* 20: 235–60.

Foucault, Michel. 1983. Subject and Power. In *Michel Foucault: Beyond Structuralism and Hermeneutics*, ed. Hubert Dreyfus and Paul Rabinow. Chicago: University of Chicago Press.

Fox, Richard, ed. 1990. *Nationalist Ideologies and the Production of National Cultures*. Washington: American Anthropological Association.

Friedman, Jonathan. 1994. *Cultural Identity and Global Process*. Thousand Oaks, Calif.: Sage Publications.

García, Ana María (producer). 1993. *Cocolos y rockeros*. San Juan: Pandora Filmes.

García, Gervasio, and Angel Quintero Rivera. 1986. *Desafío y solidaridad: Breve historia del movimiento obrero puertorriqueño*. Río Piedras: Huracán.

García, Lissette, et al. 1988. Estudio de la comunidad Mariana. Departamento de Ciencias Sociales, Escuela de Trabajo Social, Universidad de Puerto Rico, Río Piedras.

García-Canclini, Néstor. 1993. *Transforming Modernity: Popular Culture in Mexico*. Austin: University of Texas Press.

———. 1992a. Cultural Reconversion. In *On Edge: The Crisis of Con-*

temporary Latin American Culture, ed. George Yúdice, Jean Franco, and Juan Flores, 29-44.

————. 1992b. *Culturas híbridas.* Buenos Aires: Editorial Suramericana.

Garnham, Nicholas. 1993. The Mass Media, Cultural Identity, and the Public Sphere in the Modern World. *Public Culture* 5(2): 251-66.

Gellner, Ernest. 1983. *Nations and Nationalism.* Ithaca: Cornell University Press.

Gelpí, Juan. 1993. *Literatura y paternalismo en Puerto Rico.* Río Piedras: Editorial de la Universidad de Puerto Rico.

Gilroy, Paul. 1987. *"There Ain't No Black in The Union Jack": The Cultural Politics of Race and Nation.* Chicago: University of Chicago Press.

Giroux, Henry. 1993. Consuming Social Change. *Cultural Critique* 26: 5-32.

Giuscafre, Rosario. 1974. ICP busca rescatar edificio para el centro cultural. *El Mundo* (San Juan), November 3.

Glasser, Ruth. 1995. *My Music Is My Flag: Puerto Rican Musicians and Their New York Communities, 1917-1940.* Berkeley: University of California Press.

Glick Schiller, Nina. 1994. Introducing Identities: Global Studies in Culture and Power. *Identities* 1(1): 1-6.

Godreau, Isar P. 1995. The "Race" and "Color" of Strategic Ambiguity. Paper presented at the ninety-fourth meeting of the American Anthropological Association, Washington, D.C.

González, José Luis. 1987. *El país de cuatro pisos.* Río Piedras: Huracán.

González, Lydia-Milagros. 1990. Cultura y grupos populares en la historia viva de Puerto Rico hoy. *CENTRO Bulletin* (Center for Puerto Rican Studies, Hunter College, New York) 2(8): 98-113.

González, Manuel J. 1997. Nacionalismo que paga. *El Nuevo Día* (San Juan), January 25, 83.

Guevara Monge, Maribel. 1992. Estudio/Publicidad y cigarrillos. Master's thesis, Escuela de Mercadeo, Universidad de Puerto Rico, Río Piedras.

Gupta, Akhil, and James Ferguson. 1992. Beyond Culture, Space, Identity and the Politics of Difference. *Cultural Anthropology* 7(1): 6-24.

Habermas, Jürgen. 1992. *The Structural Transformation of the Public Sphere*. Cambridge, Mass.: MIT Press.

Hall, Stuart. 1991. The Local and the Global: Globalization and Ethnicity. In *Culture, Globalization and the World System*, ed. Anthony King, 19-39. Albany: State University of New York Press.

———. 1986. Popular Culture and the State. In *Popular Culture and Social Relations*, ed. Tony Bennett. Philadelphia: Open University Press.

———. 1981. Notes on Deconstructing the Popular. In *People's History and Socialist Theory*, ed. R. Samuel, 227-40. London: Routledge.

Handler, Richard. 1992. High Culture/Hegemony and Historical Causality. *American Ethnologist* 19(4): 818-24.

———. 1988. *Nationalism and the Politics of Culture in Quebec*. Madison: University of Wisconsin Press.

Harvey, David. 1989. *The Condition of Post Modernity*. Cambridge: Blackwell.

Harvey, Edwin. 1988. *Legislación cultural puertorriqueña/Legislación cultural comparada*. San Juan: Instituto de Cultura Puertorriqueña.

Hernández, Luis. 1991. The Origins of the Consumer Culture in Puerto Rico: The Pre-Television Years (1898-1954). *CENTRO Bulletin* (Center for Puerto Rican Studies, Hunter College, New York) (Winter): 38-54.

Heyes, Carleton. 1968. *The Historical Evolution of Modern Nationalism*. New York: Russell and Russell.

Hostos, Eugenio María de. 1970. *La peregrinación de Bayoán*. San Juan: Instituto de Cultura Puertorriqueña.

Humphrey, Theodore, and Lin Humphrey. 1988. *We Gather Together: Food and Festival in American Life*. Ann Arbor: UMI Research Press.

Hutchinson, John. 1992. Moral Innovators and the Politics of Regeneration: The Distinctive Role of Cultural Nationalists in Nation-Building. *International Journal of Comparative Sociology* 33 (1-2): 101-17.

———. 1987. *The Dynamics of Cultural Nationalism: The Gaelic Revival and the Creation of the Irish Nation State*. London: Allen and Unwin.

Hylland Eriksen, Thomas. 1993. *Ethnicity and Nationalism, Anthropological Perspectives.* London: Pluto Press.

Instituto de Cultura Puertorriqueña. 1993. *Patrimonio histórico edificado de la región este.* San Juan: ICP.

―――. 1990. Obra realizada por los centros culturales adscritos al Instituto de Cultura Puertorriqueña. San Juan: Programa de Promoción Cultural, Centros Culturales.

―――. 1960. *El Instituto de Cultura Puertorriqueña: Los primeros cinco años.* San Juan: ICP.

Jiménez, Félix. 1985. El arte del cambio: El país ante la nueva política cultural. *El Nuevo Día* (San Juan), July 22, 62-63.

Jiménez, Miriam. 1996. Un hombre (negro) del pueblo: José Celso Barbosa and the Puerto Rican "Race" toward Whiteness. *Centro Bulletin* (Center for Puerto Rican Studies, Hunter College, New York) (Spring): 8-29.

Johnson, Hank. 1994. "New Social Movements and Old Regional Nationalism." In *New Social Movements: From Ideology to Identity,* ed. Hank Johnson and Joseph Gusfield. Philadelphia: Temple University Press.

Jones, Delmos. 1987. The Community and Organizations in the Community. In *Anthropology in the United States,* ed. Leith Mullings. New York: Columbia University Press.

Junta de Planificación. 1995. *Informe económico al gobernador.* San Juan.

Kaplan, Flora. 1994. *Museums and the Making of Ourselves: The Role of Objects in National Identity.* London: Leicester University Press.

Karp, Ivan. 1991. Festivals. In *Exhibiting Culture: The Poetics and Politics of Museum Display,* ed. Ivan Karp and Steven Levine, 279-87. Washington, D.C.: Smithsonian Institution Press.

Kohn, Hans. 1967. *Nationalism: Its Meaning and History.* New York: Van Nostrand Reinhold.

Laclau, Ernesto. 1979. *Politics and Ideology in Marxist Theory, Capitalism, Fascism, Populism.* London: Verso.

Laguerre, Enrique. 1968. *El jíbaro de Puerto Rico: Símbolo y figura.* Sharon, Conn.: Troutman Press.

Laó, Agustín. 1997. Islands at the Crossroads: Puerto Rican-ess Traveling between the Translocal Nation and the Global City. In *The Puerto Rican Jam: Rethinking Colonialism and Nationalism,* ed. Frances

Negrón-Muntaner and Ramón Grosfoguel. Minneapolis: University of Minnesota Press.

Lash, Scott, and Jonathan Friedman. 1992. *Modernity and Identity*. Oxford: Blackwell.

Lauria, Antonio. 1991. Images and Contradictions: DIVEDCO's Portrayal of Puerto Rican Life. *CENTRO* 3(1): 92-96.

―――. 1980. Reflexiones sobre la cuestión cultural y Puerto Rico. In *Crisis y crítica de las ciencias sociales en Puerto Rico,* ed. Rafael Ramírez and Weceslao Serra Deliz. Centro de Investigaciones Sociales, Universidad de Puerto Rico, Río Piedras.

Levine, Lawrence. 1984. William Shakespeare and the American People. *American Historical Review* 89(1): 34-66.

Lipsitz, George. 1993. We Know What Time It Is: Youth Culture in the 1990s. *CENTRO* 5(1): 10-21.

LiPuma, Edward, and Sarah Keene Meltzoff. 1990. Ceremonies of Independence and Public Culture in the Solomon Islands. *Public Culture* 3(1): 77-91.

Lloyd, David. 1994. Adulteration and the Nation: Monologic Nationalism and the Colonial Hybrid. In *An Other Tongue: Nation and Ethnicity in the Linguistic Borderlines,* ed. Alfred Arteaga, 53-92. Durham, N.C.: Duke University Press.

López, Milagros. 1994. Post-Work Selves and Entitlement "Attitude" in Peripheral Postindustrial Puerto Rico. *Social Text* 38: 111-34.

López Crúz, Francisco. 1967. *Los bailes de bomba: La música folklórica de Puerto Rico*. Sharon, Conn.: Troutman Press.

Lopito, Ileana, and Howie Advertising. [1990s.] *Case History: A Story of Success* (video documentary of Budweiser promotional campaign in Puerto Rico). San Juan: Lopito, Ileana, and Howie Advertising.

Mac Aloon, John. 1984. La pitada olímpica: Puerto Rico, International Sports, and the Constitution of Politics. In *Text, Play and Story: The Construction and Reconstruction of Self and Society,* ed. E. M. Brunner, 315-55. Washington, D.C.: American Ethnological Society.

Malavet-Vega, Pedro. 1987. *La vellonera está directa*. Santo Domingo: Corripio.

Malkki, Liisa. 1992. National Geographic: The Rooting of Peoples and the Territorialization of National Identity among Scholars and Refugees. *Cultural Anthropology* 7(1): 24-44.

Mallon, Florencia. 1995. *Peasant and Nation: The Making of Post-Colonial Mexico and Peru*. Berkeley: University of California Press.

Manning, Frank, 1990. Overseas Caribbean Carnivals: The Art and Politics of a Transnational Celebration. In *Caribbean Popular Culture*, ed. John Lent, 20-37. Bowling Green, Ohio: Bowling Green University Popular Press.

———, ed. 1983. *The Celebration of Society*. Bowling Green, Ohio: Bowling Green University Popular Press.

Marqués, René. 1977. *El puertorriqueño dócil y otros ensayos, 1953-1971*. Barcelona: Editorial Antillana.

Mattelart, Armand, Xavier Delcourt, and Michèle Mattelart. 1993. International Image Markets. In *Cultural Studies Reader*, ed. Simon During, 421-37. New York: Routledge.

Maxwell, John C. 1993. Liquor Giants Increase Clout. *Advertising Age* 64 (February 15): 51.

Maxwell, Richard. 1996. Out of Kindness and into Difference: The Value of Global Market Research. *Media Culture and Society* 18: 105-26.

McCracken, Grant. 1990. *Culture and Consumption*. Bloomington: Indiana University Press.

Meléndez, Edwin. 1993. *Movimiento anexionista en Puerto Rico*. Río Piedras: Universidad de Puerto Rico.

Mercado, Rosa. 1997. "De vaqueros y sheriff." *El Nuevo Día* (San Juan), February 1, 51.

Mier, Mariano. 1993. Pero expande operaciones acá. *El Nuevo Día* (San Juan), September 16, 140.

Miller, Daniel. 1995. *Worlds Apart: Modernity through the Prism of the Local*. New York: Routledge.

Mintz, Sidney. 1989. The History of a Puerto Rican Plantation. In *Caribbean Contours*, ed. Sidney Mintz and Sally Price, 95-130. New York: Columbia University Press.

Mojica, Aguedo. 1983. *La entrega luminosa*. Río Piedras: Huracán.

Molina, Marina. 1960. "Pueblo considera actual tragedia la mayor de su historia." *El Mundo* (San Juan), September 7, 5.

Morris, Nancy. 1995. *Puerto Rico: Culture, Politics and Identity*. Westport, Conn.: Praeger.

Mouffe, Chantal. 1979. *Gramsci and Marxist Theory*. London: Routledge.

Mukerji, Chandra, and Michael Schudson, eds. 1991. *Rethinking Popular Culture: Contemporary Perspectives in Cultural Studies*. Los Angeles: University of California Press.

Muñoz Marín, Luis. 1959. Breakthrough from Nationalism: A Small Island Looks at a Big Trouble. Godkin Lectures 1-3, April 28-30. Fundación Luis Muñoz Marín, Trujillo Alto.

————. 1956. Governor's speech on April 1 before Associated Harvard Clubs, Coral Gables, Florida, quoted in "Notes on the Implementation of the Concept of Serenity by the Commonwealth of Puerto Rico." Fundación Luis Muñoz Marín, Trujillo Alto, section 5, series 17.

————. 1940. Victory speech of November 16. Fundación Luis Muñoz Marín, Trujillo Alto, section 3, series 2, speeches 1920-40.

————. 1940. Speech of November 4. Fundación Muñoz Marín, Trujillo Alto, section 3, series 2, speeches 1920-40.

Naficy, Hamid. 1993. *The Making of Exile Cultures: Iranian Television in Los Angeles*. Minneapolis: University of Minnesota Press.

Nash, June. 1995. The Reassertion of Indigenous Identity: Mayan Responses to State Intervention in Chiapas. *Latin American Research Review* 30(3): 7-42.

Nath, Uma Ram. 1986. *Smoking: Third World Alert*. Oxford: Oxford University Press.

Navas-Dávila, Gerardo, ed. 1985. *Cambio y desarrollo en Puerto Rico: La transformación ideológica del Partido Popular Democrático*. Río Piedras: Editorial de la Universidad de Puerto Rico.

Negociado del Censo Federal [Bureau of the Census], U.S. Department of Commerce. 1993. Censo de población de 1990: Características sociales y económicas, Puerto Rico, secciónes 1-2. U.S. Government Printing Office.

Negrón de Montilla, Aida. 1990. *La americanización en Puerto Rico y el sistema de instrucción pública 1900-1930*. Río Piedras: Editorial de la Universidad de Puerto Rico.

Negrón-Muntaner, Frances, and Ramón Grosfogel, eds. 1997. *The Puerto Rican Jam: Rethinking Colonialism and Nationalism*. Minneapolis: University of Minnesota Press.

O'Barr, William. 1989. The Airbrushing of Culture: An Insider Looks at Global Advertising. *Public Culture* 2(1): 1-19.

Olwig, Karen Fog. 1993. Between Tradition and Modernity: National Development in the Caribbean. *Social Analysis* 33: 89-104.

Ortiz, Laura. 1992. *Al filo de la navaja: Los márgenes en Puerto Rico.* Río Piedras: Centro de Investigaciones Sociales, Universidad de Puerto Rico.

Ortiz, María Mercedes. 1980. La politización del ICP. *Claridad* (San Juan), July 18-24, 4-5.

Ortiz Cuadra, Miguel. 1993. Líneas de crédito: Apuntes sobre el financiamiento de la Central Ejemplo y otras empresas de Antonio Roig, 1896-1933. *Boletín cultural regional este* (ICP) 5.

———. 1991. Punta Santiago: Origen y desarrollo. *El regional del este,* July 25-August 21.

———. 1986. Los hacendados ante la crisis del dulce. *Revista oriente* 4: 10-66.

Pabón, Carlos. 1995. De Albizu a Madonna: Para armar y desarmar la nacionalidad. *Bordes* 1: 22-40.

Pantojas-García, Emilio. 1990. *Development Strategies as Ideology: Puerto Rico's Export-Led Industrialization Experience.* Boulder and London: Lynne Rienner.

Partido Nuevo Progresista. 1993. Compara dos mundos. Advertising placed in *El Nuevo Día* (San Juan), October 19, 24.

PECES (Programa de Educación Comunal de Entrega y Servicio). 1994. Estudio de necesidades. Study directed by Alejandro Cotté, Ivis Santana, and Noé Mojica. Graduate School of Social Work, University of Puerto Rico, Río Piedras.

Pedreira, Antonio. 1985. *Insularismo.* Río Piedras: Edil.

Pérez, Marvette. 1994. The Politics of Culture and the Culture of Politics: Nationalism, Status, and Ambiguity in Puerto Rico. Paper presented at the ninety-third annual meeting of the American Anthropological Association, Atlanta, Georgia.

Philip, Alan Butt. 1980. European Nationalism in the Nineteenth and Twentieth Centuries. In *The Roots of Nationalism: Studies in Northern Europe,* ed. Rosalind Mitchison. Edinburgh, Scotland: Donald.

Pierluissi de Rodríguez, Aura. 1989. Dos décadas del Festival Nacional Indígena en Jayuya. Jayuya: Centro Cultural de Jayuya.

Pointi, Gino. 1994. San Juan Third in Nation in Number of Murders. *San Juan Star,* January 3, 3.

Prensa Unida Internacional. 1981. "Somos un solo pueblo, una sola cultura." *El Reportero,* April 10. Rosado Collection, Archives of Puerto Rico, Institute of Puerto Rican Culture, San Juan.

Public Records, Inc. 1994. Top Twelve Magazine Advertising Categories and Brands. *Caribbean Business,* August 11, 48.

Quintero-Rivera, A. G. 1991. Culture-Oriented Social Movements: Ethnicity and Symbolic Action in Latin America and the Caribbean. *CENTRO Bulletin* (Spring): 97-104.

————. 1989. De la fiesta al festival. *David and Goliath* 18(64): 47-54.

————. 1988a. *Patricios y plebeyos: Burgueses, hacendados, artesanos y obreros.* Río Piedras: Huracán.

————. 1988b. The Rural-Urban Dichotomy in the Formation of Puerto Rico's Cultural Identity. *New West Indian Guide* 61: 127-44.

————. 1985. La base social de la transformación ideológica del Partido Popular en la década del '40. In *Cambio y desarrollo en Puerto Rico,* ed. Gerardo Navas-Dávila, 35-124.

Ramírez, Rafael. 1977. National Culture in Puerto Rico. *Latin American Perspectives* 3(3): 109-16.

Ramos, Aarón. 1987. *Las ideas anexionistas en Puerto Rico bajo la dominación norteamericana.* Río Piedras: Huracán.

Redacción Claridad. 1980. A "malletazos" contra la cultura. *Claridad* (San Juan), February 8-14, 2.

Redacción El Mundo. 1983. Leticia del Rosario: Yo seré revindicada por la historia. *El Mundo* (San Juan), June 21, 8.

Redacción El Nuevo Día. 1994. El crimen, peor que hace dos años. *El Nuevo Día* (San Juan), May 25, 6.

————. 1980. Cultura provincial. *El Nuevo Día* (San Juan), February 7, 16.

Reyes Matta, Fernando. 1988. The "New Song" and Its Confrontation in Latin America. In *Marxism and the Interpretation of Cultures,* ed. Cary Nelson and Lawrence Grossberg, 447-61. Urbana: University of Illinois Press.

Ríos, Milagros. 1996. Descontenta con Jailene. *El Nuevo Día* (San Juan), July 12, 113.

Rivera, Daniel. [1854] 1974. *Agüeybana el bravo.* San Juan: Editorial Betances.

Rivera, Ivelisse. 1996. Geografías de exclusión en San Juan. Paper presented at the second Puerto Rican Studies conference, Puerto Rican Studies Association, San Juan.

Rivera, Raquel. 1993. Rap Music in Puerto Rico: Mass Consumption or Social Resistance? *CENTRO Bulletin* (Spring): 53-66.

Rodó, José Enrique. [1900] 1967. *Ariel.* Ed. with an introduction and notes by Gordon Brotherston. Cambridge: Cambridge University Press.

Rodríguez, Sandra. 1994a. Freedom of Commercial Speech Hot Issue. *Caribbean Business,* April 7, 49.

———. 1994b. NAZCA S & S: A New Day in Advertising. *Caribbean Business,* April 21, 1.

———. 1994c. Puerto Rico's Marketing Industry. *Caribbean Business,* November 10, 1.

Rodríguez Castro, María. 1993. Foro de 1940: Las pasiones y los intereses se dan la mano. In *Del nacionalismo al populismo: Cultura y política en Puerto Rico,* ed. Sylvia Alvarez-Curbelo and María Rodríguez Castro.

Rodríguez Fraticelli, Carlos. 1992. Pedro Albizu Campos: Strategies of Struggle and Strategic Struggles. *CENTRO Bulletin* (Center for Puerto Rican Studies, Hunter College, New York) 4(1): 24-33.

Rojas Daporta, Malen. 1958a. Culpan uniones gobierno por la crisis. *El Mundo* (San Juan), September 1, 12.

———. 1958b. Dos señalan cómo aliviar la crisis del desempleo. *El Mundo* (San Juan), September 2, 24.

———. 1958c. Grupo opina unión resolvería problemas. *El Mundo* (San Juan), September 3, 27

Rosaldo, Renato. 1989. *Culture and Truth: The Remaking of Social Analysis.* Boston: Beacon Press.

Rosa Nieves, Cesareo. 1967. La bomba, la plena y el cuento popular. In *La voz folklórica de Puerto Rico.* Sharon, Conn.: Troutman Press.

Roseberry, William. 1994. Hegemony and the Language of Contention. In *Everyday Forms of State Formation,* ed. Gilbert Joseph and Daniel Nugent, 355-66. Durham, N.C.: Duke University Press.

Rowe, William, and Vivian Schelling. 1991. *Memory and Modernity: Popular Culture in Latin America*. London: Verso.

Ruaño, Lida Estela. 1997. R. J. Reynolds investing $40 million here. *Caribbean Business*, February 20, 9.

Ryan, Frances. 1994. If Opportunity Knocks—Let It In! Franchise Business is a Natural for Puerto Rican Entrepreneurs. *Caribbean Business*, March 31, 1.

Safa, Helen. 1974. *The Urban Poor of Puerto Rico: A Study of Development and Underdevelopment*. New York: Holt, Rinehart and Winston.

Said, Edward. 1993. *Culture and Imperialism*. New York: Alfred A. Knopf.

Sánchez, Calixta. 1991. Análisis cultural de los actos comunicativos en ocho festivales populares de tema agrícola celebrados en Puerto Rico de agosto 1990 a enero 1991. Master's thesis presented to the Communications Department, University of Puerto Rico, Río Piedras.

Santiago, Javier. 1994. *La Nueva Ola portorricensis: La revolución musical que vivió Puerto Rico en la década del 60*. San Juan: Editorial Del Patio.

Santiago-Valles, Kelvin. 1994. *"Subject People" and Colonial Discourses: Economic Transformation and Social Disorder in Puerto Rico, 1898-1947*. Albany: State University of New York Press.

Scarano, Francisco. 1993. *Puerto Rico: Cinco siglos de historia*. San Juan: McGraw-Hill.

———. 1989. *Imigración y clases sociales en el Puerto Rico del siglo XIX*. Río Piedras: Huracán.

Seda Bonilla, Eduardo. 1972. *Requiem para una cultura*. Río Piedras: Ediciones Bayoán.

Segal, Daniel A. 1994. Living Ancestors, Nationalism, and the Past in Postcolonial Trinidad and Tobago. In *Remapping Memory: The Politics of Time Space*, ed. Jonathan Boyarin. Minneapolis: University of Minnesota Press.

Seijo Bruno, Mini. 1980. La guerra cultural. *Claridad* (San Juan), June 13-19, 6-7.

Shohat, Ella, and Robert Stam. 1994. *Unthinking Eurocentrism: Multiculturalism and the Media*. London and New York: Routledge.

Smith, Anthony. 1986. *The Ethnic Origins of Nations*. New York: Blackwell.

Sola, María. 1990. *Aquí cuentan las mujeres*. Río Piedras: Huracán.

Sommer, Doris. 1990. *Foundational Fictions: The National Romances of Latin America.* Berkeley: University of California Press.

Stallybrass, Peter, and Allon White. 1986. *The Politics and Poetics of Transgression.* Ithaca, N.Y.: Cornell University Press.

Steward, Julian, et al. 1956. *The People of Puerto Rico.* Urbana: University of Illinois Press.

Stoeltje, Beverly. 1992. Festival. In *Folklore, Cultural Performances, and Popular Entertainments,* 261-71. New York: Oxford University Press.

Stolcke, Verena. 1995. Talking Culture: New Boundaries, New Rhetorics of Exclusion in Europe. *Current Anthropology* 36(1): 1-24.

Storey, John. 1993. *Cultural Theory and Popular Culture.* Athens: University of Georgia Press.

Stutzman, Ronald. 1981. El Mestizaje: An All-Inclusive Ideology of Exclusion. In *Cultural Transformations and Ethnicity in Modern Ecuador,* ed. N. E. Whitten, 45-93. New York: Harper and Row.

Subervi Vélez, Federico, and Nitza Hernández López. 1990. Mass Media in Puerto Rico. In *Mass Media and the Caribbean,* ed. Stuart Surlin and Walter Soderlund. New York: Gordon and Breach.

Sveberny-Mohammadi, Annabelle. 1991. The Global and the Local in International Communications. In *Mass Media and Society,* ed. James Curran and Michael Gurevitch, 118-38. London: Edward Arnold.

Symmons-Symonolewicz, Konstantin. 1965. Nationalist Movements: An Attempt at Comparative Typology. *Comparative Studies in Society and History* 7: 221-30.

Tirado, Amílcar. 1993. La forja de un líder. In Carrión et al., *La nación puertorriqueña.*

Tomlinson, John. 1991. *Cultural Imperialism: A Critical Introduction.* Baltimore, Md.: Johns Hopkins University Press.

Torrecillas, Arturo. 1994. Watermelon Intelligentsia: Intellectuals in the Party-State. *Social Text* 38: 135-47.

Torregrosa, José Luis. 1991. *Historia de la radio en Puerto Rico.* Hato Rey, P.R.: Esmaco.

Torres, Arlene. 1995. Blackness, Ethnicity, and Cultural Transformations in Southern Puerto Rico. Ph.D. diss., University of Illinois, Urbana.

————. 1994. Racial Ideologies and Puerto Rico's National Identity. Paper presented at the ninety-third annual meeting of the American Anthropological Association, Atlanta, Georgia.

Underwood, Elaine. 1993. Beer, wine, liquor: Desperately seeking an edge. *Brandweek* 34 (October 18): 62–64.

U.S. Department of Commerce (USDC). Interagency Task Force. 1979. Economic Study of Puerto Rico. Report to the President. Washington, D.C.: U.S. Government Printing Office.

Urla, Jacqueline. 1995. Outlaw language: Creating alternative public spheres in Basque free radio. *Pragmatics,* June.

Vargas, Miriam. 1991. *Artesanos y artesanías en el Puerto Rico de hoy.* San Juan: Centro de Estudios Avanzados.

Verdery, Katherine. 1991. *National Ideology under Socialism.* Berkeley: University of California Press.

Wallerstein, Immanuel. 1991. The Construction of Peoplehood: Racism, Nationalism, Ethnicity. In *Race, Nation, Class, Ambiguous Identities,* ed. Etienne Balibar and Immanuel Wallerstein, 71–86. London: Verso.

Wilk, Richard. 1995. Learning to Be Local in Belize: Global Systems of Common Difference. In *Worlds Apart: Modernity through the Prism of the Local,* ed. Daniel Miller.

Williams, Brackette. 1993. The Impact of the Precepts of Nationalism on the Concept of Culture: Making Grasshoppers of Naked Apes. *Cultural Critique,* Spring.

————. 1991. *Stains on My Name, War in My Veins: Guyana and the Politics of Cultural Struggle.* Durham, N.C.: Duke University Press.

————. 1989. A Class Act: Anthropology and the Race to Nation among Ethnic Terrain. *Annual Review of Anthropology* 18: 401–44.

Williams, Raymond. 1983. *Keywords: A Vocabulary of Culture and Society.* New York: Oxford University Press.

————. 1977. *Marxism and Literature.* New York: Oxford University Press.

————. 1973. *The Country and the City.* New York: Oxford University Press.

Williams, Rosalind. 1982. *Dream Worlds: Mass Consumption in Late Nineteeth Century France.* Berkeley: University of California Press.

Worsley, Peter. 1984. *The Three Worlds: Culture and World Development.* Chicago: University of Chicago Press.

Yadav, Alok. 1994. Nationalism and Contemporaneity: Political Economy of a Discourse. *Cultural Critique* (Winter): (191-229).

Yoshino, Kosaku. 1995. *Cultural Nationalism in Contemporary Japan: A Sociological Enquiry.* New York: Routledge.

Young, Crawford. 1993. *The Rising Tide of Cultural Pluralism: The Nation-State at Bay.* Madison: University of Wisconsin Press.

Zehr, Douglas. 1994a. What Ever Happened to Breadfruit? *San Juan Star,* September 14, Portfolio 25-27.

———. 1994b. New Guard Takes the Forefront at Lopito. *San Juan Star,* May 16, B-5.

Zenón Cruz, Isabelo. 1975. *Narciso descubre su trasero: El negro en la cultura puertorriqueña.* Humacao, P.R.: Editorial Furidi.

INDEX

Italicized page numbers refer to illustrations.